Coal and Culture

Coal and Culture

Opera Houses in Appalachia

WILLIAM FARICY CONDEE

Ohio University Press
Athens

Ohio University Press, Athens, Ohio 45701
www.ohio.edu/oupress

Printed in the United States of America

Ohio University Press books are printed on acid-free paper ∞™

12 11 10 09 08 07 06 05 5 4 3 2 1

Library of Congress Cataloging-in-Publication Data

Condee, William Faricy.
Coal and culture : opera houses in Appalachia / William Faricy Condee.
p. cm.
Includes bibliographical references and index.
ISBN 0-8214-1588-3 (cloth : alk. paper)
1. Theater—Appalachian Region—History. I. Title.

PN2273.A66C66 2005
792.5'0974—dc22

2004018401

FOR KATHLEEN, COLIN, AND AUSTIN

CONTENTS

ILLUSTRATIONS

PREFACE

Opera houses in Appalachia are unstudied treasures that provide insights into the culture of Appalachia and America. These opera houses are integrally related to popular culture, local culture, coal mining, fraternal lodges, and the society of Appalachia from the late nineteenth century through the early twentieth century. They are largely unstudied because opera houses are no longer central to our culture, and their history has been forgotten. They are not great architectural landmarks, the plays that were staged in them are rarely performed today, and the community events that took place in them are no longer memorable. Why, then, are communities across Appalachia struggling to save and restore these buildings? The answer lies in that forgotten history. Communities are once more trying to find a social center that binds people together. The opera house was that site, and can be once again. The goal of this book is to lay a historical foundation for the restoration of opera houses in Appalachia.

My goal here is not to emphasize the beauty of these opera houses or to evaluate the quality of the events staged in them. Instead, my goal is to explicate how and why these buildings were a nexus of culture for the communities in which they were located. The opera house hosted a wide variety of events. Audiences attended performances of Shakespeare's plays, participated in religious observances, and witnessed variety shows. In a single week, a spectator could experience a production of *Hamlet,* attend Sunday School, and witness *Zarrow's Pig Revue,* all at the opera house.

This book has been a personal process of discovery. I was born and bred in Appalachia, and have returned to the region for my professional career. My education and research, however, were until recently focused elsewhere. I studied the theaters of New York, England, France, Germany, Italy, and Greece. It was during a faculty sabbatical, when I was preparing for a trip to study theaters in Italy, that I had the time and inclination to look at the historic theaters in my own backyard. That exploration, which became all-consuming, led to this book. For me, however, it was not just a study of historic buildings and their context, but a personal journey of rediscovery of my own history. I have come to know and love Appalachia—its landscape, its culture, and its people.

I wish to thank the kind and generous people I had the opportunity to meet at opera houses across Appalachia. These opera houses are preserved and are being restored because of the local, Herculean efforts of such people. They opened their doors to me on weekends and evenings, eager to share their accomplishments with a fellow enthusiast. This book would not exist without their dedication. In addition, local libraries and historical societies were generous with time and resources in providing me with historical information and illustrations. In particular, I wish to thank Rick Oremus and Shirley Seckinger at Stuart's Opera House in Nelsonville, Ohio, where my fascination with opera houses began.

I also wish to thank Toni Dorfman and Vincent Cardinal, who supported my work as successive directors of the School of Theater at Ohio University, and especially Raymond Tymas-Jones, dean of the College of Fine Arts at Ohio University, who has provided me with time for this research. Ashley Maresch Bishop and Lindsay Cummings, two Ohio University students whose work was supported by Honors Tutorial College Research Apprenticeships, provided enormous help in contacting historical societies and searching through microfilms for references to opera houses. I am indebted to them for the countless gems they uncovered. Bob Winters created what I could not have started: a database for recording information on all the opera houses, with the capability to compare and synthesize data. Lorraine Wochna and Jaime Mendola researched bibliographical material in the final stages of manuscript preparation when I was far from my sources. In addition, Brenda Llewellyn, administrative associate in the School of Interdisciplinary Arts, caught countless errors in the text and helped me cope with electronically stored illustrations. The Ohio Leipzig European Center (OLEC) provided me with time and space for research and writing during two critical phases of this work.

David Sanders and Gillian Berchowitz at the Ohio University Press have been patient and supportive as I have struggled with this project. They have been an author's ideal of a publisher and editor. Nancy Basmajian and copyeditor Bevin McLaughlin of the Ohio University Press have worked through this text with care and precision and have helped me state more clearly what I meant to say all along. I am deeply indebted to their sensitive attention to detail and grace. I also wish to thank Bruce McConachie and Don B. Wilmeth, who provided me with carefully detailed comments on a draft of this text. Richard Poole has served as my opera house inspiration and mentor throughout this work.

Finally, I would like to thank my wife, Kathleen, and my two sons, Colin and Austin. They have accompanied me on opera house adventures and have endured my rants as I thought through these ideas. Colin has crawled through filth and abandoned washing machines to help me measure opera houses, and Austin has left his mark across Appalachia. Kathleen's charm was able to open up people to recollection in ways that my scholarly inquires never could. They are part of this work, and I could not have created it without them.

PART ONE

The Opera House Project

CHAPTER ONE

The Birth of the Opera House

Meredith Willson places the fourth scene of *The Music Man,* a small-town celebration of the Fourth of July, in the gymnasium of the River City High School. The presentation includes patriotic songs, stereopticon slides, and a speech by the mayor.[1] At the time the musical was first produced, in 1957, the high school gym would have made sense as the site for such an event. But for the time the scene was meant to have taken place, in 1912, the River City Opera House would have been the site for this town meeting. By the mid-twentieth century, however, the hypothetical River City Opera House and many of its real-life counterparts had been abandoned and forgotten, or perhaps razed for parking lots. In a modern musical set in a small town, placing a scene in an opera house would have seemed nonsensical. This book traces the events that placed that town meeting in an opera house and the developments that led Americans to forget about the opera house in the decades that followed.

Opera houses were central to American life from the end of the Civil War through the 1920s. Most towns and cities, from small to large, had at least one opera house. This was the golden age of the opera house, and it is no coincidence that this period was also the golden age of popular entertainment, fraternities, coal mining, and railroads. All these aspects of American life converged in the opera house. This book focuses on the life of the opera house—from its birth, through its heyday, to its demise—in the coal-mining region of Appalachia from the 1860s to the 1930s.

At first glance, an opera house in a nineteenth-century small town in Appalachia may seem unlikely, and it is this very glance that exposes the problem of this subject. How do we define "opera house," and where do we locate the opera house within fields of study? Where we place a given subject determines how we study it, what questions we ask, what methodologies we employ, and what conclusions we draw. Since little or no opera was performed in opera houses, theater historians tend to regard them as theaters. Previous studies of opera houses have focused primarily on theatrical and dramatic performances, and theater historians have recorded the plays, companies, stars, and vaudeville and minstrel troupes that performed at opera houses, along with the nature and origin of the scenery. For example, David Naylor and Joan Dillon's admirable recent book, *American Theaters: Performance Halls of the Nineteenth Century,* states, "Of course, this building may be known as an opera house, or a music hall, or a chautauqua. . . . Collectively, by us, they will always be known as *theaters,* and be no less sweet for that." Naylor and Dillon's study separates "Eastern Town Hall Opera Houses" and "Theatrical Venues in the Midwest," with an emphasis on theatrical performance, from "Revival Halls and the Chautauqua Circuit" and "Community Halls and Library Theaters," in which chapters they mention religious, educational, and community events.[2] Evidence from Appalachian opera houses, however, does not support these distinctions. All these events occurred in all the opera houses, which undermines the very notion of such categorization across America.

No doubt, theatrical and dramatic performances were important, and they played a significant role in the lives of Appalachian opera houses. But plays, vaudeville, and minstrelsy do not alone explain what made these opera houses popular. My research indicates that a roughly equal number of evenings were filled with what audiences would then likely have considered nontheatrical events. One can use performance theory to question the validity of that perception, but late-nineteenth-century visitors to the opera house probably differentiated between a union meeting or a commencement ceremony and *Zarrow's Pig Revue* or "The Midget Four in their unheard of feat of Dancing On Each Others Heads."[3]

If we are to understand opera houses, we must investigate them in the context of local culture. My goal, therefore, is to study a large group of opera houses within defined geographic, cultural, and economic boundaries: in Appalachia, in smaller towns, and in areas in which coal mining and related industries were prevalent. While opera houses were common in many American towns, they were ubiquitous in the coal-mining towns of Appalachia—precisely because these towns were formed or grew rapidly during the coal boom from the end of the Civil War through the 1920s, the same time that opera houses were popu-

Tarentum Opera House, Tarentum, Pennsylvania (1886). A larger opera house in a mining town. Photo by author.

lar. I am focusing on small- to mid-sized towns (almost all had a population between three and ten thousand) that had one or two opera houses, and this study is based on more than 125 opera houses, about a third of which are extant. In larger cities with multiple gathering and entertainment sites, the population tended to divide, or be segregated, along class, ethnic, racial, and religious lines, with each group going to a different place. But when an opera house was the only one in town, it became the crossroads of the community.

Little, if any, opera was actually performed in these buildings. An opera house was a community entertainment and meeting hall. It was used for traveling theatrical productions, which included contemporary and classical drama, melodrama, comedy, musicals, vaudeville, and even the occasional opera. But it was also used for concerts, religious events, lectures, high school commencements, boxing matches, benefits for local organizations, union meetings, and, if the auditorium had a flat floor, skating and basketball. During the early decades of the twentieth century, opera houses were retrofitted for showing silent movies. They were truly multipurpose facilities that were inextricably intertwined with the life of the community. In the era before radio, movies, television, and malls, these buildings were essential and vital.

The opera house was a community hall, used for any event that could take place in a large indoor space. What made the opera house popular was its versatility and accessibility to the community. Nearly every newspaper issue of the time contains references to recent, current, and future events at the local opera house. The frequency of these references indicates the central role of opera houses in the local culture. Not everyone attended the meeting of democratic free silver followers or the farewell recital of Professor Fowler's dancing class, but the opera house could provide something for almost everyone.

The term "opera house" is indeed misleading, and intentionally so; it provides a veneer of social and cultural respectability and avoids the stigma of the title "theater." An 1885 article in the *Dramatic Mirror,* entitled "The Name Opera House," explains this puzzle:

> Thus it comes that we have Opera Houses—Grand Houses at that—in which opera is never heard. But the name "Opera House" has another significance. To some extent it overcame the scruples and deadened the consciences of those who cared not to build or to attend "Theatres." . . . The foreign actor or artist making a first visit to our shores must marvel at our brilliant array of Opera Houses. But after he has traveled a few weeks the sham is exposed. He finds that they are only theatres, after all, and some of them shambling rookeries at that.
>
> Still, with all this mushroom growth of Opera Houses during the last ten or twelve years, the greater number are substantial, well-kept edifices, and some of them stately piles of architectural beauty. We number our Opera Houses by the thousands. The towns of 2,000 inhabitants and upward without an Opera House, Grand or otherwise, are few and far between—especially in the west.[4]

The "antitheatrical prejudice," as Jonas Barish calls it,[5] that led to the euphemism "opera house" has deep roots, but it can be traced in America back to Puritans in the colonial era. Their objections, derived from St. Augustine and Tertullian, included the actors taking God's name in vain during plays and spectators spending on theater money that could better go to churches, charities, or

Mozart's Hall, Carlisle, Kentucky (1883). A simple, small-town opera house. Photo by author.

economic development. Spectators were also spending time in theaters when they could have been working. Theater audiences were perceived as morally suspect: most of the spectators were deemed rowdy men, and any women in attendance were viewed as prostitutes.

The first recorded use of "opera house" as a euphemism dates back to 1787. The Southwark Theater advertised itself as the "Opera House Southwark" and billed its plays as "Spectaculum Vitae" to get around a Philadelphia law banning theatrical performances. *Hamlet* became "a moral and Instructive Tale as exemplified in the History of the Prince of Denmark," and *The School for Scandal* was "a Comic lecture in five parts on the Pernicious Vice of Scandal."[6] Plays became "moral lectures" or "moral dialogues." The word "theater" was associated with immorality, licentious behavior, lewd entertainment, and a simple waste of time. Thus, while a "theater" building was often banned, an "opera house" might be permitted. Other coded names included "academy of music," "museum," and "histrionic academy," each lending respectability to the building by virtue of its cultural acceptability.

Theater was also opposed by revolutionary Americans on political grounds: it was associated with England and the Royalist cause. According to Bruce

McConachie, those fighting for independence felt that the theater "fostered a desire for luxury, destructive emulation, dependence on the crown, and class division."[7] Thus Puritans and revolutionaries lined up together in opposition to theater in colonial America.

Theater did have its supporters in eighteenth- and nineteenth-century America, basing their defense on Horace's duality that theater could serve to teach and to please. Since theater could teach moral lessons in a pleasing fashion, so the argument went, it could serve as a powerful moral force. Theater was referred to as "the most powerful moral agent in society," and "a school where manners may be polished and everything learnt which distinguishes us from barbarism."[8] Specifically, many plays in the nineteenth century dealt with temperance, abolition, and religion.

This emphasis on morality was especially profound in midwestern towns, and entertainment had to conform to these local standards. Lewis Atherton points to the nineteenth-century midwestern objection to theater based on the "cult of the immediately useful and practical," but he also notes that theatrical performance appealed to the cultural aspirations of town leaders: "Most of the entertainment by necessity attempted to meet prevailing standards of taste, but always a combination of ambitious professional entertainers and culturally inspired citizens stood ready to promote 'higher' artistic and intellectual standards."[9]

* * *

Opera houses in Appalachia varied widely as to their characteristics, but had some common features. In most cases, the opera house was in a large, monumental building in the center of town, on the main street or square, usually with an Italianate facade (80 percent of the opera houses for which such information is available had Italianate facades). The buildings were commonly brick or stone, sometimes with cast-iron decoration, while smaller opera houses might be made of wood. Commonly the words "Opera House" were displayed on the cornice across the top of the building.

Most opera houses were situated on the second story; the ground floor, which was most visible and accessible to passersby, contained commercial storefronts. The opera house, which people were more likely to plan ahead to visit, was placed on the less-accessible second floor.

Entry to the second-story opera house was through a central door between the ground-floor storefronts, or through a door on the side of the building. Spectators climbed a single, wide staircase, though larger opera houses sometimes had a separate entrance and stairway for the gallery. The box office was usually at the top of the stairs, at the doorway to the opera house. Most opera

Marlinton Opera House, Marlinton, West Virginia (1909). View toward the stage from the main floor of a flat-floored opera house. Photo by author.

houses had no lobby, but when one did exist, it was simply a small area at the top of the stairs. "Retiring rooms," if they existed at all, were off the lobby.

Overall audience capacities can be determined for some opera houses from guides published for booking agents. Current seating is rarely an accurate guide to the original capacity: even if the original seats have been restored and reinstalled, the seating density must conform to modern safety restrictions, resulting in a significantly reduced capacity. In the fifty-three cases for which the opera house capacity and the town population can be determined, the relationship between the two figures is extraordinary. These opera houses ranged in capacity from 300 to 1,000, in towns with populations from 1,000 to 12,000 (most were between 3,000 and 10,000). The average capacity was 814, and the average population was 6,968. The capacity of the opera house was therefore fully 11 percent of the town's population. In some cases, the opera house could hold up to one-third of the town's people. Even granted that miners from surrounding coal camps arrived on special branch trains to attend opera house events, the ratio of opera house capacity to town population is staggering. It demonstrates vividly the popularity and centrality of the opera house in the lives of these towns.

The typical opera house, by modern standards, was small and intimate, while at the same time the largest indoor space in town. The interior dimensions of the auditorium averaged 48 feet wide and 65 feet long (from the stage to the back wall). In smaller opera houses, the main floor of the auditorium, or parquet, was often flat, with chairs that could be easily moved to the sides for roller-skating, dancing, or basketball. In larger opera houses the main floor was raked for better sight lines. The chairs had cast-iron sides and wooden tip-up seats, sometimes with cushioning. The seats were narrower than spectators are used to today, around 18 inches wide, as opposed to the modern 20.5 inches or wider.[10] The balcony/gallery had either benches or unpadded chairs. Larger opera houses commonly had a balcony, which might be broken into sections, with a dress circle at the front and gallery at the rear. The balcony was usually a rectangular block at the rear of the auditorium, but could also extend along the side walls of the auditorium. The balcony was supported from below by narrow iron pillars or suspended from the ceiling by rods. Later opera houses used internal trusses that obviated the need for supports that blocked sight lines. None of the opera houses examined here had two balconies. African Americans were probably restricted to the gallery (at the rear of the balcony), but may have been joined there by working-class whites. In some cases, primarily in states farther south in this region, opera houses were strictly segregated. In other cases, there is no clear record of strict racial segregation. Some opera houses had an orchestra "pit," but it was often just a small area adjacent to the stage, separated from the seating by a low railing.

Many opera houses had boxes on either side of the stage. Today many assume that the box seat has the worst view of the stage, and indeed the viewing angle is from sharply to one side. But sitting in one of these boxes belies this notion. Most opera houses had a forestage apron extending beyond the proscenium arch, usually three to ten feet deep (on average, just over eight feet). The primary acting area was probably a shallow oval that extended from the edge of the apron to only a few feet upstage of the proscenium arch. The stage area behind the proscenium arch was primarily for a scenic background, spectacle, and entrances and exits. On the apron, the actors were well lit by the footlights below and the auditorium lights above. The acoustics were best from the apron, in that the actor was close to the audience and shared the same space. In addition, close proximity to the audience made for ready and easy interaction. While the view from the box was from the side, these seats not only provided the best view of the actors but were the best place to be seen by the rest of the audience. One could show off one's status in society, clothing, jewels, and companions. In addition, being seen at the opera house demonstrated one's cultural aspirations, as well as support for the particular performance.

Stuart's Opera House, Nelsonville, Ohio (1879). View across forestage from a box seat, showing the sight lines from these seats. Photo by author.

The stage in most small-town opera houses was as wide as the auditorium; in other words, there was no additional wing space. In this sense, the opera house can be looked at as a large rectangular box, one end of which was raised and partially walled off for the stage. Larger opera houses had a full stage house, with wing space to the sides and a fly loft overhead, but these were the exception in mining towns in Appalachia. Scenery consisted of wings (vertical panels on the sides of the stage), borders (horizontal panels suspended over the stage), and drops (large panels at the rear of the stage). Grooves on the stage floor and overhead allowed wings to be slid on and off the stage. (See chapter 7 for a detailed discussion of the stage and scenery.) Dressing rooms were closet-sized spaces on the sides of or under the stage. Small opera houses had as few as two dressing rooms, located on the stage proper (curtained or walled-off areas backstage) or inside the wings of the proscenium arch on either side of the stage. Larger opera houses had a fully excavated basement or a separate structure to the side of the stage that would allow for larger and more numerous dressing rooms.

The stage itself was small by modern standards. The average width of the proscenium arch was 28 feet, narrower than the 30- to 40-foot prosceniums of today. These dimensions demonstrate the small size of these buildings, but they

Stuart's Opera House, Nelsonville, Ohio (1879). The original interior, showing a flat-floored, small, second-story opera house. Reprinted with permission of Stuart's Opera House Archives, Nelsonville, Ohio.

also highlight the nature of the performative events in these halls: the focus was on the performers, usually few in number, not on the spectacle. The acting area was thus quite small, perhaps 20 feet wide and 12 feet deep, but plenty big enough for the two- or three-person scenes that dominated most of the drama, as well as for recitals and speeches.

Heat for smaller opera houses came from simple stoves in the auditorium and onstage, while larger opera houses had a central furnace. The gas jets that lit the stage and auditorium in the nineteenth century also provided heat. In summer and winter, openings in the ceiling provided ventilation, releasing hot air and fumes, though most opera houses were closed during the hot summer months. Many larger opera houses had a dome over the center of the auditorium, which provided ventilation, in that hot air, smoke, and fumes gathered in its bubble and could then escape outside. In the days of gas lighting, such ventilation was essential. The *Daily Evening Bulletin* of Maysville, Kentucky, complained in 1883 that "more attention should be paid to the proper ventilation of the opera house. For a time last night the atmosphere was very oppressive."[11] And even with the advent of electricity, the heat from the light bulbs and the spectators had to be vented.

Stuart's Opera House, Nelsonville, Ohio (1879). View toward the proscenium arch, showing the enlarged theater of 1881. Reprinted with permission of Stuart's Opera House Archives, Nelsonville, Ohio.

The style of the interior decoration of opera houses varied widely, and is hard to determine accurately, given the many changes to these spaces. Most of the smaller opera houses had a simpler decor: plastered ceiling and walls with stenciling at the top and wainscoting below. Some had wooden ceilings, and while these may have been cheaper to build at the time, they have tended to endure longer than plaster. Larger opera houses had more thematic designs, often with classical touches. Areas for special decoration were the chandelier medallion and the proscenium arch, both of which had painted decorative plaster. While these opera houses seem simple and even quaint to us today, they were uniformly described during this period as splendid, spectacular, and beautiful. The classical or renaissance design motifs reflected high cultural aspirations.

The central location and monumental architecture of the opera house indicate its prominent place in local culture. Many opera houses were in buildings for fraternal organizations or town halls, while others were privately owned. The communities wanted permanent sites of theatrical entertainment, and local organizations, whether business, governmental, civic, or fraternal, answered the call. After the Civil War, buildings such as a town hall, a school, churches, and a fire station were elemental structures in a newly emerging town, indicating that it had permanence and was investing time, bricks, and mortar in its values. The town hall demonstrated the solidity of the town and the permanence of the rule of law. The school indicated that the town valued education. Churches were a sign of the town's spirituality. The fire station showed that real estate investments were secure. The opera house, part of this architectural sign system, indicated that the town had high cultural aspirations. In addition, the opera house, along with its architectural counterparts, made the town more attractive to others. Businesses were more likely to set up shop. Families were more likely to settle.

Civic leaders often advocated building a new opera house as part of town development. In Danville, Kentucky, the opera house, called James Hall, went bankrupt in 1875, and the local newspaper led the campaign for a new opera house. By 1883 the Danville Town Hall Company had formed to build one. As it happened, the company could not raise the money, so it purchased and remodeled the old James Hall.[12] In Connellsville, Pennsylvania, the *Courier* editorialized for a new opera house and publicly promoted its new investor in 1881:

> It has long been a matter of public regret that Connellsville had no hall, or opera house, suitable for the better class of entertainments, which under such favorable circumstance would not miss paying our town a visit, but which in the tatol [*sic*] absence of proper accommodations have just as resolutely passed us by. The COURIER has always contended that an opera building in this town would be a paying investment, and we are glad to be able to say to our readers this week that there is one man in Connellsville who is of the same mind and who proposes to back up his opinions with ready cash. That man is P.S. Newmyer, Esq.[13]

For the opening of the New Grand Opera House in Paris, Kentucky, in 1890, the *Kentuckian Citizen* congratulated the opera house's promoters, while at the same time emphasizing its community basis:

> With more than ordinary pleasure we congratulate our people on the completion and possession of this gem of the builder's art, our Opera House, not Clay's, Hinton's or Ferguson's, but ours the peoples house, in the city and yet of the county as by the joint liberality of both city and county friends we owe its erection. As we stand on the stage commanding a general view of the hall, noting its perfection of its symmetrical and harmonious proportions, it makes one feel that he breathes the very atmosphere of music, and that he drinks in the spirit of the immortal dramas produced by Goethe, Wagner and other illustrious compeers of the divine art. . . .

> Who was it with quiet dignity and with unswerving loyalty to the project, by persuasive appeal won many a liberal subscription to the enterprise, besides giving generously from his personal funds? None took greater interest in our city's pride than J. W. Ferguson.[14]

The *Renovo (Pennsylvania) Record* claimed full credit for the progress toward construction of an opera house in its town in 1892: "The project started by THE RECORD a few months ago, to form a corporation to build a new Opera House . . . promises to be a success," and proceeded to list the subscribers to the new corporation.[15] Subsequent articles kept readers apprised of the progress:

> It is acknowledged by all lovers of amusements that one of Renovo's greatest needs is an amusement building, with a stage, elevated seats, together with all the appointments of a first-class theatre. Our people have passed beyond the period for a plain long, narrow hall, with level floor furnished with wood seated chairs and a stage too small to admit the scenery of four-fifths of the traveling troupes. . . . It is no longer necessary to visit our neighboring cities to see the best theatrical talent. What is needed is a first-class theatre building.[16]

Funding for building an opera house came from a variety of sources: a fraternal lodge, an entrepreneurial businessman, a single wealthy benefactor, or a subscription from prominent local contributors. Paris, Kentucky, provides a model of the many ways communities funded their opera houses. The first opera house in Paris was built in 1854 thanks to a convergence of commercial, civic, cultural, and fraternal funding. It had storefronts on the first floor, a town hall opera house on the second floor, and fraternal Odd Fellows lodge rooms on the third. According to the *Kentuckian Citizen*,

> A charter has been obtained incorporating the Lodge, and provision is made for the purpose of raising the money to purchase the property, and make the improvements by a subscription of stock, in shares of $25 each. . . . The lodge will subscribe for 50 shares of stock, equal to $2,500, and the remainder, or $4,250, will have to be raised from other sources, by a subscription of stock obtained outside the Lodge, and as an inducement, the Lodge has determined to guarantee to stockholders, 4 per cent interest in the stock, the interest to commence from the time the money is paid in, the Lodge reserving the right to redeem and take in the stock at par.
>
> We would say that this will secure the erection of a Town hall of sufficient capacity for all town purposes, and those persons who are willing to spare a few dollars at 4 per cent interest, and make a sure

> investment of their money, cannot do better than subscribe for some of this stock. In truth, all who desire to see the town prosper, will, we suppose, take some of this stock, as a building of this sort, for the purpose contemplated, will greatly improve the town, and meet one of its most pressing needs,—A Town Hall.[17]

It is significant here that the promoters stressed the broader civic and town development goals of the project, as well as the immediate payoff for investors.

Some thirty years later, plans were made for a new opera house in Paris, with an emphasis on the lucrative return on the investment: "Stocks are to be about the same as the Loan Association except weekly assessments of 50 cents instead of 25 cents."[18] A week later the newspaper boasted of the progress: "The opera house scheme is booming, with about 250 shares subscribed." Several local businessmen offered sites for the new opera house. H. M. Roseberry, president of the Agricultural Bank, offered to donate property on the corner of Main and Church Streets, a prominent and central location, "provided the Company give him the lower room for banking." Griffith, landlord of Thurston House, was willing to sell his hotel, but, according to the *Kentuckian Citizen,* "there is no lack of eligible locations if the necessary stock shall be subscribed, and the outlook is very encouraging."[19] Apparently none of these offers was taken up, because eight months later the newspaper reported "A LIBERAL OFFER":

> Mr. and Mrs. Henry Turney have offered to donate to the new Opera House Company 100 square feet of their lot in the rear of the Bourbon House, on Pleasant Street, on which to build the new Opera House. This would be a most excellent site for it, and is certainly a most liberal offer. . . . If this offer should be accepted the Committee could go to work at once in erecting the building, as $18,000 has already been established, and this with the donation of a lot would be sufficient to insure a new Opera House.[20]

By the end of the following year, plans were finally in place: "The sale of tickets for the Opera House opening began yesterday morning at 11 o'clock. The line of eager purchasers extended from Dr. Brook's pill boxes to the uttermost parts of ten feet northeast of Hinton's door. The crowd was orderly and about two deep. John T. Hinton was in the lead, as usual, and looked every inch fully determined, but open to suggestions." Others are mentioned by name, with an in-joke about each one. The article concludes: "Sheriff Armstrong arrested six for being exposed to the public, and Judge Mann held over four for their appearance on the 30th proximo. While the reporter stood looking on 202 tickets were sold, not counting those that went out the back door. Truly it is to be a grand opening."[21] The next month, the *Kentuckian Citizen* announced a meeting of the Paris Opera House Company stockholders, who were mentioned by office and name.[22] Management of the opera house was still a public matter two years later, when the paper described a contentious election of directors, with opposition from the floor over finances.[23]

In Maysville, Kentucky, promoters stressed the value of an investment in the Washington Opera House; investors were to be paid back in money and tickets:

> The company proposes "to issue coupon tickets of admission to the public entertainments to be given under their auspices at the opera house now under contract, each *ticket* with twenty coupons attached, to be sold for the sum of $20 (payable in calls of $5), and each *coupon* giving the holder of the ticket admission to one entertainment," making twenty first-class entertainments selected at the pleasure of the ticket holder and always with the privilege of a reserved seat. It will be seen that this is no "begging" enterprise, but returns a fair equivalent for the money invested, and gives no one an excuse for refusing to assist in this important undertaking. It is the first call our firemen have ever made upon our citizens, and any one who has property to protect will appreciate their right to make it. The committee has already received a large number of subscriptions, and we trust we shall be able, in a few days, to publish the complete list.[24]

This opera house was unique in that it was owned by the fire department. Supporting the opera house was therefore an investment in protecting every house and business in the town.

Individual pillars of the community also funded opera houses. In Tidioute, Pennsylvania, the Grandin Brothers discovered oil on their father's timberlands, and established their own bank. Their building housed the bank on the first floor, offices on the second, and the Grandin Opera House (1872) on the third.[25] A modern history of the region noted,

> No doubt there was a degree of self interest in the Grandin's plans for the third floor of their new block. Obviously it would be very much a community ornament but one that in ways at once direct and indirect could only resound to their credit. The brothers may have been concerned with establishing their leadership among the socially and culturally minded, but they were also out to broadcast their belief that Tidioute was a highly desirable community in which to settle or in which to invest.[26]

Washington Opera House, Maysville, Kentucky (1898). A large, impressive opera house built by and for the local fire department. Reprinted with permission of Mason County Museum, Maysville, Kentucky.

In Warren, Pennsylvania, the Library Theatre (1883) was a gift to the town from Thomas Struthers, a local industrialist, to provide income to support the library. Both spaces would enrich the cultural life of the town, with the theater providing income to support the library.

Building an opera house also provided the developer with good local press. The prime advocate for the opera house in Elkins, West Virginia (1898), was given credit in a town history eight years after the opera house had opened: "Mr. Poston is the guiding spirit in this enterprise and to him much of the deserved credit to the company by its patrons is justly due."[27] A local historian of the time promoted the builder of another opera house, in Warren, Pennsylvania: "In every community there are certain striking examples among the business fraternity of

Struther's Library Theatre, Warren, Pennsylvania (1883), which had a theater and opera house in the same building, demonstrating the relationship between teaching and pleasing. Reprinted with permission of Postcard Illustrations of American Theatres and Opera Houses collection, developed by William L. Slout and housed at the Museum of Repertoire Americana, a museum at Midwest Old Threshers, Mt. Pleasant, Iowa.

that class of men whose energy, foresight and native talent have proven prominent factors in the development of their city and in fixing the relative rank which it holds among other similar centers of commerce and industry. James D. Woodward belongs to this class of men."[28] The *Athens (Ohio) Messenger* praised the construction of Stuart's Opera House in neighboring Nelsonville: "The building is not only an ornament to the town but a monument to the public spirit of its projector."[29]

The opening of an opera house frequently included an address or proclamation by the mayor, again indicating the opera house's stature in local culture. For the opening of Parshall Opera House (1870) in Titusville, Pennsylvania, the mayor indicated that he wanted his address to demonstrate his appreciation for the owner, "something adequate to this massive, magnificent and costly structure, which he has caused to be erected here; something to express our appreciation of the man who but a few months ago came a stranger to our city."[30]

For the opening of the New Mishler Theatre (1906) in Altoona, Pennsylvania, Mayor Simon H. Walker praised the owner and emphasized the importance of the structure not merely for the audience, but also as a monument in the town's landscape: "Mr. Mishler, in planning and creating such a splendid shelter for the public in its recreations and first class amusements, should be looked upon as a public benefactor who deserves and will receive the warm thanks of the people. . . . It is impossible, even for those who are not theatergoers, to be insensible to the beauty of the edifice or the importance of it as an ornament to the city."[31]

A new or remodeled opera house was something for the town to be proud of, and promoters took every opportunity to publicize its opening. The *Renovo (Pennsylvania) Record* bragged that P. H. Sullivan's New Opera House (1885) was "one of the handsomest outside of the great cities of the State. The exterior has been handsomely painted and bears a neat appearance. . . . In short, the new opera house will not only be the largest and grandest structure in the country, but it promises to attract to our town the very best traveling shows on the road, which can afford to give the best-class of amusement at such low prices as will always ensure them crowded houses."[32] A few weeks later the newspaper proclaimed, "We felt proud in realizing the fact that Renovo had at last not only the largest Opera House outside of the large cities of the State, but one of the finest in all appointments."[33] The need for keeping an opera house up-to-date is evidenced by the fact that seven years later, in 1892, the newspaper was trumpeting the need for a new opera house.[34]

Towns in the coal-mining region of eastern Kentucky were rivals in all things during the 1920s and 1930s, and this rivalry even extended to the best theater. The town of Benham, owned by International Harvester, promoted the "Building Program in Benham" in 1922: "The new brick buildings facing Benham Park, when completed, will impress visitors as a regular city square. The new theater is already completed except the roof and inside work and fixtures." The *Harlan Enterprise* article also mentioned the new store, post office, lodge hall, and medical building: "These buildings will greatly add to the welfare and enjoyment of Benham people, who already can boast of a community spirit that is, perhaps, excelled in no other coal field in the state."[35]

The neighboring (and rival) town of Lynch, Kentucky, owned by U.S. Steel, listed the "bests" of the town in 1923:

> Lynch has—
> The greatest single coal tipple in the world—
> The greatest commissary in Kentucky—
> Best theatre in Harlan County except the New Harlan Theatre—
> Cleanest mining camp in the State—
> Finest hotel in any mining town in the world—

> One of the largest and most modern equipped private hospitals in the mountains of Kentucky.[36]

Harlan, the largest town in the county, proclaimed that with the New Harlan Theatre (1922) it could "boast of a theatre building second only to the New Manring of Middlesboro in Eastern Kentucky."[37]

In Cumberland, Kentucky, an independent town, the *Tri-City News* devoted an entire section to the opening of Isaacs New Theatre (1937). The section contained the ads of businesses applauding the opening (Benham Laundry and Cleaning, Creech Department Store, Rotary Club of Cumberland, Creech Lumber and Hardware, Scotts Store, Guaranty Deposit Bank, Cumberland Bakery, Wainscott Studio, Cumberland Department Store, Watson's, Cury's Department Store, Cumberland Drug, Jack's Place), and a box with congratulations from the mayor, chief of police, city clerk, judge, and superintendent of schools. Articles boasted of the sound and projection systems, seating, facade, air-handling system, personnel, and upholstery.[38] The mayor of Cumberland issued a proclamation for the opening, which the *Tri-City News* printed: "Amusement forms a great portion of the life of every citizen and the Motion Picture Theatre is one of the cleanest and most wholesome forms of entertainment. . . . I feel it my duty as Mayor of this city, to acknowledge publicly my appreciation of an endeavor which will give so much pleasure to such a large number of our citizens."[39] An article in the *Tri-City News,* presumably a press release from the theater owner, J. E. Isaac, demonstrates the importance of the theater as a monument and an investment in the town's future, which is significant given that this theater opened during the Great Depression, and well past the peak of coal mining:

> The New Theatre in Cumberland is more than a mighty steel and concrete monument to a great ambition; it is the sincere expression of a firm belief in a community, a splendid gesture of grateful appreciation of loyal patronage. . . .
>
> It was because he believed in the future of Cumberland, that he risked his last hard earned penny in his humble theatre enterprise; it was because of his resolution to carry through with the development of new entertainment, the talking pictures, that he achieved success in his venture and pressed on to greater things.
>
> . . . The name of Isaac is known to the people of this section having furnished countless number of people the opportunity to lose themselves for the moment in the glorious world of make-belief [*sic*].
>
> The New Theatre in Cumberland is another expression of J.E. Isaac's determination to bring wholesome and fine entertainment

> within the grasp of all. It is another visible manifestation that honesty of purpose, fairness, loyalty and sincerity are still the fundamental ingredients of success.
>
> Let the new Isaac Theatre be a shrine to amusement. Let our word be your guide to entertainment. Let this theatre be your home. To be worthy of you, we have provided a theatre of home-like comfort and brilliant splendor, but more than this, we have given it life, because of the purpose that is in it. We shall never do that which may bring discredit to it. We dedicate the New Theatre, its visible structure and its unseen, but none-the-less enduring ideals, to you, our patrons and friends.[40]

Building the opera house was not enough: people had to buy tickets and attend events. Patronage at the opera house became a matter of civic pride. High attendance figures at the opera house justified its existence, reaffirmed the town's cultural aspirations, and made it possible to book better acts. Newspapers stressed the importance of local support through ticket buying for the ongoing operation of the opera house. In Paris, Kentucky, the *Kentuckian Citizen* praised the new opera house carpet and exhorted readers: "Now let our citizens patronize them [the shows]";[41] several years later it listed all the people who attended the performance on a particular night.[42] The *Carlisle (Pennsylvania) Evening Sentinel* criticized people in 1899 for not coming to the opera house: "We have the attractions, some of the best on the road, but where are the people who cried for the same?" The manager was "at a loss to know what Carlisle theatergoers really do want."[43] In Harlan, Kentucky, the *Enterprise* announced the "Second Anniversary Celebration" of its theater: "New equipment in Harlan's play house has made it one of the most modern in Eastern Kentucky. Also it has been possible to have many good shows." But the paper stressed that "to have good offerings, the theatre must have the support of its patrons."[44] In order to book some attractions, promoters had to guarantee a minimum box office. For example, in Maysville, Kentucky, the *Daily Evening Bulletin* announced that for the performance of the comic opera *La Moscotte* by Audran, "The committee who induced this troupe to visit Maysville guaranteed them the receipts would be $200. If the public desire to encourage the disposition of bringing first class entertainments to Maysville, they will give this enterprise their support."[45] Getting audience members actually to show up for their reserved tickets was as much of a problem then as now, as a petulant note in a flier for Stuart's Opera House in Nelsonville, Ohio, indicates:

> Order your seats early but please remember that the management desires that you make up your mind that you want a seat and intend to

> keep it when you order it and you will be expected to keep it after once ordering same. Not a few persons have been imposing on the management and the theater goers by ordering seats that they have no intention of keeping and then at the last moment returning same to the box office for sale, keeping other people out of the chance to get a good seat, and this must stop or all will have to pay for seats at time ordered.[46]

The opera house was central to town life in Appalachia, as demonstrated by its monumentality, capacity, and prominence in local newspapers. The construction of an opera house was a milestone in the development and solidification of a town's identity, culture, and business. The opera house staged a wide variety of events, and all segments of society came through its doors, albeit sometimes through different doors and at different times. The following two chapters discuss the important moral and architectural place the opera house occupied in Appalachian society.

CHAPTER TWO

Morality and Transgression at the Opera House

Opera houses presented a wide variety of events, from local community shows to plays to variety acts, but there were limits to what was acceptable. The opera house was central—literally and figuratively—to the town and its sense of community. As the name "opera house," as opposed to "theater," suggests, the moral stature of the opera house was an important part of its role in culture.

While opera houses in small-town America were generally free from overt censorship, they were subject to implicit community regulation. Each event existed in the context of others surrounding it and was regulated by that context. The existence of certain events excluded others. Atherton describes the community enforcement of a moral code in small towns, which "succeeded better than cities in enforcing prevailing codes because residents and visitors alike were under constant observation. Artists and showmen played up to this emphasis on morality." Locally produced events at the opera house, including benefits and religious-oriented events, also maintained this moral code: "Midwestern country towns supported both home-talent and professional companies. Audiences justified themselves on the grounds that plays were similar to church tableaus and cantatas, that part of the proceeds went for good causes, or that actors generally tried to tailor their performances to local standards of morality."[1]

Opera houses were part of a larger, pervasive emphasis on morality and family in the nineteenth century. According to Richard Butsch, antebellum American culture based the respectability of public spaces on "whether they endangered the reputation of a middle-class woman," and theaters were considered dangerous and disreputable, frequented by prostitutes, actresses, and working-class women.[2] McConachie describes this emphasis on morality in museum theaters in the period leading up to the opera houses, when the owners "promised their patrons chaste entertainment in environments closer to the church and the front parlor than to traditional playhouses." The moral appeal of museums led other producers to make theaters more family oriented by banning prostitutes and liquor.[3]

This emphasis on moral respectability is evident in many of the surviving records of opera houses. A history of Elkins, West Virginia, written in 1906 explains that the Elkins Opera House Company was formed in 1898, "to meet the requirements of those who seek recreation and amusement as well as instruction and improvement mentally."[4] The centrality of the opera house in sustaining this moral project can be seen in the mayor's dedication to the new Parshall Opera House (1870) in Titusville, Pennsylvania. He stated that the town should show its appreciation to the owner by

> making this hall a favorite resort for the intelligent, the refined, and cultivated classes of society, by patronizing the higher order of talent and genius which it is the wish and purpose of the lessees to attract here, thereby making the drama what it should be, a picture of human life from which may be drawn lessons of a character high and ennobling to the intellectual and moral attributes of man; lessons which neither the pulpit nor the press, all powerful as they are, can enforce and portray with a like conviction to the head and the heart.

The morality carried through to the style of acting employed in the opera house's opening production of *Rip Van Winkle,* for which the reviewer praised the decorum of the leading actor: "His mimicry of intoxication was superb. It was not the stagy drunkenness of 'Toodles,' for 'Rip' never staggers."[5]

Similarly, for the opening of the New Grand Opera House (1890) in Paris, Kentucky, the *Kentuckian Citizen* evoked theater history to justify the moral rectitude of the opera house: "Only the best of plays we hope will be given from the stage; those that elevate and ennoble; those that are a real benefit to those that see them. The actor's is a noble profession. The greatest of poets has said that it is the actor's duty to hold the mirror up to nature, to portray suffering, to exhibit pity, to inculcate loyalty, to teach by art the lesson of self-sacrifice. It is a noble calling worthy of the highest genius."[6]

In Harlan, Kentucky, an advertisement for the opening of the New Harlan Theatre (1922) referred to the Horatian duality in announcing, "It will be the policy of the management to arrange programs that will not only be entertaining but instructive and educational."[7] On the occasion of its first anniversary, the theater declared,

> It has always been the policy of the management of this home of "better photoplays" and wholesome entertainment to book such pictures and performances as tend to establish better morals and set better standards than to demoralize and to tear down; the aim has been to add to the education and enlightenment of the community and afford a place of amusement where even the most critical and skeptical of people could find no objection in the way of class of performances presented them.[8]

Other occupants of the opera house building also had to maintain this moral code; any unseemly enterprise in the building could undermine the status of the opera house in town culture. Opera house buildings generally contained ground-floor storefronts housing typical small-town businesses—flower shops, banks, dry goods stores, and so forth. The opera house was generally on the second floor, and the third floor contained fraternal lodge rooms or offices. The Woodward Theatre building in Warren, Pennsylvania (1912), which had a flower shop and soda grill on the first floor, had a dance hall on the third floor, but it carried an exclusionary proviso: "The room is not used as a public dance hall, but is let to societies for social occasions."[9] Presumably the societies would be those that the dominant culture deemed morally suitable, so that any dances would be appropriately decorous.

Bradford, Pennsylvania, presents an intriguing exception to this rule of moral consistency: the Wagner Opera House (1876) was considered a "respectable" place of entertainment, but the Gem Theater in the same building, behind the opera house, was considered more risqué. The audience in the Gem was thought to be lower class, and police were called in occasionally to break up fights. Thus in one building were two sites, one emphasizing morally uplifting entertainment and the other more potentially transgressive events.[10]

Newspapers overwhelmingly praised the quality and morality of opera house performances. The few examples of shows that transgressed the recognized moral boundaries provide evidence that the community did enforce the implicit social understanding and police the morality of stage presentations. The *New Straitsville (Ohio) Record* praised a 1902 performance for supporting the prevailing mode: "The recitals given by Miss Smith and Miss Hall show that the young people of our town possess much musical talent and should be encouraged and we hope that we may have more of such entertainments to listen to in future. Such things are much more uplifting and elevating than shows which are for 'men only.'"[11] In Meyersdale, Pennsylvania, the Rhoads Royal Minstrel Show, "Under Auspices of the Meyersdale Fire Department" (1913), was billed as "morally clean and entertaining to folks of all ages."[12] *Freckles,* also presented in Meyersdale (1913), was called "a Clean, Wholesome Song Play," which was "Endorsed by The Clergy of Every Denomination."[13] And an advertisement for *The Havoc* (1913) emphasized the moral lessons the play could teach:

> [The play] deals with a problem more vital than disease,
> drink or the white slave traffic.
> A POWERFUL SERMON IN DISGUISE
> With the medium of eloquent sarcasm and without a single
> offensive line it drives home a lesson that so many dramas of this
> nature have vainly sought to teach.

The link to moralizing religious sermons was made explicit: "'The Havoc' will work more good from a moral standpoint than a million Billy Sundays or reformers of that kind."[14]

In a few cases, articles warned potential audiences that the event possibly transgressed certain boundaries, while ultimately affirming the dominant moral code of the community. Prior to the Cornell Price Players' performance of *The Great White Slave Drama* (1918) at the Knights of Labor Opera House in Shawnee, Ohio, the *People's Advocate* warned, "It is guaranteed to be a good moral play, but children under 15 years of age will not be admitted unless accompanied by parent, or other suitable escort."[15] The resemblance to current restrictions on film audiences is striking, as is the affirmation of the ultimate morality of the production. The warning, with its titillating implication, also probably served to attract spectators.

Dancing carried a potentially morally transgressive quality, which had to be mitigated for the opera house. An announcement from 1879 for the "Dancing Club" in Paris, Kentucky, declared: "'The young gentlemen of our city have acquired a widespread and very enviable reputation for the perfect manner in which they get up affairs of this kind, and parties from a distance speak in high terms of the gallant attentions paid, and the hospitality shown them."[16] In another announcement for a Paris, Kentucky, event, dancing was considered morally beyond the pale. A "Social Circle" organized in 1882 by "young ladies and gentlemen of this city" was to be held at a local residence: "no dancing will be indulged in at any of the meetings."[17]

A clear distinction was drawn between morally and artistically acceptable dance performances and more explicitly sexual dance. The *Athens (Ohio) Messenger* declared in 1885, "The Young People's Dancing Club of Athens will inaugurate the new year with a grand terpsichorean entertainment at the City

Hall on New Year's Eve."[18] The grandiloquent term indicated that the dancing was morally acceptable and culturally uplifting. In Winchester, Kentucky, a fascinating account of the recital by "Mrs. Reid's Class," which was viewed by a full house "With Standing Room at a Premium," emphasized the "classical" costumes and dance of the young women, which provided moral and educational cover. The recital consisted of Delsarte dancing, a violin trio, and a Grecian drill, "which was one of the most beautiful numbers ever seen on a stage here. Each young lady was gowned in a flowing robe. . . . Miss Rawlings was a typical little Grecian Princess." Also noted was the section in which the children, whose ages were not mentioned, acted out the professions of the adults watching from the auditorium: "The hit of the evening in uniqueness was 'The Working Song,' by forty boys and girls. Each child was engaged in an occupation, little girls grinding coffee, sweeping, rocking their dolls, etc., while the little boys were busy with saws, hammers and every conceivable tool." Proceeds from the event went to the Ladies Guild of the Episcopal Church, to replace the roof, "which was recently blown off by a storm."[19] The dance was legitimated as a benefit for the church, and also as a way for the young to rehearse the acceptable gender stereotypes of their elders.

In towns dominated by the mining industry, some performances and dances strayed from acceptable moral codes and went late into the night, such as the 1933 production in Shawnee, Ohio, of "Sunny Side Up." It was announced as "a musical vaudeville in 7 big acts at the K of P [Knights of Pythias] Hall, tonight . . . Dance after show from 10 to ??"[20]

On the other hand, some performances set up expectations of moral transgression that they did not fulfill. The 1899 performance of the "European Sensation Burlesque" at the Ariel Opera House in Gallipolis, Ohio, "was quite a dissapointment [*sic*] to many who had the idea that it was to be a wild reckless, thrilling, high-kicking, skirt-lifting affair, that might shock the modesty of ladies." The same author was critical of the production, however, for its "too free use of the word d—n."[21] In Middlesborough, Kentucky, the management was concerned in 1902 that advertised promises might actually be fulfilled, and took pains to reassure the town that it would police an upcoming show: "The management of new theatre announce that notwithstanding the sum what [*sic*] lurid style of advertising for the Fannie Hill sho [*sic*] which is here next Monday night, nuthin [*sic*] indecent or in any degree offensive to the most refined taste will be permitted. The sho [*sic*] will be clean or be cleaned up."[22]

In a few cases, performers at the opera house did offend the town's morality. At the Ariel Opera House in Gallipolis, the comedians in *McDoodle and Poodle* (1896) were "vulgar, and some of the players were a trifle wicked."[23] In New Straitsville, Ohio, a performance by "the lady minstrels" succeeded in "disrupting" this predominantly coal-mining town: "At least our public morals received such a shock that they will not recover for some time."[24] In Maysville, Kentucky, the *Daily Evening Bulletin* reported in 1882 that a performance was banned because of its potential moral transgression: "The entertainment by Sullivan's Hibernian Blonds [*sic*], announced to be given at the opera house next Saturday will not take place. A lot of hand bills distributed about the city indicated that the exhibition would be of an improper character, and influenced Mayor January to refused [*sic*] to grant a license to the troupe."[25] The police attempted to prevent Duncan Clark's Female Minstrels (1892) from performing in Washington, Pennsylvania, because of their bad reputation. Clark posted a hundred-dollar bond to ensure that the show would be morally acceptable and was allowed to proceed with the performance, with police stationed in the opera house and the women performing in long dresses.[26]

After film became part of opera house entertainment, the morality of its depictions was also subject to regulation. The New Harlan Theatre announced in 1922: "It will be the policy of the management to arrange programs that will not only be entertaining but instructive and educational. Serial pictures have been reduced under present management from three per week to one each week, and an effort has been made to provide such serials as will be interesting and in a measure educational."[27] The concern over the social implications of risqué film and vaudeville was especially notable in the *Winchester (Kentucky) News* in 1911:

> Some measures should be taken by the managements of the various vaudeville and picture theatres towards the uplifting of the moral status of the motion picture shows throughout the country.
>
> A mother sends her small, wayward boy to a picture show thinking thus to keep him out of mischief, and in many cases the influence exerted by the pictures shown has a greater tendency to corrupt the boy than would that of half a dozen evil companions. Sin and degradation are exploited before the unfolding minds of our boys and girls, many times in rosy hues, and often there is an absolute lack of a moral lesson.
>
> . . . The motion picture shows have a influence which cannot fail to tend towards the corruption, if not of the acts, then surely of the pure young minds of the children who attend them.

The author goes on to advocate that motion pictures be "regulated and selected with judgment and only clean, wholesome and moral pictures shown."[28]

Some shows deliberately promoted sexually oriented material. This could mean simply featuring women in advertisements, such as in the *Meyersdale (Pennsylvania) Republican* photograph in 1912 of women lounging, with the caption,

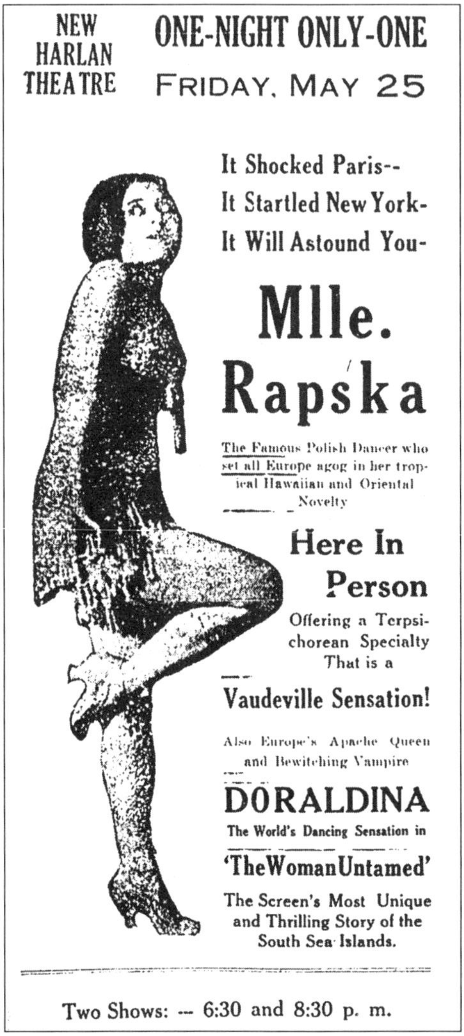

Advertisement for a vaudeville show in Harlan, Kentucky, in 1923, demonstrating the more sexually suggestive material in a mining town in the 1920s. From *Harlan (KY) Enterprise.*

"Some of the Beauty Chorus with 'MUTT AND JEFF.'"[29] In other cases, the sexual emphasis was more explicit. It is significant that the examples of shows cited here are from the 1920s, all taking place in Harlan, Kentucky, in a building called a "theater," not an "opera house." By the 1920s, there had been a loosening of strict moral codes, allowing for more overt sexual content and obviating the need for the "opera house" euphemism; and Harlan had a reputation as a tough mining town. A newspaper advertisement in the *Harlan Enterprise* with a photograph of women in a chorus line was underlined with the captions, "Geo. E. Wintz's

Advertisement for a vaudeville show in Harlan, Kentucky, in 1923. From *Harlan (KY) Enterprise.*

MODELS OF 1925 with NYRA BROWN, American Beauty" and "EVERY MODEL A PERFECT 36."[30] Another Harlan advertisement featured a picture of girls in bloomers called "THE PALM BEACH GIRLS."[31] An advertisement for "VAUDEVILLE" at the New Harlan Theatre proclaimed,

> Special Scenery and Wardrobe, New Spicy Vaudville [*sic*] talent—
> Cast of fourteen people (Mostly Girls) . . .
> 12—FLAPPERS—12[32]

A help wanted advertisement in Harlan, Kentucky, offered employment to local young women, using the cover of family values:

> WANTED AT ONCE
>
> Girls that can sing, to join Family Vaudeville and Musical Comedy Co.; also girl piano player; good pay; work year round; show going to Florida for the winter. Call for Mr. or Mrs. Dunbar, Kelly Hotel, Sunday afternoon.[33]

Outright scandal enmeshed the opera house in Pithole, Pennsylvania, in 1865–66, demonstrating the opera house's potential for morally liminal status and the ultimate enforcement of the dominant moral code. Mlle Brignoli was a popular local performer, playing the violin and singing, but a handbill accused her of abandoning her husband and two children. She denied the accusation and continued performing in the opera house and singing in the local Catholic church on Sundays. The manager kept her on and inserted a note in the program: "Her valuable services are still to be employed for her and our benefit. Furthermore, her efforts to please will be rewarded by a benefit at no distant date." The editor of the *Daily Record* supported her cause, emphasizing her morality and religion:

> Mlle. Brignoli, pretty and graceful dancer and singer, who conducts herself with propriety, goes to church regularly and spreads her apron frequently for contributions from her many masculine admirers, seems to have a disagreeable appendage—a husband.
>
> He, wanting to share her fortune published an address to the people of Pithole, which if true would be as disgraceful to him as to her. The Catholics have taken it up and her friends have purchased several hundred tickets and showered her with triumphant applause.

But during her benefit performance someone stole her purse, sixty dollars, a gold watch, and a locket from her dressing room. She was subsequently eased out of the opera house and then dropped out of sight.[34]

Audience behavior was also subject to community regulation at the opera house. If the opera house was to be a morally safe zone, the social code had to be enforced in the auditorium as well as onstage. According to Lawrence W. Levine, late-nineteenth-century audiences were lectured on proper behavior in order to enforce a new moral code: "Nothing seems to have troubled the new arbiters of culture more than the nineteenth-century practice of spontaneous expressions of pleasure and disapproval in the forms of cheers, yells, gesticulations, hisses, boos, stamping of feet, whistling, crying for encores, and applause." Once audiences had been properly trained, the behavior changed: "The passive politeness that came to characterize audiences in American theaters and vaudeville houses after the turn of the century became familiar as well in the movie houses that soon dotted the nation. . . . These were far from the raucous, independent audiences of the nineteenth century."[35]

This trend toward creating and enforcing a code of morally acceptable audience behavior can be explained by what Mary Ann Clawson calls "the imposition of decorum and the feminization of theatre audiences,"[36] or what Levine dubs "the cult of etiquette."[37] Theaters were "regendered" in the course of the nineteenth century, according to Butsch, as theatrical performance was domesticated into family entertainment, audiences became feminized at matinees, and audience behavior was tamed. By the mid-nineteenth century, audience behavior was more regulated by managers, and women felt freer to go to the theater.[38] There was still a clear gender distinction in the perception of audience behavior at vaudeville performances: "boys" were perceived as perpetrators of gallery pranks, while "ladies" acted as censors.[39] Etiquette books promoted new feminized standards for theatergoers, including a prohibition on drinking and gaming.[40]

Tony Pastor and B. F. Keith, two early innovators of vaudeville (see chapter 9), are often credited with advancing this new code of audience behavior. According to Levine, Keith and Pastor "promised audiences unprecedented comfort and courtesy," but "they demanded order and decorum in return."[41] A sign in Keith's theaters read:

> Gentlemen will kindly avoid the stamping of the feet and pounding of canes on the floor, and greatly oblige the Management. All applause is best shown by the clapping of hands.
>
> Please don't talk during the acts, as it annoys those about you, and prevents a perfect hearing of the entertainment.[42]

On one occasion at Keith's theater in Providence, Rhode Island, those seated in the topmost gallery were making noise, which elicited the following response, according to Keith's account:

> I stepped out onto the stage and explained to those portions of the audience that it would not be allowed to continue these demonstrations any longer. I said, "You can't do that here. . . . I know that you mean no harm by it, and only do it from the goodness of your hearts, but others in the audience don't like it, and it does not tend to improve the character of the entertainment, and I know you will agree with me that it is better to omit hereafter." As I walked off, I received a round of applause from the whole house including the gallery. And that was the last of the noise from the gallery gods.

Sign prohibiting tobacco use in Marlin's Opera House, Brookville, Pennsylvania (1886), where audience behavior was subject to newspaper criticism. Photo by author.

In this theater, men were required to put out their cigars, and women had to take off their hats. According to Keith: "The public needed to be educated in these matters." Ushers acted as the in-house police, enforcing promptness and silence. They carried signs around the theaters with admonitions regarding smoking and hats. Keith seemed to feel he had been successful when he wrote, in 1898, "The character of the vaudeville audience has notably improved in recent years."[43]

The architecture of opera houses was also transformed to reflect and enforce this new emphasis on morality: the pit, formerly an area primarily for men to stand or sit on benches, was transformed into the orchestra section, with seats for middle-class spectators of both sexes. All the opera houses examined here exhibit this architectural transformation. Changes in lighting technology also affected audience behavior. Gas lighting, an innovation in the early nineteenth century, allowed the auditorium to be partially darkened, and electric light allowed for an auditorium lit only by the reflected light from the stage. This lighting differential focused the audience's attention on the stage, if for no other reason than that it was hard for spectators to see each other. According to Clawson, "Theatre thus became less a social and more a spectatorial event."[44] With the combination of orchestra seating, a darkened auditorium, and rules of behavior, audiences became passive consumers of entertainment.

The creation of the opera house, then, was the creation of a feminized space, as Clawson observes:

> The shift toward gentility and decorum was also an attack on the theatre as a men's club. Entrepreneurs who initially realized that the presence of women guaranteed the respectability of their theatres now recognized them as a lucrative new market. By 1900 they constituted a major audience presence at vaudeville shows, now promoted as family entertainment, and at legitimate-theatre performances, increasingly defined as the special province of women audiences.[45]

The result was a building with a sharp gender distinction: a feminized space in the opera house below and a masculinized space in the fraternal lodge above (see chapter 6).

While opera houses did not have dozens of ushers, as did Keith's theaters, the same changing codes of audience behavior were evident. The *Jackson (Ohio) Standard Journal* criticized spectators at the high school graduation ceremonies at the Grand Opera House in 1883: "The only thing to mar the enjoyment of the commencement was the conduct of a lot of idiots in the gallery. These should have been dragged out of the building."[46] *Penalty of Pride,* performed at the New Straitsville (Ohio) Opera House in 1904, was "a complete success," according to the *Record*. However, "the performers were handicapped by the intolerable noise that was kept up and allowed to exist by the Opera House management. Strenuous action is necessary to quell these disturbances or the people who pay their money to patronize the shows will 'cut them out.'"[47]

The audience of 1890 in Marlin's Opera House in Brookville, Pennsylvania, was chastised by the *Jeffersonian Democrat* following the production of *Mother Goose* by the Young Ladies' Missionary Society of the Presbyterian Church: "We regret the necessity of calling attention to the disorder in the gallery the first night. It seems to us that some measures should be taken to stop this annoying feature of all our public gatherings. Young men and boys who disturb audiences should know that they mark themselves as unfit to go where respectable people are."[48] The statement implies that the opera house is a place for respectable people; hooligans should be excluded or their behavior controlled.

Behavior in Brookville presumably did not improve; the newspaper escalated the attack by identifying an offending public official at a performance: "One of the disgusting and disagreeable things was the indecorous and ungentlemanly iuterruption [*sic*] of Mr. Joseph Davis by unearthly noises from the gallery, part of which, we are informed was made by a borough peace officer. If the charge is correct the Council should remove the guilty party and put in his place someone who will help preserve the peace instead of create disorder."[49]

There are no further records of criticism in Brookville until nine months later, when the *Jeffersonian Democrat* seemed to realize that the attacks were ineffective, and that the opera house manager should be the new target. At a performance of the "Stanley Macy 'Kindergarten' troupe," "The order in the gallery [was] the most disgraceful ever had in any house in Brookville. No landlord would permit such order in his barroom; and if the management expect the public to patronize them they will have to see to it that the right men are there to keep order. Some of the 'toughs' amused themselves by spitting on the people down in the parquet."[50] Presumably the opera house should be a far cry from the barroom, a socially liminal zone that would not even tolerate such behavior.

Three months later, the *Jeffersonian Democrat* writer again chastised the audience, this time for its behavior at the high school commencement: "There was fairly good order, but at times the noise, especially in the gallery, was annoying to those who wished to give special attention to the exercises. When the next commencement comes 'round the gallery should either be closed or persons should be placed there to see that absolute quiet is observed when the pupils are reciting their exercises."[51] This statement makes explicit the exclusion of undesirable people and/or the direct control of audience behavior. The writer was also critical of latecomers to the ceremony: "Another inconvenience, and more than that, annoyance, is to have persons coming in after the exercises have commenced. It is disturbing to those present who desire to hear and enjoy the program, and worrying to the performers. Miss Ames' salutatory was marred greatly by the noise of persons entering late, and the reading of her original poem . . . was almost spoiled to a large portion of the audience by the noise in the gallery."[52]

The role of women at the opera house demonstrates the gendered nature of this struggle over behavior. Women were perceived as improving the demeanor of opera house audiences in Athens, Ohio, according to an 1886 article in the *Messenger:* "The very large number of ladies that have been in attendance at the several political meetings" at the opera house "exerts a noticeable beneficial influence on the order and civil bearings of such promiscuous assemblies."[53] Presumably attendees of male-only events had been misbehaving, and their conduct was elevated by the presence of "the ladies." For a Republican meeting at the opera house in the Athens City Hall, the *Messenger* noted: "We are authoritatively authorized to extend a special invitation to the Ladies to contribute the morale of their presence."[54]

The nature of some events may have constrained women from attending. The audience was entirely male for an exhibition boxing match (1898) in Gallipolis, Ohio,[55] and a women's club (see chapter 8) opposed a boxing match in Nelsonville, Ohio. A woman's place was apparently not at a boxing match.

Some events were specifically billed as being "for the ladies," emphasizing their moral rectitude. In Maysville, Kentucky, the *Daily Evening Bulletin* announced that the Armstrong Minstrel Troupe (1882) "will give a refined entertainment, free from the least exhibition of coarseness. The ladies are invited to be present and they are assured they may do so safely."[56] The following year, "Howorth's Double Show Grand Hibernica" promised "more fun without vulgarity than any company on the road."[57] At the turn of the century, the *Daily Evening Bulletin* promoted the Holman Opera Company as "elegant, chaste and refined in every particular. Everybody must attend, ESPECIALLY THE LADIES."[58]

Women's hats, however, were an area of behavioral struggle in the opera house, especially considering the large fashionable hats of the period. The Ohio legislature even passed a law banning women from wearing large hats into theaters and opera houses.[59] The *Maysville (Kentucky) Daily Evening Bulletin* reflected this concern:

> We admire the custom of the ladies removing their hats. Any old tousled head of natural hair looks better than a great big turkey feather or ostrich plume.
>
> Right in front of us was the biggest hat of the biggest kind. Every hat in the orchestra circle went down except that one on that beautiful head a few short inches in front of us. The fair owner looked to the right—to the left—and not so much as a high back comb obstructed her view.
>
> Then she turned around nervously and looked behind her.
>
> Her gaze rested for one brief second on the forlorn looking chub behind her, whose eyes were turned upward in an attitude of prayer and supplication, trying to read John I. Winter's ad. near to the top of the drop curtain.
>
> A second hurried glance to the right and left and down came that hat—God bless her.[60]

A reporter from the *Louisville Courier-Journal* visiting Paris, Kentucky, in 1893 found the hat behavior more creditable: "Paris is a good show town . . . A feature worthy of emulation everywhere is the ladies' cloakroom and here the offending hat is laid away until the opera is over and nobody is plagued into profanity by dodging around to see what is on the stage. That is worth the price of admission."[61]

African Americans had more than their behavior constrained: if they did attend integrated events (as opposed to the specifically black community events described in chapter 8), they were segregated into the "colored balcony," as existed in Paris, Kentucky.[62] In other cases, such as in "model" towns in Kentucky, companies built completely separate entertainment sites for blacks.

Native Americans were considered a curiosity at Marlin's Opera House (Brookville, Pennsylvania) in 1890, when the *Jeffersonian Democrat* took special note that "Pawnee Bill and several of his Indians attended the Uncle Tom's Cabin show . . . and were quite a curiosity to many present."[63] The comment suggests that Native Americans at the opera house were notable exceptions to the audience norm. (In addition, it is intriguing that they attended *Uncle Tom's Cabin.*)

Some opera house performances featured female impersonators, which could be considered transgressive today but seems to have been readily accepted by nineteenth-century opera house audiences. According to Laurence Senelick, female impersonators were a common part of variety theater by the mid–nineteenth century: "audiences accepted, with varying degrees of enthusiasm, the ambiguous figure of the adult male decked out in seductive feminine frippery. . . . By 1860 the female impersonator was a fixture of the entertainment world." Female impersonators were especially prominent in minstrel shows, which had all-male casts, and were interpreted as simply another of the wide variety of white caricatures of African Americans featured in minstrelsy. Female impersonators performed dances derived from the Jim Crow dance and later the "Topsy" character derived from *Uncle Tom's Cabin,* "rubber-legged acrobatics with limbs concealed in absurd frills and furbelows" or "spastic antics."[64]

After the Civil War, female impersonators evolved into a specialty role: the male soprano, who was a respectable, refined "yellow gal" of minstrelsy. These characters were considered harmless and beyond reproach, which was significant in a time when display of women's bodies was an important part of other more risqué forms of variety theater. This context of female impersonation is critical to its reception. According to Senelick, female impersonation was socially acceptable if it was part of a morally respectable framework, for example in minstrelsy or vaudeville, but not in the more questionable variety shows: "By 1900 refined vaudeville had leached the specialty of any overt sexuality. As a solo act emphasizing technical expertise and quick-change, and sandwiched between other displays of virtuosity, it remained safely within the theatrical frame."[65] Thus female impersonators at opera houses could be considered morally acceptable, provided they occurred in the proper performative frame.

Two minstrel groups in Maysville, Kentucky, included female impersonators: McIntyre, Heath and Bellmont's Mammoth Southern Minstrels in 1882 ("Roselle, in his female impersonations, is a good card, and makes his changes rapidly"[66]) and Baird's Mammoth Minstrels in 1883 ("Ace Leroy, one of the best female impersonators in the burnt-cord field"[67]). In Winchester, Kentucky,

Ariel Opera House, Gallipolis, Ohio (1895), where the management of the opera house became an issue of public debate. Photo by author.

"Gilbert AtLee Eldridge, the impersonator" (1909), performed at the opera house under the auspices of the Ladies' Aid Society of the First Christian Church: "Fourteen different characters will be represented."[68] And in 1914, the Oil City, Pennsylvania, opera house presented "Miss Lilly Gaston, widely known as the best and greatest male impersonator, who sings and dances in the garb of a man, possesses several medals of honors from such people as King George of England, also the Czar of Russia, in commendation of her clever acting."[69]

Finally, the management of the opera house was central to this social understanding. While the opera house may have been in a privately owned building (commercial or fraternal), the opera house manager was a de facto public official, in that he (generally) was in charge of booking touring events and acting as a gatekeeper for locally produced events. The extent to which the opera house manager was subject to public debate is clearest in Gallipolis, Ohio.

The management of the Ariel Opera House was a hotly debated issue in 1898; newspaper articles complained about the quality of performances and advocated that the current manager be fired and a new one hired. The *Tribune* criticized one production harshly and extended the denunciation to the manager himself: "If this is the kind of entertainments our Opera House managers are going to turn loose on our citizens this season, it would be better that the doors be closed." The author added that the theater company, however inferior, agreed with his assessment: "The manager of the Leon Washburn Minstrel Company was strong in his condemnation of the management of our Opera House. He said that it is the most badly managed house that he has visited in all his years in the show business." (The writer did add, however, that the minstrel company could also "improve matters by having a better show.")[70]

A few months later the newspaper lobbied directly for a new manager: "Gallipolis playgoers are certainly getting it 'in the neck' this season. What the Opera House needs is a competent manager, one who will only book good shows and sidetrack the 'snide ones.' It is a question who is the manager of the house, but nevertheless the fact remains that he is incompetent. Give us a new manager or close the house." And, indeed, the opera house had a new manager the following season.[71]

These issues of management and moral transgression come together in an incident in Nelsonville, Ohio, when the manager of Stuart's Opera House booked a production of *September Morn* during the 1920–21 season. He billed it as "racy" and local churches succeeded in drumming him out as manager.[72] In this case, the social understanding was broken, and the transgressor was banished.

Events at the opera house were subject to community regulation. Those that upheld the dominant, family-oriented code were praised. Those that transgressed the perceived boundaries were criticized or banned. Audiences similarly had to conform to a code of behavior, with transgressors publicly singled out. While the opera house was a crossroads of the community, and staged the life of that community, traffic on the stage and in the auditorium was tightly controlled.

PART TWO

The Opera House in Context

CHAPTER THREE

The Opera House in the Landscape

In order for the role of the opera house in its local culture to be understood, the opera house must be located within the landscape of that culture. The field of landscape studies, a branch of geography initiated in the early 1950s by John Brinckerhoff Jackson and practiced by D. W. Meinig, Peirce F. Lewis, Richard V. Francaviglia, and others, can be helpful here. The goal of cultural landscape studies is to better understand culture through the examination of what Jackson calls "*synthetic* space, a man-made system of spaces superimposed on the face of the land."[1] As Paul Groth explains, "*Landscape* denotes the interaction of people and place: a social group and its spaces, particularly the space to which the group belongs and from which its members derive some part of their shared identity and meaning. All human interaction with nature can be considered as cultural landscape."[2] According to Meinig, landscape is "not something to look at but to live in."[3]

The discipline of cultural landscape studies "seeks to understand the lives of ordinary people," according to Meinig.[4] Given the use of the opera house by ordinary townspeople, landscape studies may be used to examine the opera house in the context of its local culture. As Lewis notes, "Elements of a cultural landscape make little cultural sense if they are studied outside of their geographic (i.e., locational) context."[5]

The ordinary quality of opera houses in the town landscape is precisely what makes cultural landscape studies a helpful methodology. The focus is on how people use "ordinary" landscapes, such as the

Cotrill's Opera House, Thomas, West Virginia (1902), as it appears today under restoration. The opera house is the tall building left of center, blending into the street facade. This is a typical mining town street, as it snakes between a stream and a steep hill. Photo by author.

main street, company town, garage, mobile home, and road, "to establish their identity, articulate their social relations, and derive cultural meaning."[6] Vernacular landscapes are seen as "crucibles of cultural meaning and environmental experience,"[7] since "all human landscape has cultural meaning."[8] Lewis is adamant on this point: "Most items in the human landscape are no more and no less important than other items—in terms of their role as clues to culture. Thus, the McDonald's hamburger stand is just as important a cultural symbol (or clue) as the Empire State Building."[9]

The approach of cultural landscape studies is particular, historical, and contextual, suggesting questions such as the following: What is the overall city layout? Where is the opera house located in the city? What buildings are located near the opera house? Who owns the opera house? Where in the building is the opera house located? What other facilities are also in the building? Does the audience enter the theater through a single, common entrance or through separate entries? What is the relationship between the public and private places? What is the opera house used for besides theatrical performance? Is the audience a diversified representation of the community or made up of a single ethnic, religious, or gender group?

Marlin's Opera House, Brookville, Pennsylvania (1886), showing the opera house (left) as part of the street facade. The tall windows on the second and third floors are clues to the existence of an opera house inside. Photo by David L. Taylor.

The opera house was one of the major public buildings in town, along with the town hall—in some cases, it was in the same building as the town hall. The opera house usually stood at or near the town center, on or near Main Street, which Francaviglia calls an "architectural climax of two- and three-story buildings," with the "highest density of buildings in the town."[10] Politically significant buildings, such as the courthouse, town hall, armory, and jail, as well as culturally significant buildings, including stores, hotels, barbershops, restaurants, banks, and the opera house, surrounded the square.[11] This public space at the center of town was the "container" or "frame" for the political and cultural life of the town.[12] The opera house did not stand alone, but operated in the political, economic, and social context of these other vital buildings.

These Appalachian opera houses were primarily in towns dominated by coal mining. Coal mining produced distinctive patterns of urban landscape, and therefore affected the location of the opera house and its relation to the landscape. For example, the pattern of streets can tell the story of the town's development, as Francaviglia observes: "Are the communities clustered, scattered, or

Stuart's Opera House, Nelsonville, Ohio (1879) (*right of center*), showing an opera house on a town square. Note the tall windows on the second floor. Reprinted with permission of Stuart's Opera House Archives, Nelsonville, Ohio.

located in any particular pattern? Are these communities laid out in regular, geometric patterns, or helter-skelter?"[13] Company "model" towns, such as Benham, Kentucky, tended to have a more rectilinear layout, as well as a planned uniformity: "A mining district usually has less visual variation from location to location, and within any particular location, if one company is in control. Normally, companies try to achieve the greatest degree of design control possible, including regularity of street pattern layout and architectural design of all structures and buildings. . . . The result is a predictable visual order and regularization of design."[14] Independent towns, such as Cumberland, Kentucky, tended to have more "visual variety," because there was no centralized town design. Geography also determined a mining town's development: "Its crooked, winding, narrow main street, irregular, postage stamp-size lots, and maze of narrow side streets tackling the steep hillsides impart a sense of mystique and beauty that early speculators probably never anticipated."[15]

The commercial district of a mining town tended to be larger and more densely packed than that of a comparable nonmining town, because there were more single males who were dependent on others for goods and services. Francaviglia suggests that looking at the relationship and density of these elemental structures can reveal the nature of the town's origin and planning:

> The location and design of institutional buildings (such as town halls, miners' unions, schools and churches) say much about the organization of public or social space in mining towns. The density of construction, competition for commercial space, paucity of flat space on which to build, and emphasis on intense indoor social activities such as drinking, gambling, and carousing may result in relatively little open space being set aside for parks and squares, especially in those mining towns that developed in the nineteenth century.[16]

Opera houses were located not merely in a physical landscape, but also in a notional location—in the heads of town residents. Lewis observes that "any landscape is composed not only of what lies before our eyes but what lies within our heads."[17] Kevin Lynch, who developed this model of the "image of the city" in dwellers' minds, defines certain elements of the image:

1. Paths: "the channels along with the observer customarily, occasionally, or potentially moves," including streets, walkways, transit lines, canals, and railroads.
2. Edges: "the linear elements not used or considered as paths by the observer," such as boundaries, linear breaks, shores, edges of development, walls, barriers and seams.
3. Districts: "the medium-to-large sections of the city, conceived of as having two-dimensional extent, which the observer mentally enters 'inside of,' and which are recognizable as having some common, identifying character."
4. Nodes: "the strategic spots in a city . . . the focus and epitome of a district, over which their influence radiates and of which they stand as a symbol."
5. Landmarks: reference points, including buildings, signs, stores, mountains, towers and domes.[18]

This model is helpful in understanding the location of the opera house in the town and its role in local culture. The opera house was on a major path (main street) and in a defined district (the center of town). It served as a node in that so many lines of the community crossed through the opera house, given the diverse range of townspeople attending events. The opera house was a landmark in that the building was architecturally prominent.

Fisher Opera House, Zaleski, Ohio (1884), originally, and to this day, the tallest building in Vinton County, Ohio. Photo by author.

Many opera houses served as reference points in the community. Countless advertisements refer to the location of businesses in relation to the opera house. Shawnee, Ohio, for example, held a parade in 1918 in honor of the young men going off to war, and the prominence of the opera house is evident from the description of the parade route, which went "over the principal streets and halted on Main Street in front of the K. of P. [Knights of Pythias] opera house, where a splendid program was rendered."[19] The importance of the theater in Harlan, Kentucky, is shown in a 1922 article referring to it as "the largest building in Harlan except for the court house."[20] The list of the most important buildings in Benham, Kentucky, refers, in order, to the theater, store, post office, lodge hall, and medical building.[21]

Marlin's Opera House, Brookville, Pennsylvania (1886). View from an opera house window to the city hall, showing the proximity of these two essential buildings. Photo by author.

Marvin Carlson draws a distinction between "urban facade" theaters and "urban hub" theaters that can be helpful in understanding how these opera houses functioned as nodes and landmarks. According to Carlson, a facade theater is "a single element in the facade streetscape of the modern city . . . a row of contiguous facades." These theaters had a commercial basis, as Carlson makes clear: "The most valuable part of the structure was the ground-floor facade, where the store made its critical contact with potential customers and attempted to attract them inside."[22] This row of buildings that included the opera house was usually detailed, formal, and distinctive, with a repetition of styles; all the buildings were fewer than four stories tall.[23] While large urban facade theaters were often closely integrated into an architectural continuum, not distinct or calling attention to themselves,[24] small-town opera houses were distinct and designed to function as landmarks. The ground floor, which was most visible and accessible to passersby, contained storefronts. The opera house, for which people would more likely plan ahead, was placed on the less-accessible second floor. In the fraternal buildings, the top floor was reserved for the organization's meeting rooms, with the two lower floors providing the income to make the building self-supporting.

Pierce Opera House, Sharpsville, Pennsylvania (1871). View from an opera house window to the owner's house. Photo by author.

Opera houses in town halls are examples of Carlson's urban hub theaters, which were characterized by "physical isolation," with multiple views of the building "that made these public monuments both landmarks and nodes."[25] Like the public theaters of Greece and Rome, these opera houses "were major civic monuments, which held prominent positions in the urban text."[26] These opera houses can also be compared to a description of an ideal theater written in eighteenth-century France: "It ought to be isolated on all sides and therefore situated in the middle of a square. . . . This square should be entered by several streets, the main ones aligned with the main lines of the edifice, so as to es-

Twin City Opera House, McConnelsville, Ohio (1892). An example of an opera house as an urban hub. The building also housed the city hall, and was situated on the central town square. Photo by Joseph M. Berman.

tablish suitable vistas, in order that those who are arriving can easily enjoy its aspect."[27]

The prominent position of the opera house in the town landscape is quite evident in the opera houses studied here. Murphy's Theatre (1865), in Pithole, Pennsylvania, was, at three stories tall, the largest building in town,[28] and the Fisher Opera House (1884) in Zaleski, Ohio, was—and still is—the tallest building in Vinton County. The opera house in Tarentum, Pennsylvania (1886), was in the largest commercial building in town, with stores, a skating rink, and a dance hall.[29] Many opera houses, including the Condron Opera House (1873) in Hollidaysburg, Pennsylvania, were on a corner of the central town square.[30] The Benham Theater (Kentucky, 1922) was on the town square, along with the school, church, and company store. Several opera houses were built close to the city hall or courthouse: Mozart's Hall (1883) in Carlisle, Kentucky, is on the main street across from the courthouse; the Nova Theatre (1937) in Cumberland, Kentucky, is across the street from city hall; the Harrodsburg Opera House (Kentucky, 1905) faces the main street, surrounded by the city hall and the fire station; the Winchester Opera House (Kentucky, c. 1880) is one block from the courthouse; Marlin's Opera House (1884) is on the town square in Brookville, Pennsylvania, across from the courthouse, and in the downtown's largest privately owned

Winchester Opera House, Winchester, Kentucky (c. 1880). An example of a prominent opera house on a corner in the center of town. Reprinted with permission of Postcard Illustrations of American Theatres and Opera Houses collection, developed by William L. Slout and housed at the Museum of Repertoire Americana, a museum at Midwest Old Threshers, Mt. Pleasant, Iowa.

building. Hoof's Opera House (1889) of Point Pleasant, West Virginia, was on the main street near the post office and major hotel. The Elkins Opera House (West Virginia, 1898) was on a prominent corner, near the major hotel, city hall, and the railroad station. Thirteen of the opera houses studied here were actually in the same building as the town hall: examples are the opera houses in Athens, Ohio (1874); McConnelsville, Ohio (1892); Chesterhill, Ohio (1908); and Fairmont, West Virginia (1870). In Buckhannon, West Virginia, the opera house (1854) was in the courthouse; when the room was not needed for circuit court it was used for speeches, lectures, religious meetings, school commencements, and performances.

In other cases, the opera house was close to the owner's house or primary business. The Pierce Opera House (1872) in Sharpsville, Pennsylvania, overlooks the owner's house, as well as the church he attended, and the Tabb Opera House (1909) in Mount Sterling, Kentucky, was located right behind Tabb's coal and feed yard.

Opera houses, like other buildings on main streets after 1850, tended to be designed in a formal, Victorian Italianate or Gothic style, which provided a "sense of permanence and confidence."[31] Francaviglia describes the "high style"

Einstein Opera House, Blairsville, Pennsylvania (1904), showing the large scale of the opera house building in the town landscape. Photo by author.

of elemental structures in mining towns: "Town halls, opera houses, and fire stations were also likely to be impressive storefront-style buildings with towers and cupolas. Being rather prosperous, truly cosmopolitan, and fairly civic minded, mining towns abounded in impressive institutional buildings. Generally, mining communities are richer than surrounding nonmining towns in buildings that reveal cultural diversity."[32] Architectural detailing, in the form of metal trim, iron columns, window details, and cornices, was readily available and affordable after the Civil War, because foundries built to make weapons could be retooled for making standardized cast-iron architectural treatments.[33] Continuous rows of columns, pediments, and cornices gave towns a sense of grandeur, even if they were false fronts: "When constructed side by side along Main Street, they tended to make the streetscape appear far more impressive, and rather more complete, than it actually was."[34] In this continuous facade, certain buildings stood out as "exclamation points"—buildings with turrets, oriels, bay windows with towers.[35] As monuments designed to attract attention, opera houses were frequently such exclamation points.

The opera house's relationship to the community can also be seen in the other businesses and offices in the opera house building. The Washington Opera

Grand Opera House (*center*), Portsmouth, Ohio (date unknown), demonstrating the scale and centrality of the opera house. Reprinted with permission of Postcard Illustrations of American Theatres and Opera Houses collection, developed by William L. Slout and housed at the Museum of Repertoire Americana, a museum at Midwest Old Threshers, Mt. Pleasant, Iowa.

House in Maysville, Kentucky, was owned by and also housed the town fire department. The old opera house had burned down, and the fire department raised the money for a new one. In this way the fire department deflected potential criticism for the loss, gained a revenue source for its building, and could claim credit for supporting the cultural life of the community. In turn, the opera house was inoculated against moral charges, since it provided income for the town's fire protection. Architecturally, the fire department was prominent in the building, with its entrance in the center of the facade, flanked by stores. Upon the opera house's opening the *Daily Evening Bulletin* declared it "a handsome improvement and a monument to the enterprise of the Washington Fire Company."[36]

Businesses housed in the opera house building were central and essential to town life, and, as described in the previous chapter, had to uphold the town's moral code. The Knights of Pythias Opera House in Shawnee, Ohio (1881), housed the offices of *The People's Advocate* newspaper, as well as the lodge's meeting rooms. The Carlisle Opera House building in Carlisle, Pennsylvania (1898), also housed a barber shop, billiard room, and bowling alley, with the opera house on the second floor and Masons' meeting rooms on the third floor.[37] The Grandin Opera House in Tidioute, Pennsylvania (1872), had the Grandin Brothers' bank on the first floor, as well as the Andrews and Company Hardware and Well Fitting Store, for the oil industry of the region, and the Bolard Brothers Drug Store. The second floor was used for offices, including that of the town newspaper, and the opera house was on the third floor.[38] Walton's Opera House in Stanford, Kentucky, housed the town's post office and a restaurant. Hoof's Opera House in Point Pleasant, West Virginia (1886), contained the mayor's office, the telephone company, and apartments. Finally, the Struthers Library Theatre in Warren, Pennsylvania (1883), contained, as the name suggests, the town's public library, as well as stores and the post office.

In all these cases, the opera house was central to the town landscape and culture and functioned as a node and landmark in the town. It was one of the elemental structures that marked a town's mature stage of development and demonstrated its cultural aspirations.

CHAPTER FOUR

The Opera House in a "Strange Land"

The location of these opera houses in Appalachia is integral to their nature and identity. These opera houses emerged during coal mining, railroad, and population booms in Appalachia. They were a place for the people of Appalachia to gather across generational, class, religious, and racial lines. Opera houses are therefore central to understanding Appalachia, and vice versa.

Geographers and historians have argued for years over what constitutes Appalachia, but the states studied here are included in any assessment, with the occasional exception of southeast Ohio. Appalachian studies emerged in the second half of the twentieth century as a discrete discipline, and the field has provoked great debate over whether the people in the region share common traits. One author conducted a metastudy of the literature on Appalachia, and found that certain traits were frequently applied to the people: independence, religious fundamentalism, strong family ties, life in harmony with nature, fatalism, traditionalism, honor, fearlessness, allegiance, suspicion of government, and born trader.[1] Others find these terms to be generalities that steamroll over the differences and diversity of the region, and perhaps meaningless when applied to a large population across a wide region.

The idea of Appalachia as a defined region was formed in the 1870s, when Appalachia was discovered by "local color" writers. In 1873, Will Wallace Harney wrote a travelogue entitled "A Strange Land and Peculiar People" for *Lippincott's Magazine;* 125 short stories and 90 sketches were published over the following twenty years about life in

Appalachia.[2] Appalachia and its people were perceived as deviant and "other" compared to the dominant culture and perceived norm of the United States. Appalachia was terra incognita, and all the more fascinating because it was within the United States. Appalachia captured writers' and readers' imaginations because it became identified with the people and habits of America's past. William Goodell Frost, president of Berea College in Kentucky and one of the "inventors" of Appalachia, called Appalachians "our contemporary ancestors" in 1899. One reason for this perception of Appalachia's cultural separation from the United States was its physical isolation. The mountainous terrain complicated travel and communication to and from the rest of the United States and within the region itself. Attaining a sense of community with the rest of the country and with fellow Appalachians was difficult. The opera house played an important role in bringing peoples of the region together.

The period under examination here, the 1860s to the 1930s, is especially significant in terms of this perceived otherness of Appalachia. This was a time of rapid changes for native-born white Americans, filled with social and economic traumas: reconstruction, rapid industrialization, growth in the number and size of cities, migration from the southern United States to the north, immigration from southern and eastern Europe, labor conflict, political scandal, and populist agitation for reforms and the redistribution of wealth. Whites reacted with Jim Crow race laws, anti-immigration laws, and strict labor laws.[3] In a country that increasingly perceived itself as being unified and homogeneous, Appalachia was perceived as different, "in American but not of America."[4]

Appalachia was a relatively undeveloped and unpopulated area as recently as 1870. Farming was common in the region through the first two-thirds of the nineteenth century, but by 1865 some unproductive farms were already being abandoned.[5] The region's hilly terrain was not well suited to farming, especially with the introduction of machine-powered tractors in the twentieth century, and mining became more lucrative. Fueled by the coal industry, the area developed rapidly following the Civil War through the early decades of the twentieth century. Following the Great Depression and the decline of coal mining, many areas slowly returned to their natural state. It is ironic that while many now view development as unidirectional—from undeveloped to developed—Appalachia has experienced zigs and zags. Development was slow and steady from roughly 1800 to 1865 and exponential from 1865 to the 1920s; the latter period was followed by a sustained reversal of fortune. Thus many areas in Appalachia were far more developed, with a greater population, more industry, and more towns, a hundred years ago than today. Industry and people have moved away and towns have disappeared. The boom period for Appalachia—the 1860s to the 1920s—is precisely the era of the opera house.

Before the coal-mining era, people in rural Appalachia lived on subsistence farming, producing enough food for survival but not enough to sell for profit and a living wage. Appalachia had the largest percentage of self-sufficient farms in the United States from the early 1800s to the early 1900s, and as late as the 1930s Appalachia had the highest concentration of low-income farms.[6] During the nineteenth century, according to Crandall A. Shifflett, life for Appalachian farmers "deteriorated . . . into a desperate struggle to make a living." Subsistence farming "was not the Arcadian myth of a care-free, independent, untrammeled yeomanry, but an endless round of work and struggle against the forces of population growth, shrinking farmsteads, and limited opportunities."[7] The difficulty of farming in Appalachia, with its hills and thin, rocky soil, was a reason why many Appalachians preferred coal towns to subsistence farming, despite the dangers and uncertain employment of mining. Coal mining offered a new hope; as the wife of one miner observed, "People found mining to be a nice way to make money."[8]

Industrialization, via coal, the railroads, and other industries, transformed the society and economy of Appalachia following the Civil War. Ironically, the period of Appalachia's industrialization was also the time that Appalachia was being discovered by local color writers, who proclaimed the region's unsullied natural state. Railroads carried lumber and coal out, but also brought new manufactured goods into the region: food, dry goods, furniture, supplies, and merchandise from mail-order catalogs. This once isolated region became connected with the rest of the country through the telegraph and telephone. The infusion of money and immigrants into the Appalachia area brought banks, newspapers, running water, sidewalks, and fire departments. One of these developments was the opera house, with sites of entertainment being common as the frontier moved west and towns were formed.

Coal was not the only industry in Appalachia. Salt and iron were among the first industries in the area, and they contributed to the development of the coal industry: coal was used to fire the salt brines in the early nineteenth century, and after the salt industry declined, coal mining took its place. Iron furnaces operated in the 1870s and 1880s. Iron ore was prevalent in Appalachia, and charcoal was used to fire the furnaces initially, followed by coal. Clay products, including brick, tile, sewer pipe, and conduit, were manufactured beginning in the 1870s. Many workers were also employed by the railroads, an industry interdependent with coal mining.

Opera houses were filled with an exploding population during the mining boom. Roughly 200,000 people lived in the central Appalachian plateau in 1870, and the population reached 1.2 million by 1920.[9] To look at one of the first coal regions in Appalachia, Ohio's Hocking Valley, the seven townships that made up the coal region had a population of 9,502 in 1870, and by 1900 the population had reached 38,646.[10] In Nelsonville, the major town in the Hocking Valley, the population in 1870 was 1,080, and in ten years it nearly tripled, to 3,095. By 1910 it had doubled again, reaching 6,082, and then it slowly fell in the 1920s following the collapse of the region's coal economy.[11]

The first miners were Appalachian natives, primarily of Scottish, Irish, and German backgrounds, who had previously been farmers and tradesmen. But as coal production boomed in the late nineteenth century, operators needed more labor than the mountains could provide. Company agents traveled to the southern United States and to Europe to recruit new laborers, with the largest increase in immigration occurring between 1890 and 1910. The early foreign immigrants came from the British Isles and Canada, with increasing numbers from Germany and Scandinavia in the 1880s. Immigrants from southern and eastern Europe (Italians, Poles, Hungarians, Russians, Czechs, and Slavs) arrived in the last two decades of the century, as did African Americans from the southern United States. In Pennsylvania, for instance, the number of immigrants tripled between 1890 and 1910. In West Virginia, there were only one thousand immigrants in 1880, but by 1910 the figure had risen to between twenty and thirty thousand.[12] Lynch, Kentucky, had a population consisting of more than twenty nationalities, including Germans, Hungarians, Austrians, Serbs, Poles, Greeks, Italians, Croats, Albanians, Bulgarians, Mexicans, and Russians. In Lynch, 25 percent of the mine workers were American-born and white, while the rest were African American or from Eastern Europe.[13] The peak of immigration came just before World War I, and after the onset of war many immigrants returned to Europe to fight.[14] Some towns remained ethnically homogeneous, such as the company town of Stearns, Kentucky, which claimed that in 1926, "native-born whites constituted 99.6% of the total population."[15]

The influx of immigrants forever changed traditional mountain culture,[16] from one that was relatively homogeneous to one that was racially and ethnically diverse. This diversity also enriched life at the opera house. In larger cities, ethnic groups erected buildings for business, social, and entertainment activities, resulting in segregation along ethnic, racial, color, and religious lines. But in smaller, mining-oriented towns, one opera house was the site for all the town's activities. Some activities may have been implicitly or explicitly segregated because they appealed to only one group or excluded African Americans, but many events attracted broader audiences. In either case, lines from all over the community crossed at the opera house, and virtually everyone entered its doors.

African Americans played a major role in Appalachian coal mining, especially after immigration from Europe trailed off in the 1910s. Mining agents traveled south to recruit blacks to work the mines, and while most blacks came voluntarily, some were sent from prisons in boxcars.[17] Until 1870 the number of African Americans in the region was very small (14,360 in central Appalachia in 1870), but it increased steadily: 30,226 in 1890, 64,251 in 1910, 88,076 in 1920, and a peak in 1930 of 108,872.[18]

Most African Americans in Appalachia worked in the coal industry. In 1870, only 36 percent of the African Americans in Appalachia lived in the coal-dominated counties, but by 1920 almost all (96 percent) were concentrated in coal areas. Most African Americans in Appalachia lived in West Virginia, which had 69 percent of the region's black population and 62 percent of the black miners in 1920.[19] African Americans also formed a significant portion of the state's population; 39 percent of West Virginia's coal miners were African American in the early 1900s.[20] With the drop-off in coal operations after 1930, the African American population of Appalachia declined, as people left for jobs elsewhere and blacks were laid off in disproportionate numbers.

African Americans were often ostracized because of white racism and fear of unemployment. Blacks and European immigrants (especially from southern and eastern Europe) were brought in by operators in order to break strikes and upset union solidarity. In addition, operators often preferred immigrant labor to white or black American labor, because the immigrants were considered more dependable, harder working, and more easily controlled.[21] Owners felt they could foment dissension among miners by employing blacks and immigrants, setting one group off against another. For instance, in 1874 mine operators brought African Americans to Ohio's Hocking Valley mines as strike breakers, though the newly arrived workers were unaware of their role. The conflict that ensued was racial, but economics and job security surely played a part.[22] That event was still on the mind of R. M. Gibson when he wrote *The 1907 Photographic History of New Straitsville:*

> Perhaps the most striking contrast plainly evident to the observer is the utter absence of Southern European immigrants. No "Riff-Raff," Negroes, Hungarians, Italians, or so-called cheap laborers have ever been permitted to reside in the town. One disastrous attempt was made during the big strike of 1874 to import negro strike breakers, but the honest Straitsville miners, numbering among their ranks native born Americans, sturdy sons of Scotland and England, the sociable Irish, and the thrifty Welsh, resented this intrusion so bitterly and vengefully that no other attempt to force cheap labor in the mines has ever been made. So strong is the Union sentiment that a "black leg" or "scab" is an abomination in the sight of a citizen of Straitsville.[23]

Segregation and discrimination were evident in the layout of coal towns. Separate minority housing districts often were given derogatory names such as

Hunkytown, Little Italy or Dagotown, Colored or Nigger Town, Spanishtown, and so on. Most towns were racially segregated, with separate housing, schools, YMCAs, sports teams, movie theaters, restaurants, and saloons for whites and blacks. For example, a study of Benham, Kentucky, from 1920 notes, "The Negro population is in a segregated district,"[24] and a 1915 picture shows "two views of the Benham Y.M.C.A. for colored folk."[25] But in small mining camps of two to five hundred people, life may have been more integrated. And even if a town was segregated, a small size meant that people lived near each other and worked together. Towns with small populations sometimes had integrated sites of recreation.[26] While opera houses may have had separate and segregated audience areas, restricting blacks to the balconies, there is no evidence of separate opera houses. This may have been a reflection of the small size of these towns; large cities did have separate entertainment and community sites, including opera houses, based on race, ethnicity, and income.

The ethnic variety of the coal industry produced a social pyramid, with Anglo-American mine owners at the top and beneath them a managerial class, mostly of northern European descent. Blacks almost never had positions of authority, and whites refused to work for black supervisors. Management was especially segregated. In 1927, for example, there was only one African American supervisor in Appalachia out of a total of seven thousand. A black could work in a supervisory role only if he was leading other blacks. At the bottom of the pyramid was a wide range of ethnic minorities, holding the most physically taxing and dangerous jobs.[27]

Coal mining is the focus of the following chapter, but the industry's control of Appalachia is relevant here. The large mine fields of Appalachia were owned and controlled by absentee coal barons and corporations. For example, Justus Stearns and his son Robert Lyon Stearns cofounded the Stearns Coal and Lumber Company, bought 107,000 acres in Kentucky and Tennessee, and built the town of Stearns, Kentucky, and the Kentucky & Tennessee Railroad. International Harvester and U.S. Steel owned Benham and Lynch, Kentucky, respectively, neighboring and rival coal towns. All these towns had opera houses or theaters, which were owned and controlled by the companies.

Timber and mineral buyers arrived in rural Appalachia with what seemed to natives like buckets of money for land considered worthless. In many cases, the buyers wanted only the mineral rights, leaving the owner with the belief that he still controlled everything on the surface. Many residents were unaware of the true value of their land and were eager to sell. Others sold because the title to their land was unclear, and they were threatened with dispossession. Land passed from longtime mountain residents to absentee owners. Some speculators resold the land to developers, while other buyers were agents of mining companies, including International Harvester, U.S. Steel, and Ford. In 1892 Kentucky, absentee owners possessed 80 percent of the mineral lands in Bell County, and more than 60 percent in Harlan, Leslie, Letcher, and Rowan Counties. In 1900 in West Virginia, outside capitalists owned 90 percent of the coal mines in Mingo and Wayne Counties, and 60 percent in Boone and McDowell Counties. In 1923, nonresidents owned more than 50 percent of West Virginia land and 80 percent of the total land value of the state.[28]

Through this ownership, coal barons controlled the politics and economy of Appalachia. Powerful absentee owners dominated state governments, and most sheriff deputies were paid by coal operators. In politics, nepotism, corruption, killings, stuffed ballot boxes, and stolen elections were commonplace. Between 1888 and 1924, all West Virginia governors were coal company officials or men chosen by the coal barons. The coal barons bribed state legislators, who left their industry largely unregulated.[29] According to Ronald D. Eller, "Those who controlled the jobs also controlled the political system, and those who controlled the political system used their power to exploit the region's natural wealth for their own personal gain."[30] The region's economy became dependent on the coal industry, to the benefit of the industry and not the population. For example, coal lands were underassessed, so the mines provided little in tax revenue for public services.[31] In 1921 a West Virginia judge testified before the U.S. Senate, declaring, "We think and live coal. If you take our coal from us, we shall go back to the days of bobcats and wilderness. Coal is our existence."[32] According to Walter Precourt, "The coal barons aimed at nothing less ambitious than the total domination of the state government as an assurance of the continued profitability and freedom from regulation of their industry," while miners lived "in a state of virtual peonage because of their indebtedness to the company store, tyrannized by gun-carrying private guards."[33]

The model of internal colonialism is helpful in understanding the class, economic, and political structure of the coal-mining region of Appalachia. Harry Caudill, writing in the mid–twentieth century, was one of the first to describe the region in these terms, calling it "the last unchallenged stronghold of Western colonialism."[34] Robert Blauner, who is widely cited on the concept of colonialism, defines it as "domination over a geographically external political unit most often inhabited by people of a different race and culture, where this domination is political and economic, and the colony exists subordinate to and dependent upon the mother country." He defines the colonialization process as having four steps:

1. "A forced or involuntary entry."
2. "A policy which constrains, transforms, or destroys indigenous values, orientations, and ways of life."

3. Administration "by members of the dominant power."
4. Racism, consisting of "social domination by which a group seen as inferior or different . . . is exploited, controlled, and oppressed socially and psychically by the superior group.[35]

In Appalachia, this process began in the mid-1800s, before coal extraction became the dominant industry. Industrialists knew that coal was there; the problem was that local Appalachians owned the land. The locals were in the way, and something had to be done with the people in order to get at the coal. Outsiders used Appalachian otherness and poverty to justify acquiring and exploiting local land, as well as relocating and exploiting the workers, as Precourt describes: "The process of denigrating local populations for purposes of exploitation contributed to the poverty stereotype. . . . The Appalachian way of life did not fit the market model; it was therefore lacking; it was therefore in need of salvation by outside industrial interests. Indeed, the poverty label places people, socially, in the need-of-help role."[36] Jack Weller points out that the outside interests were able to achieve colonial domination, to label this work as "progress," and to blame any problems on the ignorance or deficiencies of the Appalachian people:

> Appalachia is simply our American example of how we use colonization powers in the economic realm all over the world. We strip an area and its people of their wealth under the guise of "developing" them, saying all the time of course that without this development look where they'd be. Yet in essence, we are robbing them of their wealth, impoverishing their people, controlling their economy, politics and people, meanwhile growing rich and powerful in the process. . . . Appalachia is indeed such a colony—a mineral colony, if you will.[37]

As outside capitalists gained control of the means of production in Appalachia, colonialism entailed specific and far-reaching changes in the lives of the people of Appalachia. Harlan County, Kentucky, for example, was colonized in the 1910s and 1920s, resulting in radical changes in the lives of traditional mountain people, according to Paul Frederick Cressy:

> Instead of the security provided by the older self-sufficient agriculture there was substituted the instability of industrial employment. A man's livelihood now depended on fluctuations in the national economy which were entirely outside his control. The miner worked when there was demand for coal, but he was left destitute when the demand declined as happened during the depression of the 1930s. The mountain

> man also had to surrender the freedom and timeliness which he had enjoyed on his isolated farm for the routine of mine whistles and fixed hours of work.[38]

The miner was dependent on the outside forces that controlled wages, scrip, the company store, politics, and law. He was therefore dependent on the industrial market of the United States, but, as Precourt points out, he was a specialized and isolated worker, with no other source of labor: "During the times of unemployment, therefore, the miner was economically defenseless; he was dependent on, but not well integrated into a market industrial way of life."[39]

All these factors—the development of the coal industry in Appalachia, the growth in population and diversity, and the internal colonialism—led to the development of the opera house and played roles in the life of the opera house. These towns would not have existed, or would not have grown, without the coal industry. There would have been no audiences without the population explosion. The diversity of events at opera houses reflected the diversity, and segregation, of Appalachian communities. And many opera houses were owned, like everything else in these towns, by the coal companies.

CHAPTER FIVE

King Coal and the Opera House

The opera houses with which this book is concerned lie in the coal-producing region of Appalachia. Coal mining spurred the development of Appalachia just at the time that opera houses were becoming popular in America. Thus, virtually every mining town in Appalachia had an opera house between 1870 and 1930. Without coal, these opera houses would not exist, and understanding their relationship to coal mining is therefore essential.

The availability of coal was crucial to industrial development in the nineteenth century. Coal fueled the American industrial revolution, and remained a cheap source of energy in the decades surrounding the turn of the century. After the Civil War, coal was burned in locomotives, factories, and ships, as well as in electric power plants, homes, and iron and steel mills. By 1885, coal had replaced wood as the leading source of energy in America, with mining levels reaching 110 million tons and doubling again in less than twenty years. By the turn of the century, the United States was the world's leading coal producer, at 243 million tons. Demand for coal increased significantly after 1900, and again in 1915, when factories were powered up for war supplies. The height of the coal industry came in 1923, with 700,000 men working in 12,000 mines and an annual production of one billion tons.[1]

Coal was king in Appalachia between 1890 and 1930. Coal mining was concentrated in Pennsylvania, Ohio, and Illinois until about 1890. West Virginia was the next state in which coal was exploited on a massive scale, starting around the turn of the century. Coal mining in

Kentucky came later, beginning in the 1910s, but assumed a dominant position quickly. By 1930, Appalachia produced 80 percent of the coal in the United States.[2]

Coal was not the only, or even the first, extractive industry in Appalachia. Between 1890 and 1920, timber was a major industry, and it provided the first nonfarming work for many people in Appalachia. Timber also survived in a symbiotic relationship with coal, providing lumber for propping up coal mines. In addition, when the timber had been exhausted on their land, owners frequently turned to exploiting the coal underground. For example, the Stearns Coal and Lumber Company, which originated as a lumber company in Michigan, moved to Kentucky in 1903 with combined timber, coal, and railroad operations.[3]

Mining development occurred in five phases, according to Francaviglia, and this structure is helpful in understanding the role of the opera house in mining development. The first stage is exploration, in which potential mines are prospected. The second is initiation, the boom period of mining, typically lasting fifteen years, in which the owner invests in the site and the richest areas are mined. Opera houses were typically built during this phase. The third phase is diversification, typically lasting twenty-five years, when improvements in technology make it possible to exploit lower grades of ore. The fourth period, intensification, involves mining low-grade ore with open-pit or surface mining, resulting in massive reworking of the landscape over a period of forty to fifty years. In the end comes cessation, caused by the exhaustion of the ore deposits and the rising costs of production. The corporate investment is liquidated and the mines are flooded, ending all mining operations.[4]

Railroad construction was an essential part of mining development. Coal needed railroads to reach the markets, and railroads needed something to haul. Indeed, the same investors often put money into both mines and railroads.[5] In the period immediately following the Civil War, there were few railroads in Appalachia. The West Virginia coalfields were connected to national markets by the Norfolk & Western Railroad after 1881, and the company offered financial incentives to investors in mines and company towns along its routes. Railroads entered Kentucky through the Cumberland Gap in the 1880s, but did not reach the coal counties of Harlan, Letcher, and Perry until the beginning of World War I.[6] Railroads led to development not merely by taking coal out, but also by bringing building materials and supplies in. The entrance of the railroad into Appalachia therefore marked the end of the pioneer phase of coaling and the end of the region's isolation.[7]

The rapid expansion of the railroads also made possible the golden age of the opera house. Touring theatrical companies took advantage of the new routes, and 1,300 troupes were traveling around the United States by 1896. Rail-

Benham Theatre (*left of center*), Benham, Kentucky (1921). The theater faces the town square, along with the post office, city hall, company store, medical building, and school. Photo by author.

road expansion also made touring more profitable, because producers were able to book their shows into a chain of small towns as they traveled between major cities without long layovers between performances. In turn, this availability of touring shows prompted towns to build opera houses.[8] In mining areas, there was also an extensive network of branch lines to bring coal from outlying fields to the major town for regional and national distribution. These special branch trains were used to bring miners into town for major shows at the opera house.

Many miners lived in company towns, especially in the southern Appalachian coalfields. A 1925 survey by the U.S. Coal Commission found that 80 to 90 percent of West Virginia miners lived in company towns; in Kentucky the figure was 64 percent. In Ohio, which had more established towns prior to the exploitation of the coalfields, only 23 percent of miners lived in company towns.[9] The period when company towns were most common coincides exactly with the heyday of the opera house, and many opera houses were built in company towns.

Company towns existed for sound practical and economic reasons. Coalfields, especially in West Virginia and Kentucky, were in areas that were largely undeveloped prior to the era of coal mining. The mines were often far from established towns, and therefore lacked the infrastructure of housing, stores, schools, and so on. For example, until the Harlan County, Kentucky, coalfields were developed, the area was extremely isolated, consisting largely of self-sufficient farms that were a two-day wagon ride over rough mountain roads from the nearest railroad. Rapid development began in 1911 with the arrival of the railroad to export coal from the newly opened mines. In 1914, one million tons were shipped out; by 1921, this figure had reached seven million tons; and during 1928 and 1929, fifteen million tons of coal came out of Harlan County. The population reflected this surge in development. In 1910 there were just over ten thousand people in Harlan County; the population tripled in ten years, and doubled again in the next decade, reaching over sixty-four thousand in 1930.[10]

Coal operators needed to house and feed these miners, so they developed coal camps. As the coal companies sought to attract and retain workers, they had to provide the further amenities of a town.[11] The goal of the town was quite simply to attract and retain labor.[12] According to Robert F. Munn, the majority of company managers "clearly regarded the company town as a necessary evil, to which a prudent manager devoted as little time, energy and money as possible. Most company officials appear to have known little and cared less about the living conditions of their employees." The reason owners invested in their towns was to attract a workforce that was "responsible, sober and stable"—and nonunion.[13] The company town was intended to be a well-run business that would increase profits.

Company towns went through three phases of development, according to Shifflett. In the pioneer phase, railroad construction often came in advance of the town, with only the men needed to lay the rail beds. This was followed by a coal camp with temporary housing consisting of tents or boardinghouses. Next came the paternalistic phase, which occurred mostly between World War I and the Great Depression. It was during this phase that major town construction occurred, including construction of the company store, offices, and houses. The first recreation facility built was usually a saloon. As families moved in, an opera house and/or an all-purpose recreation building with a theater, pool hall, and bowling alley would be added. In order to encourage a stable family life, some companies built a school and churches. Finally, company towns declined from the 1930s to the 1960s.[14]

The size and quality of company towns varied widely, though most were small, with fewer than one thousand people.[15] According to Ronald L. Lewis, company towns ranged from "crude coal camps erected on 'gob piles' to model towns with all the modern conveniences and a benevolent owner-operator."[16] Most camps/towns were crowded affairs, quickly thrown together in narrow valleys, with acid runoff from mines that polluted the drinking water, coal dust

Stearns Opera House, Stearns, Kentucky (c. 1910). The opera house was in the building with the peaked roof to the right (at the rear), adjacent to the company store and other company-owned buildings. Photo by author.

trapped in the air, few roads, and no sewage disposal. For example, a study published in *American Child* in 1920 found, "Without exception, all the small Harlan County operations which were visited are located on a stream-bed in a narrow valley with wooded hills rising abruptly on either side."[17] In the small camps and meager towns there was little opportunity for recreation other than the saloon, gambling, and violence.[18]

Company towns were under the sole control of the coal company, which owned everything in the town, including houses, schools, streets, churches, and recreation facilities. The company built the town, was the landlord, provided the police force, built the churches and stores, and provided all other services.[19] Workers had to live in company-owned houses, with six to eight people in a four-room house with no running water and no inside bathroom.[20] Cressy states, "The miners had no voice in governing these villages nor any sense of local responsibility."[21]

Some companies went further than the basic requirements and created model towns. Companies made major investments in model towns for a variety of reasons: to compete for skilled labor, as a public relations offensive, to make a display of benevolence, and to resist unions.[22] With the immigration of workers

Lynch, Kentucky, Main Street with model homes, strung along the narrow valley. Reprinted with permission of Appalachian Archives, Southeast Community College, Cumberland, Kentucky.

from the 1890s onward, operators wanted a more stable workforce that was less likely to move to other jobs. Towns became more family oriented in order to attract and keep workers.

International Harvester and U.S. Steel were large companies with sufficient capital to invest in the model towns of Benham and Lynch, Kentucky. The coal mines and therefore the towns had stability because the mines were "captive": their sole market was the steel mill owned by the parent corporation.[23] In model towns, houses were better constructed than in other company-owned towns, and several plans were available, all with electric lights and running water. The catch was that the miner had to be working for the company. If he quit, or was fired or laid off, he and his family had to leave.[24] The company built schools, churches, recreation facilities, lodge halls, poolrooms, libraries, playgrounds, athletic fields, and graveyards.[25]

An examination of Stearns, Kentucky, reveals the control a company had over a model town. The company owned everything except the United States post office, although the post office was in a company building and the postmaster was a part-time company employee. Stearns had its own government, utilities, waste disposal, maintenance and repair facilities, police, and fire pro-

Victory Theatre, Lynch, Kentucky (1919), a company-owned theater in a model town. Reprinted with permission of Appalachian Archives, Southeast Community College, Cumberland, Kentucky.

tection—all provided by the company. It was a feudal society, with houses of standard construction. The State Bank of Stearns was owned by the company, as was the Stearns Hotel, which was rebuilt in 1922 after the fire and labor massacre of 1908 (see below). The opera house, also owned by the company, was in the center of town, adjoining the company store. The *McCreary County Record,* the company-owned newspaper, declared, "It is a model town maintained by the Stearns Coal and Lumber Company. A bank, a newspaper, a hotel, a theatre, churches and a modern school building are included among its attractions and advantages."[26]

One of the most famous, and most studied, model company towns is Lynch, Kentucky, built, owned, and operated by U.S. Steel, with all the coal going to its factory in Gary, Indiana. Lynch was founded in 1917 and had two thousand buildings and a population of ten thousand by the mid-1920s. Lynch was a "self-contained community," with all the amenities of a model company town, including a recreation center that housed a theater.[27] Lynch had one of the nation's largest coal-mining plants, and in February, 1923, it broke the world record for one-day coal output at a single operation.[28] The headline in the *Harlan (Kentucky) Enterprise* read "Lynch Breaks World's Record":

> The tremendous work in the up-building of the city itself, as well as the immense scale of coal mining, should be a matter of pride, and a boast to any County in the State. . . .
>
> Big things are being done in Lynch. . . .
>
> Yet, remember, that the city itself, while every attention has been lavished upon it, is only secondary to the real intention; a means to the real end—The Mining of Coal. . . .
>
> Lynch is the Greatest coal Producer in the World. . . . [It] has broken the world's record. Let Harlan County and Kentucky know what we have done at Lynch. Let's Boost ourselves.[29]

The landscape of the town of Lynch is typical of many mining communities. The town covered all the available flat land and then climbed up the sides of the valley, resulting in a long and narrow town. A coal-industry publication praised the company's control of the town's real estate and design: "Everything required for comfortable living in the ordinary large town would have to be furnished by the United States Coal & Coke Co., so it was fortunate that all the property was owned in fee simple and there were no outside lots or owners to create embarrassment in laying out the town."[30]

Wages, employment, and working conditions for coal miners—the potential audience at the opera house—were uncertain at best and downright poor at worst. Coal mining was the most dangerous job in the United States, and as electricity and machines entered the mines it became yet more dangerous, with more dust and greater chance of explosions.[31] Miners worked in the dark with explosives in the midst of coal dust and dangerous gases, while coal cars darted through narrow tunnels. Overhead were tons of shifting rock held up by wood. Mines in southern West Virginia were the most dangerous: between 1890 and 1912, mines in this area had the highest death rate in the coal-producing states, five times higher than the rate in any country in Europe. The death rate among miners in West Virginia was higher than that among the American soldiers serving in Europe during World War I.[32]

Faced with powerful owners and dangerous working conditions, coal miners organized to establish their rights. Various miners' unions and organizations existed in the late nineteenth century, and in 1890, Ohio miners from the Hocking Valley met in Columbus to form the United Mine Workers of America. Workers wanted more social freedom, better wages, improved working conditions, the elimination of mine guards, equitable prices at the company store, and the right of free assembly.[33]

Victory Theatre, Lynch, Kentucky. Reprinted with permission of Appalachian Archives, Southeast Community College, Cumberland, Kentucky.

But Appalachia was a hard area to organize. Early mountaineer miners were not interested in being organized, and owners were strongly resistant to unions. According to Thomas F. Ford, "The history of labor organization in the mines and mills of the Appalachian region is one of blood and violence."[34] Mine wars erupted every decade between 1893 and 1933.

For example, R. L. Stearns worked incessantly to keep labor unions out of his company town in Kentucky. At Christmas, 1908, three labor organizers in Stearns were ordered to leave; following their refusal, a gunfight erupted in which a U.S. marshall and two local lawmen died. The organizers holed up in the Stearns Hotel and could not be drawn out. Stearns's solution was to set fire to the hotel, so the organizers could be shot as they escaped the burning building.[35] In 1922–23, the United Mine Workers tried to organize Stearns as part of an effort to organize all of eastern Kentucky. Although there was no violence in Stearns this time, all the miners who participated in the effort were fired and blacklisted. Neither they nor any members of their families could work for Stearns again. In 1934–35, during the nationwide economic depression, the United Mine Workers came back to Stearns. There was no resistance from the company, but the miners were working only one to two days a week.[36]

The relationship between mining unions and the opera house is clearest in Shawnee, Ohio, where the opera house building was owned first by the Knights of Pythias and then by the Knights of Labor, both worker-oriented fraternal societies. In 1893, a circular was distributed to "miners of Sub District 1. of District 6, United Mine Workers of America," regarding an annual meeting to be held in the Knights of Labor Opera House the following month.[37]

Wages for coal miners rose faster than the cost of living, but remained low by current standards. As the demand for coal increased, the demand for labor and earnings also increased. Between 1890 and 1929, the peak years of coal mining, workers enjoyed a 92 percent increase in real annual income, and wages increased 169 percent between 1890 and 1923, when miners' income peaked.[38] But miners were prey to economic fluctuations to a greater degree than workers in other industries. Many mining families suffered with frequent unemployment and were left destitute because of nationwide economic depressions that cut the demand for coal and influxes of new workers that drove down labor costs.

Miners were paid not by the hour, day, or week, but by their production: the amount of coal they extracted, usually at a rate of fifty to eighty cents per ton around the turn of the century. A miner might earn anywhere from seven to fifteen dollars per day, depending on output, with workdays lasting ten to twelve hours. In 1901, for instance, a coal miner in Athens County, Ohio, earned an annual average wage of $1,045, but by 1910 an excess of workers had cut that amount to $418.[39] And at any given time, 15 to 30 percent of the miners were unemployed.[40]

While miners were not flush with money, these figures do indicate that the opera house offered affordable entertainment. At the turn of the century, a miner would have to move one-quarter to one-half ton of coal for the cheapest seat in an opera house, or one and one-quarter to two tons for the most expensive. Put a different way, the miner would have to work, on average, about fifteen minutes for the cheapest seat, and about an hour for the most expensive.

Company stores were notorious for using monopolistic tactics for increased profits. Workers were often paid in scrip, which was redeemable only at the company store or other company-owned facilities. Workers had no choice but to purchase all their goods at inflated prices. Company stores were often a necessity during a mining camp's initial establishment. Few independent businesspeople would open up stores for an isolated, risky mine with a small population. On the other hand, companies often refused to allow independent stores in order to maintain a monopoly. For workers, the company store was convenient, but often there was no alternative. In some cases, companies lost money at the mines but made their profit through the company store.[41] In 1877, one operator made only $287 from its mine, but gained a whopping $22,000 from its store.[42] The profit from the company store may have been one reason operators encouraged an excess of labor: The miners and their families had to buy food whether or not they were employed

The company store also served as the hub of town life, offering a wide variety of merchandise and a place to socialize. It was almost always situated near the center of town, along with the commissary (where equipment was sold), barbershop, post office, and business offices.[43] The connection between the coal companies and the opera house is demonstrated in a turn-of-the-century postcard from Nelsonville, Ohio, that shows the Sunday Creek Coal Company Store on the ground floor of the opera house building. Likewise, photographs of Stearns, Kentucky, show the opera house and the company store in the same building.

Churches and schools were also central to life in coal towns. Churches suggested permanence, respectability, and restraint, so it was in the company's self-interest to encourage their development. A church provided a sense of belonging and unity, and strengthened the social organization. Early mining camps, most of whose residents were single men, had no churches or schools. In time, companies began to seek a more permanent, family-based labor force, so they provided schools and churches, along with the opera house, as part of the transition from mining camp to town. Often the company fronted the money for the school building and the teacher, then repaid itself by deducting a fee from miners' wages.[44] In Lynch, Kentucky, U.S. Steel contributed the land and half the construction costs for churches. In other cases, the operator constructed the church and leased it to various denominations. The coal company held title to the building, however, giving it leverage in church affairs.[45]

In times of a tight labor market, operators realized they needed more than wages to keep a stable workforce, and many built family recreation sites. George Wolf, manager of Winding Gulf colliery in Kentucky, suggested that the owner build amusement sites rather than houses, since there were already twenty-six houses empty: "Do something to make people better satisfied," he advised. He also pointed out that the company was obligated to match the five hundred dollars that people had raised for a church. Wolf proposed a whites-only church (as well as a separate school for African Americans): "We are the only operation in Winding Gulf without a single church for whites."[46]

In Lynch, Kentucky, U.S. Steel erected the Victory Building, also known as the Number One Amusement Center or the Y, which was tightly controlled by the company and racially segregated.[47] This was a three-story wood-frame building with bowling alleys, restaurant, poolroom, dance hall, lodge hall, and

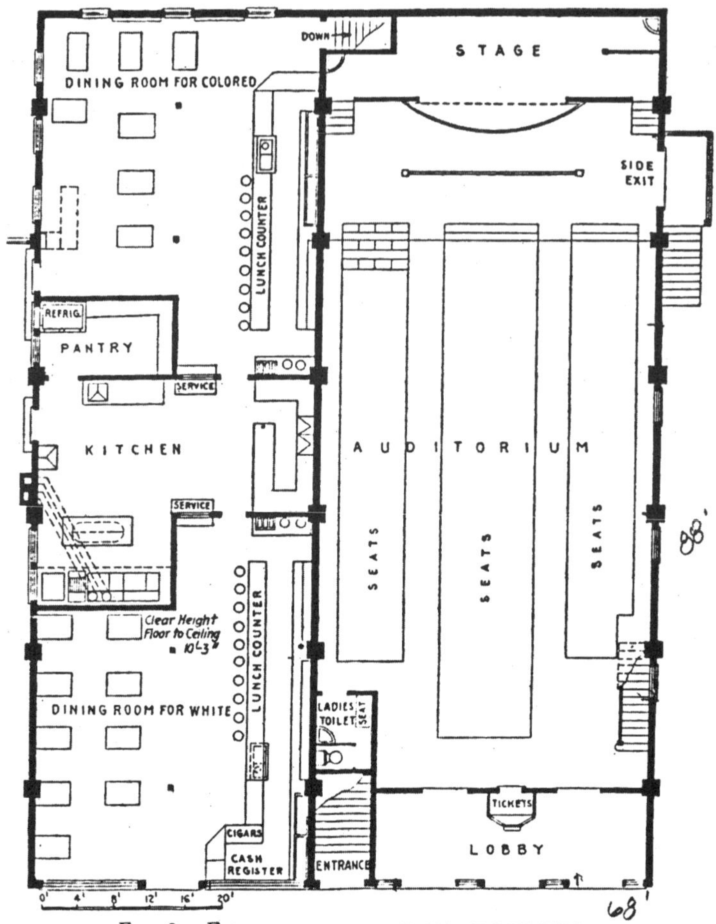

FIG. 9.—FIRST FLOOR OF AMUSEMENT BUILDING.

Ground plan of the Victory Theatre, Lynch, Kentucky (1919), showing the separate dining facilities for blacks and whites. Reprinted with permission of Appalachian Archives, Southeast Community College, Cumberland, Kentucky.

theater. The dance hall was leased to a "colored man" on Friday nights for dances, and the manager sponsored dances every Thursday night for whites. There were also meeting rooms for the segregated clubs and social organizations of the town, as well as for ethnic organizations of Croatians, Italians, and so on. According to an article in a coal-industry journal, there was also a restaurant "where both white and colored are served in separate rooms, from one kitchen." The theater, which sat 450, showed movies, concerts, and vaudeville shows. It had a separate gallery "which is used by colored people, the ground floor being reserved for the whites."[48]

Managers believed that company-sponsored recreation was valuable as a way to counteract the appeal of alcohol and prostitution. While saloons were among the first businesses to open in independent towns, saloons were forbidden in company towns, and alcohol was made hard to obtain. In addition, company towns forbad houses of prostitution and independent stores. Replacements for saloons included YMCAs with soda fountains, bowling alleys, theaters, and swimming pools—"wholesome and inexpensive recreation."[49] A coal-company publication reveals the nativist sentiment that ascribed less wholesome pastimes to foreigners: "Lack of social centers and the favorite pastimes of his homeland, drive him to the saloon, drinking club, or 'speak-easy,' in any one or all of which he can receive plenty of enlightenment upon the question of 'personal liberty' and kindred subjects. . . . It represents the foreign side of the problem which, when taken with the native born side of the proposition, forms a complexity of human relationships difficult of solution."[50]

Movies provided more than just entertainment. The operators felt that movies could influence miners and their families, either positively or negatively, as part of the overall system of control. According to one mine operator, "The miner seems to be more easily reached through the eye than the senses, and this makes the picture a powerful moral and educational agent." Another operator felt that movies "would teach the miners to 'dress in better style' and teach them 'better manners.'"[51] Operators were careful in booking movies, however, and often censored them. A Kanawha County, West Virginia, operator intended "to give [the miners] pictures having an educational value, avoiding the lurid, unreal wild-west type." It was common to avoid violent movies, out of the fear that they would lead to violence. A Boone County, West Virginia, operator was concerned about "all these here niggers carrying high-powered rifles." He testified to an investigating committee of the United States Senate: "Those little boys who are about 10 years old; he wants to be known as a bad man, and he goes to the rotten moving-picture shows that pretends to represent the western bad man, and he gets a pistol, and he goes off and wants the people to believe that he is bad. He gradually grows up to be a gunman."[52] A showing of *The Little Church around the Corner,* which the advertisement called "A special coal mining picture," at the New Harlan (Kentucky) Theatre in 1923 certainly offered what the operators wanted: mining and morality.[53]

An article in *American Child* from 1920 provides a revealing overall picture of entertainment in coal towns:

> The commercial amusements were limited to motion picture shows found in three camps and planned for in two others, pool rooms found in one camp and an occasional traveling carnival.

> The motion picture theatres were commonly open three nights a week, Monday, Thursday and Saturday; prices were 10 and 15 cents. One theatre had a balcony to which negroes were admitted. Many children attended these shows regularly and a number of them in addition went in to Harlan theaters. One group of three small boys went to Harlan every Thursday night to see the Wild West serial films. If they went oftener than once a week they said they could not remember them all—"it gives us too much to think about."
>
> The class of film shown at the camps, according to teachers, miners and managers, is very fair; comedy films and serials were the most popular, and the children were quite familiar with the leading actors in both fields. In Harlan Town a censorship board was established, last year by action of the city council. It is composed of five women. The ordinance provides that this board shall examine and pass on all picture films before public presentation and shall eliminate anything tending to be of an immoral or improper nature. The board, however, does not view the pictures before they are shown. Films arrive in Harlan only a few hours before they are to be exhibited. Rejection then would leave the proprietor in a position of having to pay for a picture for which he would be unable to secure a substitute; very likely he could not open his theatre at all that evening. These conditions of film distribution may have helped determine the policy of the board. The policy adopted is to make it plain to the proprietors that they must select and insist upon getting good pictures from the distributors. A Harlan pastor said, "The mere fact that there is a board and that these women have access to the shows at any time keeps a fairly high standard of film showing." The mayor concurred in this opinion.
>
> Pool rooms had been closed by the manager in one camp because of the gambling and fights which took place there and in the one village where they were still to be found they bore a very bad reputation. The Kentucky state law provides that no minor shall be allowed in a pool room without written authorization or without parent or guardian, but the law is generally disregarded.[54]

Coal mining in Appalachia declined beginning in the early 1920s, and then dropped off sharply in the 1930s.[55] Shipbuilders turned to oil, hydroelectric plants began to replace coal-fired plants, and cheap oil came out of Texas. The mechanization of coal mining also meant that more coal could be produced with fewer workers. Between 1920 and 1922 there was a drop in coal production of 164 million tons and a drop in employment of two hundred thousand jobs.

The population in coal-producing regions of Appalachia had doubled in the previous decade, leaving many out of work. The rest of the 1920s was disastrous for the coal market, with seventeen hundred fewer jobs each month for ten years, followed by the crash of 1929.[56] According to Eller, "By 1930, unemployment, destitution, and despair stalked the coal fields."[57]

This decline also led to the death of company towns. Confronting overproduction, poor earnings, and an uncertain future, coal companies were eager to cut back on nonessential spending. There was no longer a shortage of workers, and consequently no need to compete for them. In addition, by the mid-1920s, there was no longer a need for miners to live within walking distance of the mine. With the advent of paved roads and automobiles, miners were more inclined to live in nearby independent towns with more facilities than the best model town could provide.[58] Model towns declined from the 1920s to the 1950s, and many towns ceased to exist after World War II.[59] With their demise, the opera houses also closed.

CHAPTER SIX

The Opera House in the Fraternity

Many opera houses were situated in fraternal lodge buildings and had a symbiotic moral and cultural relationship with the fraternity. The fraternity provided a location for the opera house; the opera house provided culture to the lodge and the community. And the fraternity and the opera house depended on a project of upholding each other's and the town's sense of respectability.

A common model was a building with storefronts on the ground floor, an opera house on the second floor, and fraternal lodge rooms on the third floor. The stores and opera house provided income for the fraternal lodge, making the building economically self-supporting. The lodge also provided the community with an opera house, fulfilling part of the mission of the fraternal organization to enhance cultural life, to create opportunities for self-improvement, and to maintain moral respectability. The opera house therefore aided the finances and the image of the lodge.

The golden age of fraternal societies, 1870–1930, was, not coincidentally, also the golden age of opera houses. According to Clawson, "Fraternalism was a project that captured the nation's imagination." Fraternal orders were a "numerically massive and widely distributed presence" in late-nineteenth-century America,[1] with separate orders for natives, immigrants, men, women, Catholics, Protestants, blacks, whites, adults, and children.[2] Estimates of the number of separate organizations during this period range from 150 to 800, with membership estimated at 5 million in 1896 and 30 million in 1920. In 1896, almost one-third of the adult population were members of a lodge, and in 1920 half of all adult Americans belonged to a lodge. In the 1930s, with the Great Depression making it harder for members to keep up with dues and other membership expenses, fraternal organizations declined, and many buildings were sold. For example, the Red Men lost 300,000 members between 1925 and 1940, and the Pythians lost more than half a million.[3]

There were many kinds of fraternal organizations, but they all had certain features in common. They employed rituals that were organized around levels of membership. Each organization had elaborate initiations, with what C. Lance Brockman calls "secret rituals administered by incremental degrees, funeral services that confronted both individual and collective mortality, and elaborate hierarchical structures with exotic titles."[4] Fraternal organizations also strived for the moral edification and self-improvement of their members. Finally, they were not based on a single trade or business; instead members ranged across a variety of professions.[5]

The buildings for fraternal organizations, like other opera house buildings, were massive structures intended to be landmarks. Masonic buildings were called "temples" and, according to Lynn Dumenil, were designed

> on relatively secular lines, resembling such public buildings as courthouses and libraries of the period. . . . The effect they desired was monumental. Descriptions of the buildings emphasized their massive quality, equating size and bulk with evidence of the permanency and stability of Masonry itself. . . . The temple was classed with such major public buildings as the courthouse, a bank building, and schools. . . . [Temples] stood as imposing symbols of the wealth and permanency of Masonry.[6]

The meeting rooms in the lodge were set up according to a predetermined form of the given order, based on its ritual, with little variation from one lodge to another. The placement on the third floor was not merely for the economic reasons stated above, but also to remove the lodge rooms from the sights and sounds of the street. The members were not to be distracted, and snoopers could not peer in or listen to the rituals. The design of the room was, in some form or other, usually revivalist—in some cases Gothic or Egyptian—which, William D. Moore notes, "artificially separated the room from the time period in which it existed." In all ways, the lodge room was "an alternative realm set apart from day-to-day reality."[7]

One reason that the golden ages of opera houses and fraternal organizations coincided was that both represented a national concern with building a sense of community, including through games, sports, politics, and drinking.

Harrodsburg Opera House, Harrodsburg, Kentucky (1905), which was also the lodge for the local Odd Fellows and was adjacent to the city hall. Photo by author.

Fraternal organizations appealed to Americans during this era because of their emphasis on fellowship. In short, the lodge was a place for men to gather, socialize, and express their comradeship. In small towns, the lodge's social and entertainment events, including dinners and dances, were significant, since there were fewer attractions than in large cities. According to Dumenil, "The lodge was a respectable gathering place, filling the gap between exclusive clubs of the wealthy and the saloons of the poor."[8] The physical proximity of the lodge, the town's primary social site, to the opera house, the one source of entertainment in many towns, did not happen by chance.

There were also practical benefits to membership in a fraternal order. Members received sick and death benefits, and in some cases a home when they became indigent and/or elderly. Members also gained social and economic prestige, and the fraternity conferred a sense of respectability that could provide business and political connections, especially when members were traveling. Dumenil observes, "Men saw in Masonry the opportunity to associate with leading citizens, but they also sought Masonry as a badge of respectability."[9]

Members gained this reflected respectability because of the moral emphasis of fraternal organizations. Masonry in particular offered members, according to Dumenil, "identification with a religious and moralistic organization that upheld societal norms." The most important tenet of Masonry was self-improvement based on "sobriety, thrift, temperance, piety, industry, self-restraint, and moral obligation." This philosophy was socially significant in that it offered members "identification with the values honored in the middle-class world of late-nineteenth-century America."[10] For example, members of the Knights of Pythias in Shawnee, Ohio, following the fraternity's national norms, could not be saloon owners or liquor dealers; if it was discovered that a member did own a saloon, the lodge would hold a "trial," and the defendant would be forced to quit his business or the lodge. Pythians in Shawnee were also required to be civil to each other in public. One member was accused of swearing at another member, and another confessed to "acting in an unpythian manner."[11] The projects of fraternal orders and opera houses coincided in this emphasis on moral respectability. That opera houses and fraternal orders were popular in the same era, and were so frequently in the same building, is testament to this fact.

Ritual activity was central to all fraternal organizations, and included rituals for initiations, funerals, and cornerstone laying. The rituals varied from one society to another, but all, according to Dumenil, were "heavily infused with religious symbolism and allegories."[12] Societies competed for members by revising their rituals to make them more appealing. Clawson observes that these spectacular rituals turned fraternities into "providers of something approaching mass media entertainment. . . . They were marketing a standardized entertainment product that was reproduced socially and organizationally rather than electronically, as radio, films, and records would be." The difference between these lodge rituals and modern mass media, however, was that fraternal entertainment was "based upon face-to-face communication among people already known to each other." Instead of today's passive viewer, "the nineteenth-century lodge brother participated as actor rather than spectator in the ritual performance." Again, the connection between the activities in the lodge room upstairs and the opera house downstairs is clear: "The nineteenth-century lodge bears a marked resemblance to more traditional forms of popular culture in that it was an organizational vehicle through which its members *made their own entertainment,* through their active engagement in the dramatic events."[13]

Despite the rhetoric of equality, these societies were segregated on the basis of class, race, and gender. The most significant societies were composed primarily of white, primarily Protestant men of British and northern European background. According to Clawson, the egalitarianism was "made possible by the exclusion of women, blacks, and ethnic minorities from the relevant social universe, a universe whose boundaries fraternal institutions helped to demarcate and guard. . . . . The fraternal order was not . . . a neutral social arena in which some people happened, in random fashion, to unite as brothers. Rather, it was a form of association with a particular history and content, based on deeply grounded social and cultural assumptions."[14]

Fraternal organizations were more culturally pluralistic from the 1860s through the 1880s, accepting immigrants and allowing rituals in languages other than English. This changed in the 1890s, with a rise in immigration from southern and eastern Europe and a resulting increase in nativist sentiment. Lodge members had to be white, and Masons and Odd Fellows lodges became recruiting grounds for the Ku Klux Klan during the 1920s. Blacks set up separate societies paralleling the white groups, but they were not always sanctioned by the national organizations.[15] In 1915, ten thousand African Americans in West Virginia belonged to at least one social club or fraternal society, and by 1922, membership reached thirty-three thousand, representing half of the black population. The appeal was the same as for whites: social interaction, respectability, and insurance. Mining companies encouraged fraternal membership among blacks and allowed space in town for social clubs. The companies felt that the fraternal societies could relieve boredom and provide a respectable, "moral" alternative to the illicit activities the miner operators assumed blacks would otherwise participate in. Social clubs also encouraged middle-class and antiunion views. According to one black state official: "They stand for a high degree of morality, for peace, law and order and progress. They teach industry and thrift. . . . More than any other agency working among negroes, they have taught them the value of unity."[16] For example, the *Paris Kentuckian Citizen* reported, "The colored population of Paris have shown commendable zeal in the organization of societies and making efforts to educate, christianize and cultivate tastes calculated to give their race a correct idea of what they owe to their Creator, to themselves, and to Society." The paper listed the members of the "colored Odd Fellows of Paris," and observed, "The above societies are officered by some of the most intelligent and influential of the colored men of Paris, are prosperous and doing good work."[17]

Women were also excluded from the traditional lodges. As Dumenil observes, "Indeed, one of the most striking aspects of the lodge room was its maleness." The lodge was an "escape from women" and a place "where men might gather for relaxed fraternal camaraderie."[18] The creation of a specifically male space, both physical and institutional, is significant, according to Clawson, with its goal "to promote solidarity among men, to make them aware of their separation from women, and thus to enforce and facilitate the exercise of masculine power. . . . Fraternal orders not only offered an alternative social space for the expression of male solidarity, but dignified and idealized it by means of rituals that excluded women and celebrated the creation of specifically male social bonds."[19]

Male organizations grew in opposition to what has been called the "cult of domesticity" in the nineteenth century, which gave rise to such organizations as the Woman's Christian Temperance Union that was attacking men's right to drink. According to Kenneth L. Ames, "The home, the arts, the church, and the theatre were all feminized to varying degrees. By the early twentieth century, many men were reacting to this far-reaching feminization of former male strongholds." One such reaction was the growth of fraternal lodges as a model of male society in which "the traits of male culture were enshrined and often exaggerated."[20] In other words, the men ruled the lodge rooms upstairs, while the opera house was the feminized space downstairs.

These gender-charged spaces are related to wholesale changes in American culture in the late nineteenth century—in what Dumenil calls "an increasingly complex and disordered world." The economy, technology, railroads, and industry were all subject to radical changes. The balance of power also shifted, as national corporations grew more powerful at the expense of local communities, causing economic and political instability. The workforce was also changing in America, with a new white-collar world of office workers and new immigrants arriving in the 1890s from eastern and southern Europe, primarily Jewish and Catholic. Men found comfort in the traditions of secret societies as an escape from the social disruption of the modern world. Segregated white fraternities were a homogeneous asylum for American men of northern European descent in an increasingly heterogeneous world: "Confronted with a world apparently composed of many conflicting standards, the individual sought in group identification a means of finding others who shared his ideals."[21]

As women challenged these male organizations, fraternal societies were forced to allow women into events or create parallel women's organizations.[22] In the 1860s and 1870s, societies founded "Women's Auxiliaries" that "mitigated women's resentment of the order," Dumenil notes, "as it allowed them to duplicate their husbands' experience of secrecy, ritual, and sociability."[23] These auxiliaries included the Daughters of Rebekah (Odd Fellows), Pocahontas (Red Men), Pythian Sisters (Knights of Pythias), and the Order of the Eastern Star (Masons). That these organizations were not independent, but subservient to the male societies, is shown in the membership requirements: to join, one had to be wife or daughter to a society member.

Some of the fraternal organizations in coal-mining regions were specifically related to labor, in particular the Knights of Labor and the Knights of Pythias. The Knights of Labor was founded in 1869 and quickly became a leading radical force for organizing the American working class, with almost three-quarters of a million members in 1886; after 1886, membership rapidly declined. The Knights of Pythias was founded in 1864, originally as a secret society for government

Knights of Labor Opera House, Shawnee, Ohio (1881), later the home of the Knights of Pythias. Photo by author.

clerks, though membership was later broadened. Labor-oriented fraternal societies mobilized and organized workers prior to the widespread founding of labor unions—in particular, for this area, the United Mine Workers. Fraternal societies were, aside from unions, the organizations most accessible to workers.[24] For example, the Shawnee, Ohio, chapter of the Knights of Labor, founded in 1876, owned the Knights of Labor Opera House, which was the site of many labor meetings for coal miners. The Knights of Pythias chapter in Shawnee was founded three years later and shared the building with the Knights of Labor. With the national decline of the Knights of Labor, the local Pythians bought the building in 1902, and the building then became known as the Knights

Knights of Labor Opera House, Shawnee, Ohio (1881). Close-up of insignia on facade, showing both the *P*(ythias) and the *L*(abor). Photo by author.

of Pythias Opera House.[25] To this day, the facade of the building displays the K of P insignia, with the letter *L* peeking through beneath the *P.*

Other lodge events engaged members of the community and gained broad recognition. Masons regularly held St. John's Day celebrations, with speeches, toasts, dinner, and a grand ball. New Year's Eve parties, lodge anniversaries, and the installation of officers were big events in the life of any lodge.[26] For example, in Paris, Kentucky, the elections of officers for the Masonic Lodge and Odd Fellows were regularly listed in the *Kentuckian Citizen.*[27]

In Shawnee, Ohio, fraternal gatherings were events for the entire town. According to the *People's Advocate,* March 7, 1902, "was a day to be long remembered in the annals of Pythianism in our town." There was a parade with a brass band, and "one hundred and twenty five Uniformed Knights were in line making a most beautiful pageant with their swords, plumage and epaulettes." The day concluded with a grand ball and supper at the Knights of Pythias Hall.[28] Clubs used Native American names and regalia for exotic appeal, and in Shawnee "the Sun had just began to rise when Shawnee was astir, dressed in holiday attire, and waiting to receive the Red Men and Pocahontas from all parts of District 45." Everyone was "escorted" to the Knights of Pythias Hall "to register and receive a souvenir badge of the Pow-wow." The reception was moved to the opera house because there were too many people for the lodge rooms, demonstrating the cozy relationship between the fraternity and the opera house.[29]

Opera houses and fraternal orders were made for each other. They advanced the same causes: moral respectability, self-improvement, social interaction, and entertainment. Their temporal existence during the same period, and their physical existence in the same building, was no accident, but evidence of the regional forces at work within both organizations.

PART THREE

The Opera House in Action

CHAPTER SEVEN

Thunder and Lightning at the Opera House

Opera houses in Appalachia emerged out of a frontier tradition of showboats and traveling theatrical troupes. In the last decade of the eighteenth century and through the early decades of the nineteenth century, theatrical companies moved west with the frontier. By 1830 people in cities and towns along the Ohio and Mississippi Rivers were able to experience theater, whether resident or traveling. Some of the early performances west of the Alleghenies were in Kentucky: Washington in 1797, Lexington in 1808, and Louisville in 1815.

In the early nineteenth century, communities desired entertainment, and performers saw the frontier as a lucrative opportunity, but there were few suitable venues for performance. Schools and churches were potentially available in some towns, but many refused on moral grounds to rent their facility for theatrical use, though some allowed lectures or concerts. The answer was a portable theater that could easily be moved from town to town. So, before the boom in railroad construction, theatrical troupes traveled by the best means available: water. Each troupe carried—or rather, was carried by—its own theater in the form of the showboat. Many of these floating theaters were grand and fully equipped, complete with stage machinery and an auditorium with all the amenities, while others were more modest.

The creation of the showboat is generally credited to William Chapman, who put his family and theater on a boat and floated it downstream from Pittsburgh to New Orleans in 1827. Showboats became especially popular in the 1840s and 1850s. While the Civil War halted the showboats' activity, they quickly resumed business and multiplied thereafter, remaining popular until the early twentieth century. For almost a hundred years, showboats brought urban entertainment to many large and small towns east of the Mississippi, and were sometimes permanently moored in larger cities. According to Philip Graham, "The showboats had come into being to serve a region where civilization had been slow to penetrate, especially where the non-physical forms of entertainment, such as the drama, and the social niceties of living were retarded by the environment."[1]

Showboats were commonly run by a family, an arrangement that made economic and moral sense: it held down labor costs and could be used to counter the criticism of theater on moral grounds. Showboats advertised their fare as "Family entertainment, BY families, FOR families."[2] In the showboat, a family performed onstage for families sitting in the auditorium. This emphasis on moral respectability prefigured that of the opera house.

A showboat was usually a flat-bottomed barge, one hundred feet long and sixteen to twenty feet wide, with a shoebox-shaped structure on top, roofed decks on the ends, and narrow walkways along the sides. Early showboats had no power of their own, but were pushed by a steamboat or propelled with paddles. Doors in the front opened onto a small corridor, with offices and living quarters on either side, leading to the auditorium itself. The auditorium was long and narrow, seating somewhere between eighty and two hundred. The seating consisted of simple benches, though the front rows sometimes had cushions, backs, or both. Sometimes there was a small balcony that held about twelve rows at the rear and one row along each side. There was often a box with about four seats on each side of the stage. The stage was small, even by nineteenth-century standards: about eight feet deep and fifteen to eighteen feet wide. There was a roll curtain at the front of the stage, painted with an exotic locale or a mythological scene, with panels advertising local merchants. The scenery onstage consisted of simple flat wings on either side and a roll drop at the rear. The stage was lit by oil or candle footlights and a chandelier in the auditorium, which remained lit throughout the performance. The simplicity of the rectangular room, with a raised stage at one end and a balcony at the other, prefigured the form of many small-town opera houses. In some cases, the audience sat on the canal bank under a tent, looking at a stage on the boat's deck.[3]

Upon a showboat's landing in a town, a family member beat a drum to announce the arrival, while another posted bills with the performance information. Performances consisted of plays, vaudeville, minstrelsy, songs, dances, and jokes. Jim Stauffer, a member of George Stuart's troupe on the Hocking Canal in Ohio, recalled his days with the company: "Arriving at a town which had been posted with bills a few days or a day or so before, we would disembark, put up our tents and generally showed to enormous crowds. The novelty of the show attracted hundreds at every point."[4]

Stuart's showboat is emblematic of the shift from showboats to opera houses. About 1869, George Stuart made a fateful decision to move his showboat from Ohio's Hocking Canal to the Erie Canal in New York. J. Sheldon Scott, who performed in the band at Stuart's Opera House, attributed the move to Stuart's ambition and the showboat's popularity, but Ohio's deteriorating canals, which were losing out to the competing railroads, may have provided another reason. Floods, cave-ins, low water, and long, cold winters were all destructive to the canals, which needed constant and expensive upkeep. Initially such maintenance made economic sense, but a national struggle ensued in midcentury as to which mode of transportation would prevail: canal or railroad. The latter emerged victorious after the Civil War, and the canal system ran into the ground. Whether or not canal problems influenced Stuart's decision, Scott records that Stuart

> engaged a lake steamer to tow the theater from Cleveland to Buffalo. This had been done successfully many times previously, but the Stuart voyage met with disaster. About halfway to Buffalo a sudden storm arose, and high waves began buffeting the two craft. Canal boats were not built to withstand such stresses. The hull of the showboat disintegrated and sank, with the loss of all its contents; and the family and troupe barely escaped with their lives. The loss of all his possessions seems to have cured the Stuarts of their liking for a floating playhouse.[5]

Stuart returned to his hometown of Nelsonville, Ohio, and opened an opera house there in 1879. Stuart's showboat career thus neatly coincided with the canal era; the destruction of his showboat occurred as canals were dying out; and his ensuing opera house venture coincided with the coal boom.

The last third of the nineteenth century saw a boom (interspersed with a series of busts) in America's economy, population, railroad building, coal production, and theatrical production. All these are interrelated and all led to the golden age of the opera house. Local economies had to generate the surplus capital to pay for opera houses and opera house tickets, and in this region of Appalachia the money came from coal and related industries. Railroads carried the coal out and brought new cultural influences in. Immigrants to Appalachia provided the labor for the coal and the audiences for the opera houses. By 1880, according to an estimate by William Winter, there were approximately five thousand theaters in thirty-five cities and towns across America. Touring theatrical productions were able to reach this far-flung network of opera houses and theaters because of the growth of railroads across the United States and, in particular, the completion of the transcontinental railroad in 1869. In 1850, the

United States had only 9,021 miles of railroad tracks, and one could not travel directly from New York to either Albany or Boston. By 1860 there were 30,000 miles of track, and by 1910 the mileage had increased to 240,293. In 1905, the United States had one-third of the world's train tracks.[6]

Until the Civil War, local stock companies, which were resident in a single theater, provided theatrical entertainment for cities and towns. Each town had its own troupe of actors who performed in all the plays, with the theater managed by a local manager. Star actors did tour, but did so on their own, performing with the local troupe of actors and using the theater's scenery.

After the Civil War, resident companies relied more and more on visiting stars. Audiences came to theaters to see star performers, and local managers realized they could charge higher ticket prices. But the managers also had to pay more for the stars, so they had to make budget cuts elsewhere, including in wages for other actors and sets. Traveling stars found that local theaters could not always be relied on for quality scenery and supporting actors, so they started traveling with their own sets and supporting casts, initially consisting of one or two other actors and then developing into an entire company. Audiences enjoyed the touring companies: many had grown tired of the familiar faces of the stock company, and they liked the stars, frequent change of plays, and high production values of the touring companies.[7]

These professional "combination companies," complete with stars, full cast, and scenery, were able to reach towns all over America by rail. Producers used the network of rail lines to book their shows into a series of small towns in between larger cities, avoiding long delays between performances. This rail system made touring more profitable for producers, and the availability of touring shows encouraged towns to build opera houses.

The change from resident stock companies to combination companies began about 1870, when producing organizations in New York began to send shows to theaters in major cities around the United States. Combination companies reached small towns across America in the 1870s and forced out the local stock companies in the process. During the 1871–72 season, there were fifty permanent stock companies in large cities, but by 1880 that figure was down to seven or eight; the resident stock company was essentially gone. The height of the combination system was around the turn of the century, when 250 to 300 productions toured each year to reach a vast nationwide audience.[8]

Local theaters essentially became booking houses for touring companies, which duplicated the original New York production of a show and were billed as "Direct from Broadway." The problem for combination companies was complexity: trying to book 250 companies into 5,000 theaters. The result was frequently chaos, and especially difficult for local managers who traveled from all over the United States to Union Square to negotiate with New York producers. Company managers frequently cancelled bookings at the last minute if a more lucrative offer came along. In self-protection, local managers often booked two shows for a single night, figuring that at least one would show up.[9] For example, in New Straitsville, Ohio, the *Record* reported in 1902, "Our opera house manager . . . has been unfortunate this year. He has had half a dozen extra good shows to cancel their dates."[10]

The solution for local managers was to establish theatrical circuits, which were groups of neighboring theaters on a single railroad route. A circuit increased their bargaining power, decreased the chance of cancellations, and made it less expensive to book productions. The growth of a theatrical industry also led to a new role in the theater: the booking agent, a professional middleman who negotiated between the circuits and the producers. A booking agent could set up a well-planned route for both theaters and shows, avoiding costly jumps and layovers. In order to increase their power, then, agents wanted sole control to book shows into a given theater, which opened the door to the monopolistic Theatrical Syndicate.[11]

The trend in late nineteenth-century theater was toward centralized control of bookings for actors and theaters. By the 1890s, there were two major theatrical agencies, which merged with other agencies in 1896 to form the Theatrical Syndicate. The Theatrical Syndicate monopolized the theater business for the next fifteen years, until it was supplanted by another monopoly, the Shubert Brothers. The Theatrical Syndicate established its control not only through the chain of theaters it owned, but also by establishing exclusive booking rights with the smaller theaters. In a short time, the syndicate took control of most theaters in large and small cities and was able to force non-syndicate theaters to sign up or close. By 1904, the syndicate controlled over five hundred theaters.[12]

Like other turn-of-the-century "trusts," the syndicate could set booking fees without competition. The syndicate could dictate what plays were produced, with what actors, and at which theaters. If a theater manager or actor rebelled, he or she could be frozen out of the business by being denied bookings or work.

This centralization and monopolization of theater around the turn of the century paralleled the same trend in other industries. The shift was to centralized control, a division of labor between management and production, a standardization of the product, and the control of growth by big business. After the Civil War, the answer to economic chaos and instability in areas of commerce, whether oil, sugar, liquor, or theater, was the same: to create a monopoly or trust, with control of the industry by a few people in order to integrate production and distribution. The economy had been faced with unstable prices, competition, and periodic gluts, so the goal was to "rationalize" the market by eliminating competition and setting prices. While it is easy, in looking back, to see the Theatrical Syndicate as evil, it promoted itself as a stabilizing force in booking. The syndicate would end rivalries, provide a steady supply of shows, eliminate the need for local managers to make expensive trips to New York, eliminate empty theaters, and create economic and efficient routes with no jumps or layovers.[13]

Between 1898 and 1905 groups of independent producers tried to break the syndicate's control. Harrison Grey Fiske and Minnie Maddern Fiske, his wife, tried during the 1898–99 season, and David Belasco from 1903 to 1905. Finally the Shuberts succeeded in the years after 1905, when they joined forces with Belasco and the Fiskes. In the next decade the syndicate and the Shuberts fought for control of the American theaters in a series of wars and truces. Both groups built or signed up competing theaters in major cities, resulting in a glut of theaters. The Shuberts broke the syndicate's sole control in the 1910s and established their own monopoly.[14]

Towns across Appalachia were part of this national trend of opera house and theater construction after the Civil War. Opera house stages differed in detail, but there were common features in the overall architecture. The opera house stage was usually flat, though some were raked, sloping gently toward the audience, with one to three trapdoors. Among the opera houses studied here, the average proscenium was 28 feet wide and 22 feet high. The average depth of the stage was 27 feet, including an apron between the front curtain and the footlights that was an average of 8 feet deep. Offstage, on each side of the proscenium arch, was an average of 17 feet of wing space. A paper read to the Architectural Association in 1883 gives an indication of the national norm at the time, stating that the proscenium width should be 30 feet, the height should be 35 feet, and there should be 15 feet offstage on either side of the proscenium.[15] Thus opera houses in Appalachia were generally somewhat smaller than the national model, and many were quite small.

At the front of the opera house stage was a drop curtain, which was the most elaborate piece of scenery. It was harmonized with the interior of the theater, and usually showed a romantic or idyllic scene, with a painted frame and swag curtains.[16] Small theaters generally could not afford to hire a scene painter on staff; instead the theater manager ordered scenery from the catalogs of major scene houses, such as Armbruster (Columbus, Ohio), Lee Lash (New York), and Twin City Scenic (Minneapolis).

Each opera house had a stock of common sets that were reused from one production to another. Stock exterior scenes were referred to as "timber" (a forest) and "town" (a street scene), and other scenes may have included a rocky

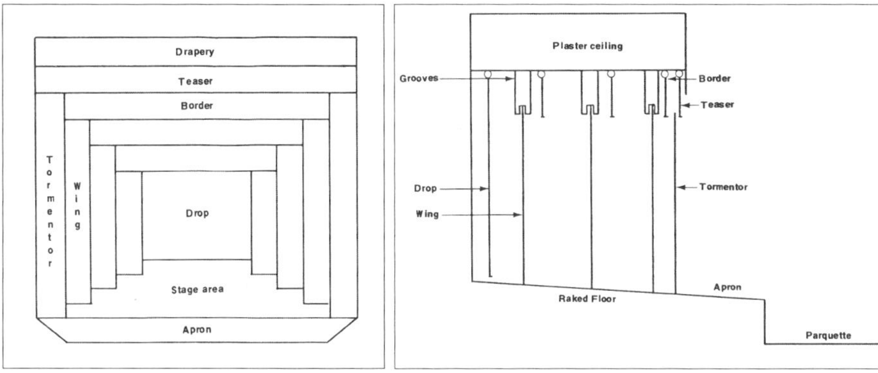

Sketch showing the scenic units of a typical opera house stage. Reprinted with permission of Warren County Historical Society from *The Grandin Opera House, or Theater on the Kerosene Circuit, 1872–1904* (Warren, PA: Warren County Historical Society, 1973).

Woods backdrop, an example of typical stock scenery of an opera house. Reprinted with permission of Great Western Scenic Company Collection, Performing Arts Archives, University of Minnesota Libraries, Twin Cities.

mountain pass, a garden, and a palace. The most common interior sets were a front room and a back room, as well as possibly a Gothic interior, a cottage, a chamber, a palace, a prison, and a conservatory. Each set consisted of two wings, which were painted panels at the sides of the stage; cut drops, which were cutouts of trees or clouds; and a backdrop. All the details on the scenery were painted, and not built up three-dimensionally. Even the shadows were permanently painted on the scenery. This recycled scenery sometimes became too well known to local audiences, as was the case in Buchanan, Michigan. In 1889, the *Berrien County Record* commented that the Rough Opera House management should "shoot the woodpecker on the stump in the rural scene, or make him catch the bug he has been chasing for the last ten years. . . . If there be anything the American people enjoy it is an occasional change."[17]

Stagehands could change the scenery by sliding the framed wings in and out of a set of tracks on the floor and overhead. The system was simple to operate, and little could go wrong. It was cheap and quick to install, and could be used in theaters without an overhead fly loft of ropes and pulleys. In addition, this system had incredible endurance: it dates back to the Italian Renaissance, and continued in America into the early twentieth century.

Gas was the dominant form of lighting during this period and was used for general lighting of the stage. Gas jets were arranged as footlights at the front edge of the stage, border lights above, and bunch lights behind doorways. Gaslight was brighter than the oil light and candlelight that preceded it and was also more controllable. An operator could dim, but not fully darken, the auditorium.[18]

Calcium, lime, and electric arc lights were used for spotlights and special effects. These spotlights heated small pieces of lime or calcium, and in an electric arc the electricity leaped, or arced, across a small gap. In each case, an intense point of light was produced that could then be focused for use as a bright accent on stage. Electric incandescent light was introduced after 1885, and had the advantages of generating less heat and no fumes, and being less of a fire hazard. As initially installed, rows of electric bulbs simply replaced gas jets in the footlights, borders, wings, and auditorium. Gas was still kept as a backup in many theaters, however, since electricity was initially not reliable. Gas was still used exclusively in many opera houses at the turn of the century, but by 1910 most theaters were fully electric.[19]

A major part of the show at the opera house consisted of special effects, and the stage was filled with machines designed for this purpose. For example, five different effects might come together to create a storm. A rain machine created the sound of rainfall by means of a wooden cylinder with dried peas inside; when it was rotated the peas struck against wooden teeth inside the cylinder.

Marlin's Opera House, Brookville, Pennsylvania (1886). Backstage, showing grooves for changing scenery. Photo by author.

Another cheap, portable rain device was a child's hoop covered in brown paper with bird shot inside; when it was tipped from side to side, the bird shot rolled around. The illusion of visible rain could be produced by vibrating fine, polished wires strung vertically across the stage. A wind machine consisted of a drum with protruding flanges and covered in loose fabric. When the drum was rotated, the flanges brushed against the fabric, creating the sound of wind, which could be regulated by the speed of the rotation. A more portable device was a simple hose whirled around in the air. Thunder could be produced by many means, depending on the resources of the opera house. The thunder sheet, a sheet of iron suspended backstage, could be shaken for a roll or sharp crack of thunder. A thunder drum consisted of a box covered in calfskin that was beaten with a stick. A rumble cart, filled with heavy material and rolled on irregular wheels, could create the sound of far-off thunder. A crash of thunder could also be created from a box filled with hundreds of pounds of junk and chain; when the trapdoor at the bottom was opened, the debris dropped onto an iron plate. The thunder run was the most expensive and timber-rattling storm effect, with cannon balls running down troughs backstage. Lightning could be produced by burning magnesium, as in flash photography, or with flashes from calcium or electric lights.[20]

Other common special effects included the illusion of moving water, such as a lake, river, or ocean, which was created with each wave made of a separate piece of fabric; each piece was waved from the sides of the stage, producing an undulating effect. A water effect could also be created with cylinders laid across the stage and covered with stiffened canvas patterned like threads on a screw; the cylinders were then rotated by a crank on the end. The sound of the water could be created by rolling bird shot or pebbles around in a tin-lined box. Snow could be depicted with small pieces of paper dropped from the flies or with a snow cradle, which consisted of a muslin trough cut with slits; when the cradle was rocked above the stage, the paper slipped out. The sound of carriage wheels could be produced with a small carriage backstage run over a wooden track. Overall, special effects were critical to performances at the opera house. According to Garrett Leverton, "Nothing was too difficult to be attempted. Buildings burned, men dived into lakes, snow fell, rain came down in sheets, the wind howled, thunder roared, cannon and rifles boomed, and each manager vied to outdo the others in this field."[21]

Theatrical production and special effects were prone, however, to breakdowns, then as now. A local Oil City, Pennsylvania, production of the military drama *Allatoona,* presented by the Sons of Veterans, featured one hundred people on stage, as well as "Horses, Brass Band and Drum Corps! New Scenery! New Music! Calcium Light Effects." But the play dragged on so long that the farce intended as an afterpiece, *Oil Exchange Bull Ring,* had to be cancelled. The battle scene in the local Grand Army of the Republic production of *True Blue* "did not pass without casualties, as some of the troops engaged in firing shot too low and the wax wads did damage to the faces and hands of those in the foremost ranks."[22]

Though this was the golden age of popular entertainment, life was difficult for actors, who worked in a clearly hierarchical structure. At the top were the stars, who received the highest salaries and gained the best amenities. They were followed by the leading actors and actresses, who aspired to be stars. The principal lead played opposite the star; the female star had a male lead, and the male star had a female lead. The leads depended on their good looks and cultured manner for their careers. Juvenile leads ranged in actual age from teenagers to adults in their thirties and provided dramas with romantic intrigue and comic subplots. Other leading actors might have specialties as heavies, comedians, character actors, old men, or grand dames. Utility actors ranked below the leading actors; these were stage novices doing bit parts and helping out backstage. They also functioned as "walking gentlemen and ladies," filling out scenes visually and sometimes adding a few lines. At the bottom of the hierarchy were chorus girls and supernumeraries, the latter working in crowd scenes and nonspeaking roles.[23]

The combination system of the late nineteenth century resulted in higher and more dependable salaries for actors. In a first-class company performing in large cities, the leading men and women earned $75 to $250 per week, with comedians or character actors earning about $100; juveniles, ingenues, old men, and other supporting actors earning $30 to $75; and utility actors $12 to $18. Actors in a second-class company, such as would probably play in Appalachian opera houses, rarely earned more than $50 per week, and most earned $30 to $35. An 1894 study estimated that the average actor earned $35 per week for 25 weeks, resulting in an annual salary of $875. This compares with average salaries during the same year for manufacturing workers at $386, clerical workers at $278, postal employees at $919, and ministers at $824. Actors were therefore in the "modest middle class," with leading actors and actresses more well off. Nonetheless, all had to confront periods of extended unemployment.[24]

The ethnicity of American actors during this period was overwhelmingly native-born white. This Anglo-American dominance remained unchanged during the nineteenth century, despite the waves of immigration from eastern and southern Europe. According to Benjamin McArthur, the majority population feared "that this country's racial stock was threatened, and they sought reassurance that the Nordic race was still in command. The theatre gave this support . . . by offering a procession of actors and actresses who were models of Anglo-Saxon gentility and femininity. By contrast, ethnic roles remained safely subordinate, being predominately low comedy."[25]

The age range of male actors was similar to that of men in other professions, but almost half of all actresses were under twenty-five. Many women retired upon marrying, and few remained in theater after age thirty-five. On the other hand, women faced fewer barriers in the theater than in other professions.[26] An incident from the opera house in Winchester, Kentucky, illustrates, perhaps melodramatically, the travails of one such actress:

> ACTRESS SUFFERS DURING THE PLAY
>
> Miss Beulah Poynter is Assisted By Physician While on Stage
>
> Very few, if any, of those in the audience that witnessed the performance

> of Miss Beulah Poynter last night at the Opera House in Lena Rivers will believe that at the time she was playing the part of Lena, with her many happy as well as sorrowful moments, she was suffering almost beyond human endurance from the effects of an operation that was performed some weeks ago.
>
> At two different times during the performance a physician had to be called on the stage to give her a hyperdermic [*sic*] to strengthen her, so that she could play out her part. The physician that attended her said that he never saw any one in his life suffer as much as she did and still be able to hide it as well as she did on the stage.[27]

Opera houses in Appalachia provided communities with human-scaled spaces that were capable of showing great spectacles. Audiences relished the traveling shows and homegrown talent. But the opera house was also a flexible space that could house the wide variety of community events that made it central to the local culture. These events are explored in the following chapter.

CHAPTER EIGHT

(Per)Forming the Community at the Opera House

The opera house was a nexus of entertainment, politics, and community. Only about half of the events in opera houses were conventional theater, that is, comedy, melodrama, vaudeville, minstrelsy, and so on. The other half of opera house presentations consisted of a variety of community events. Even among the presentations that could be considered conventional theater, many were school plays or local variety shows that were closer in nature to community events than to professional theater. To understand how these halls nested in the local culture, these community events must be given due attention. These local events put the town onstage, literally and figuratively, forming and performing the town's cultural memory.

American culture expects separate venues for different kinds of events: popular, "low culture" entertainment, "high culture" performance, and community gatherings. In small towns a hundred years ago, however, the opera house was the single gathering site, and a spectator could see an example of each kind of event there in a single week. The opera house was the site of variety entertainment, such as *Hoity Toity, A Trip to the Moon,* and *Liberty Belles.* Lecture series were common. And the opera house was used for performances of Shakespeare's plays and legitimate (though rare) operas. Thus, when the spectator came to see *Hamlet,* she could remember that this was also the site of *Zarrow's Pig Revue* and "the world's largest Sunday School." Some members of the community might have heard a "cogent and eloquent plea for unmodified woman suffrage"[1] at the opera house or attended a "colored convention."[2] The opera house was the single site for all these socially legitimated, intergenerational events, crossing gender, racial, religious, and political boundaries. The inclusion of this rich variety, however, also created and enforced a certain moral universe that excluded other events.

Before schools had gymnasiums and auditoriums, they used the opera house for a variety of student events, including alumni reunions, school plays, and basketball. Other instructional groups also used the opera house for end-of-term recitals, including dance, music, and gymnastics. College and high school commencements were an annual event that brought multigenerational families to the opera house. Before the advent of widely accessible college education, a high school commencement was a significant coming-of-age event attended by parents, relatives, and friends, who might account for a significant portion of the community. And when staged at the opera house, graduation could take on an air of spectacle, as at the graduation of the Bourbon Female College at the Paris (Kentucky) Opera House: "Some members of the class in flower bedecked swings suspended by means of ropes around which seasonal blooms had been braided were swung out from the stage by other members of the class being graduated while all the class sang a chorus 'Moonlight and Roses.'"[3]

Commencement at Marlin's Opera House doubled as a benefit for the Brookville, Pennsylvania, public schools: "In our opinion this is the most important event transpiring in our community each year, and we believe its importance should be recognized by all our people by giving the exercises a vast attendance. . . . The admission charged is not for the purpose of making money for any person's benefit, but is devoted to purchasing apparatus for the schools, when any balance remains after paying expenses."[4]

In Maysville, Kentucky, public school examinations were staged at the opera house and were reported day by day in the *Daily Evening Bulletin:* "The examination of District school No. 1" was noted, with the report the next day that "the pupils acquitted themselves with credit and furnished evidence of patient and careful training." After another exam at the opera house, the teacher was singled out for public praise: "The exercises were very interesting and indicated a marked progress of the pupils during the past school year. Prof. Wilson is a very thorough teacher [and] has done his work carefully and well."[5]

The opera house was also a site for addressing contested political, racial, gender, and religious issues. Political parties held rallies, and local, state, and national politicians lectured at the opera house. For instance, in Glouster, Ohio, in 1896, "The democratic free silver followers of the valley held a meeting." Apparently there were so many democratic free silver followers in the valley that "the opera house was quickly filled," creating a need for "an overflow gathering, which assembled at the platform near Hotel Bishop."[6]

An opera house in a city hall (for example, those in Athens, Ohio, and Buckhannon, West Virginia) was often used for political speeches, rallies, debates, and lectures. Politicians running for office addressed national, state, and local issues. Topics included temperance, taxes, and gun control ("We have read no speech in advocating of the Second Amendment that is more likely to prove more effective than one recently delivered by Hon. Mills Gardner").[7]

The ready flow between the opera house and city hall is evident in records concerning two towns in Kentucky. In Winchester, Kentucky, the opera house was promoted for use as the new city hall: "The opera house would be capital as a city hall, where everybody who comes to town could see it and we all would be proud of it."[8] It is evident here that the opera house was a city landmark, and also was considered a sufficiently respectable site to be the seat of city government. In Paris, Kentucky, two thousand people showed up for the Republican convention at the courthouse, which could only seat one thousand, so the event was moved to the opera house.[9] The opera house was a culturally legitimated site and recognized as the largest gathering place in the city.

Watching election returns was a form of entertainment and a box-office draw for the opera house. In Winchester, Kentucky, the *News* ran a string of advertisements:

> AUDITORIUM HALLOWE'EN MASQUERADE, Saturday Night, OCTOBER 31st, Prize for most graceful skater and best masqued couple now on exhibition . . . Seven Lap Race Between Monkey and Coon.
> CHILDREN'S Masquerade Saturday Afternoon, from 2 to 5 P.M. $5 skate book for best masqued girl under 15; for best masqued boy, $5 skate book.
> Election Returns at Rink Tuesday Night, Nov. 3rd, Skating Until 10 P.M. Returns until 1 P.M. Admission 25c. Skates Free.[10]

> THE AUDITORIUM will give full Returns of the Election on Tuesday Night. Each dispatch will be read as it is received. You can come and enjoy Skating and at the same time hear all about the Election. Don't forget the Masquerade, To-Night.[11]

These advertisements consistently emphasize the currency of the election information, the admission fee charged, and the other, simultaneous entertainment. According to Atherton, these gatherings are indicative of the community spirit of opera houses: "The election was an excuse for people of both parties to attend a midnight show together, not the culmination of weeks of marching, arguing, and even fighting by those who would be present."[12]

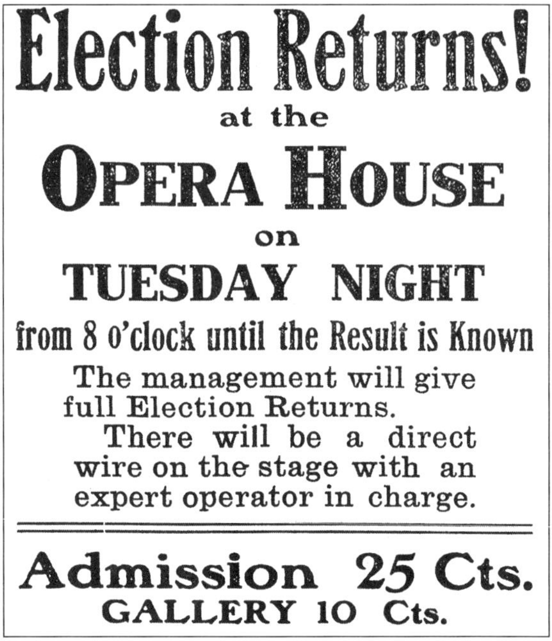

Advertisement for election returns at the Winchester Opera House, Winchester, Kentucky, 1908.

The opera house was also a site for the formation and performance of identity within the broader culture. Women's suffrage was a major political issue in turn-of-the-century America and was a subject of debate at the opera house. For example, Susan B. Anthony lectured at Wagner Opera House in Bradford, Pennsylvania, in 1892 on behalf of the Woman's Christian Temperance Union. The *Era* reported, "Notwithstanding the shortness of the notice, long before the hour announced people began thronging to the place of meeting and when 3 o'clock arrived every available seat in the house was occupied. Standing room was soon out of the question and hundreds went away unable to gain admission." Anthony spoke about "the necessity of the ballot for women, in carrying out the social and moral reforms they desired."[13] Similarly, an 1894 lecture in Athens, Ohio, under the auspices of the Woman's Christian Temperance Union, concluded with a "cogent and eloquent plea for unmodified woman suffrage," which "evidently enlisted the warm sympathy of her hearers."[14] Women also organized frequent balls, charity events, and temperance meetings. On the other hand, women were excluded or discouraged from attending other events, including variety shows and sporting events, because they were morally suspect (see chapter 2 and below). But women may also have been unable to attend because of the time of events at the opera house, which might have conflicted with societally imposed obligations. For political stump speeches in New Straitsville,

Ohio, in 1903, "only a few ladies and children [were] present. It was not the fault of the ladies that they were not there in great numbers but the hour of the day (about 5 P.M.) which made it inconvenient for them to attend."[15]

The opera house was also a site for African American community events, some of which were explicitly political in nature. For example, African Americans in Athens, Ohio, held the first "colored convention of the county" in 1879 "to discuss what part, if any, they would have in the present somewhat mixed political county affairs." The convention concluded with "entire unanimity in the determination to work till the close of the election as unceasingly and as cordially for the success of the straight Republican county ticket as for the State ticket."[16] In Winchester, Kentucky, the "colored Republican Club" met at the skating rink (a space culturally allied with the opera house).[17] African Americans also used the opera house for fraternal meetings, as when "The Green Hill, colored, Lodge of Good Templars, of Athens," held a fair at the city hall opera house in Athens, Ohio, in 1879.[18]

African American balls and masquerades were also popular at the opera house, as indicated in the "Colored Column" in the *Winchester (Kentucky) News* in 1908. The column includes a listing for a Halloween "mask carnival" at the Hippodrome, in which "all skaters that contend for prizes wil [*sic*] be in mask." First prize went to the woman with the "most perfect mask," and second prize to the man with the "most grotesque mask."[19] While these events were predominantly black, they were also charged with the tensions of the racist culture. In Carlisle, Pennsylvania, African American masquerade balls were held at Rheem's Hall for entertainment and to raise money: admission was charged to spectators, who were mostly white. At the end of a ball in 1878, whites "threw shot around the hall, broke a window, and sprayed the room with bi-sulphate of carbon." The *Herald* described another black community event, a picnic held by the "colored" Odd Fellows' lodge at Williams' Grove: the excursion train "numbering four coaches, [was] filled with big and little darkies, and onc hash car. . . . Our town was pretty well deserted of its colored population." The picnickers then went to Rheem's Hall for dancing.[20]

The opera house was also used for white-sponsored racially charged events. In Bradford, Pennsylvania, the Ku Klux Klan met in the Wagner Opera House in 1924, protected by a large crowd outside.[21] The manager of Stuart's Opera House in Nelsonville, Ohio, rented the hall for a lecture in the 1920s, only to discover that it was actually a Ku Klux Klan rally. He canceled the meeting, but on the night it was to have been held he had to walk home through a gauntlet of Klansmen.[22]

The most terrifying demonstration of racism at the opera house was a lynching. In 1911, the town marshal in Livermore, Kentucky, fearing that a black man suspected of a shooting would be lynched, hid the suspect in the abandoned opera house until he could be transferred to a county jail. A lynch mob formed and found the hidden man. According to the report the following day in the *New York Times,*

> The shooting of the Negro was done in a weird scene. Against the wall were props, long unused, and bare windows, and startled from their night's rest rats scurried across the floor. Against such a backdrop the Negro was bound hand and foot and placed in the center of the stage. Many of the lights when the current was turned on refused to burn, and in the semi-darkness, the mob, silhouetted against the theatre walls, awaited the signal of the leader. When it was given, fifty guns fired in unison, one piercing scream was heard, and their work was over. The lights were then extinguished, the curtain lowered, and the mob filed out.[23]

Kirk Fuoss has found other articles about this event that describe tickets being sold, with the price of the ticket dependent on where one sat and how many bullets one fired. Fuoss doubts reports that describe the tickets, curtain, and lights, and suspects that the murder took place in the dressing room where the man was found. He theorizes that antilynching activists and reporters exaggerated their accounts of the incident.[24]

Ethnic groups from the dominant culture gathered more benignly at the opera house. Scots commonly celebrated Robert Burns at the opera house, holding annual all-night parties at the Knights of Labor Opera House in Shawnee, Ohio.[25] In 1918, for example, "the 159th anniversary of the birth of Robert Burns, Scotland's National Poet, was celebrated in the K. of P. opera house . . . under the auspices of the Scotch Lassies Club" with entertainment, a ball, and supper. The event was "larger than ever, and as usual the good time continued throughout the entire night."[26] The Croatin Club of Lynch, Kentucky, "an organization composed of the best of the foreign populace," was especially proud to present "Signor Tino Pattiera, a tenor singer from the province of Dalmation in Jugo-Slavia, who has just recently acquired international fame. . . . The appearance of so noted a singer in the mining town of Lynch is wondered at and was arranged for only following the persistent efforts of the Croatin Club."[27] The audience was "large and enthusiastic," and, the newspaper reported, "Lynch citizens feel proud of the fact that this is the first place in the state in which Signor Pattiera has given a concert and that their city is only one of two places in the state where he will sing, Louisville being the other. Moreover this is the first time since the memory of man runneth not to the contrary that a grand opera star has ever given a concert in a mining town in the United States."[28]

Artist's rendering in the Paris newspaper *Le Petit Journal,* in 1911, of the lynching at the Livermore Opera House. Reprinted with permission of Special Collections and Archives, Margaret I. King Library, University of Kentucky.

Music offered an opportunity for people to participate in local presentations at the opera house. In Shawnee, Ohio, for example, Welsh singers were prevalent, and a 1908 advertisement for the "EISTEDDFOD OF THE WELSH CHURCHES" at the Red Men's Opera House offered prizes of up to a hundred dollars in a variety of categories, allowing numerous community groups, large and small, young and old, male and female, to win.[29] An announcement in Corry, Pennsylvania, proclaimed, "COMMUNITY SING PROVES GREAT SUCCESS" at the Rex Theatre in 1919, and linked the event to patriotic feelings for soldiers in World War I: "Roy Gourley, who spent some time with the soldier boys at Camp Grant and later was working, under the Y.M.C.A. with the soldiers overseas . . . was in charge."[30]

While admission may have been charged for these community events, organizers emphasized the goal of fund raising, rather than profit making. The announcement from the *Jeffersonian Democrat* for the Marlin Opera House in Brookville, Pennsylvania, is typical: "The admission charged is not for the purpose of making money for any person's benefit, but is devoted to purchasing apparatus for the schools, when any balance remains after paying expenses."[31]

Winchester, Kentucky, had a long-term fund-raising campaign in 1911 for a new hospital. The organizers presented a "good moving picture show to aid the hospital fund" at the opera house, as well as speeches regarding the hospital. A listing of the plays for later that week in the *News* reminded readers: "Remember one half of the proceeds go to the hospital fund."[32] Because the events at the opera house benefited local organizations, citizens were frequently urged to attend out of a sense of civic duty. A *Winchester News* article entitled "WE SHOULD WAKE UP" exhorted:

> It has been several days since we have heard of the hospital movement. Is it possible that the interest in this project which is to mean so much towards the growth and improvement of our city, is on the wane? . . . We are told that a number of Winchester citizens attended a theatrical performance in Lexington, cheerfully paying train fare and the price of choice seats, all of which could not possibly benefit any but themselves, and that on the same evening at the Opera House in Winchester was given an attractive entertainment twenty per cent. of the proceeds of which was to go towards the hospital fund.[33]

Similarly, in Maysville, Kentucky, citizens were urged to patronize Washington Hall, which was owned by the local fire company, with income benefiting the fire department:

> Every one of the citizens should feel it incumbent upon himself to attend these entertainments. Besides having the satisfaction of witnessing the performance of a first-class troupe with the play properly put on the stage, they will also be contributing to the organization which has been at great expense built up a hall worthy of a city the size of Maysville. The few cities that can boast of a fire department that is as efficient and prompt in responding to a call for subduing the fire king as our department [*sic*]. And we should not let this opportunity pass to extend to them substantial aid which they at present so need. Let the house be crowded every night.[34]

Plays could also be presented as community fund-raising events, such as the "Home Talent Play to Be Produced at Donges Theater for Benefit Civic League" in Meyersdale, Pennsylvania, in 1913. The announcement in the *Republican* stressed the morality of the show, perhaps because, while drama was morally suspect, the civic league should not be: "'Golden Gulch' is not a shooting play, nor is it of the lurid type."[35]

Minstrel shows were also popular benefits, with the headlines from 1907 in Meyersdale, Pennsylvania, declaring

LADY MINSTRELS DO RIGHT WELL
Burnt Cork Artists From the County Seat Performed in Donges Theatre.
AUDIENCE NOT LARGE, BUT APPRECIATIVE.

The local flavor of the events was stressed in the description: "Even the editor of this paper who was the butt of some of the jokes is willing to admit that the ladies are to be complimented."[36]

Locally produced theatrical shows were also fund-raisers, but advertisements stressed the comparability to professional productions. When a local talent show "for the Ladies' Auxiliary of the Y.M.C.A., at Donges theatre" (1907) in Meyersdale, Pennsylvania, raised $250, the newspaper noted, "This entertainment proves that Meyersdale has plenty of home talent and that they have no need to go out of town and employ strangers to drill such entertainments."[37] Members of a local minstrel group in the same town and year were praised for being comparable to professionals: "The boys made a very fine appearance and looked like real minstrel men."[38] A flier for a local benefit production of *Ten Nights in a Bar Room* in Glouster, Ohio, in 1906 declared:

> "Ten Nights in a Bar Room," produced by a home talent company in Gordon's opera house, Saturday night, March 3, was up to the expectations of all, and those participating are deserving of the praise they received. Each one was a thorough master of his part and played it like a professional. In fact it was far superior to some shows that have traveled on the road for years and that charge an admission of 50c. The play has clearly demonstrated that Glouster has some talent of no mean ability and the people are justly proud of it.[39]

Women were responsible for many of these benefits; an announcement in 1882 stated, "The ladies of Maysville have decided to present at the opera house at an early day, 'The Smith Family,' which will be found most amusing."[40] The female "Junior Masonic Order" in Harlan, Kentucky, presented "Round The Clock with the De Molay" in 1924, billing it as a "local talent show: A Musical Comedy Novelty With 300 in the Cast. 36 Extreme Novelty Features—Absolutely New and Different from Anything That Has Ever Been Shown in Harlan Before . . . [with] Unsurpassed electrical effects."[41]

One of the most fascinating benefits was a mock trial held at the Winchester, Kentucky, Opera House in 1911 under the auspices of the Hart Chapter of

Flier for *Belles of Blackville,* a benefit performance at Stuart's Opera House, Nelsonville, Ohio. Reprinted with permission of Stuart's Opera House Archives, Nelsonville, Ohio.

the Daughters of the American Revolution, for the benefit of a proposed new hospital. The first *News* articles stressed the comic quality of the event:

> Fun! Fun! Fun!
> Let no innocent man escape. At the great
> 'MOCK COURT TRIAL' . . .
>
> One of our most citizens [*sic*] will be charged with Breach of Promise. Regular court rules. Startling developments. Ludicrous situations. Local hits. An evening of refined fun.[42]

Another article promoted the fictitious lurid intrigue of the trial: "No wonder there is deep interest when so important a question is at stake, as to whether the affections of fair woman shall be trifled with, her heart rent asunder and her future blighted, with no redress whatever." The article listed the town dignitaries—including court officials who would participate, proving "That this Mock Court Trial will be no light affair"—and concluded, "The jury to be empanelled if the lawyers do not kill each other before the trial begins."[43] The morally acceptable nature of the event is secured by the fact that it is offered as a benefit for the Daughters of the American Revolution, in the same place as a "Free Lecture on Christian Science."[44]

Another form of community event at the opera house were balls of various types, including "the Leap Year ball and supper given by the Ladies of Athens" in 1880,[45] and "calico masques" offered in 1885 and 1886 by the Nelsonville Dancing Association at Stuart's Opera House.[46] There is certainly a performative quality to a ball, especially one attended in costume—at which the partier is presenting him- or herself to others—so that each individual is simultaneously spectator and performer.

Richmond, Kentucky, held a ball with a social and political intent: to unite the community after the Civil War. The invitation stated: "You are respectfully invited to attend a masquerade ball to be given by the young men of Richmond, at Green's Opera Hall, Richmond, Ky." According to a local historian,

> At midnight came the unmasking. There were surprises and laughter and much hand-shaking. Sons of Union soldiers danced with daughters of Confederates, all unknown to each other until the paper masks were dropped to the floor. There was some embarrassment of course. Young people met and danced who had not spoken since the outbreak of the late war. Men too old to dance sat around the walls and talked freely and with friendliness without knowing each other until the mask was dropped.[47]

The opera house was also used for local religious events, both because it was a large, centrally located auditorium and, perhaps, because it was a way for churches and preachers to reach a wider audience. The staging of religious events at the opera house also demonstrates the importance of maintaining the moral rectitude of the venue. Other, nonreligious events, such as theatrical performances, could not be allowed to tarnish the building's character. If religious services were to be held in the opera house, it could not also be the site of sexually oriented entertainment, or even drama that was anything less than morally edifying. The opera house was used for Sunday school classes, church services (when a local church was being repaired, as in Marlinton, West Virginia, and Athens, Ohio), religious lectures ("Truth with the Bark Off,"[48] "Two Salvations But No Second Chance"[49]), religious drama (*Passion Play*), and religious school presentations.

Advertisement for lectures at the Knights of Pythias Opera House, Nelsonville, Ohio, 1924.

Public events that might otherwise have been held at the church also occurred at the opera house, including weddings and funerals. In Oil City, Pennsylvania, the 1885 marriage of Prince Flatow, a contortionist with Pullman's Boston Dime Museum and Theatre, to a local young woman was described prominently in the *Derrick*, a local newspaper. The account is worth quoting at length, given its emphasis on the performative nature of the wedding, including the curtain's rising and falling, the cast of characters (including biographies), the set, the musical accompaniment, the costumes, and the ovation. While these performative aspects are latent in any ceremony, the fact that the wedding occurs here on a stage brings the performance to the fore:

> All the chairs were occupied, and as for the gallery it was packed to suffocation, and many were turned away. The regular programme was enacted and as the curtain was rung down on the last act there was a noticeable uneasiness among the audience which plainly indicated the intense interest felt concerning the great event of the evening, namely the marriage of Prince Flatow and Miss Gray. (It might be well to mention here that Miss Hattie H. Gray is a resident of Meadville, and has relatives and friends in both this city and Franklin. She and the Prince have been engaged for some time, and it was only when the museum exhibited in Meadville, three weeks ago, that the novel idea of being married on the stage was talked of.) All preparations having previously been perfected, the audience was not kept long in waiting.
>
> As the curtain rose the stage was discovered set as a parlor, with handsome furniture and decorations. Flowers and flags ornamented the room, and on a stand in the center of the stage were a number of beautiful baskets and designs of flowers. As the wedding march, composed for the occasion by Prof. Church, was begun by the orchestra, little Dot and little Pearl Pullman entered, strewing flowers before the bridal party, which entered, marched once around the stage and

> formed in two lines, ladies at one side and gentlemen on the other, with the bride and groom in the centre. Justice Luman Stevens then stepped forward and the marriage service was gone through with. As the happy pair were pronounced one and the groom kissed the bride, a storm of applause arose, which continued until the curtain fell. The bride was beautifully dressed in a rich blue satin dress with lace trimmings, while the groom wore the conventional broadcloth. The bridesmaids were all charmingly attired and the whole presented a pretty picture.[50]

In Harlan, Kentucky, a wedding took place in the projection room of the movie theater during a showing:

> UNIQUE WEDDING AT THEATRE
>
> When Couple are United in Film Booth as Wedding Runs on Screen
>
> "The End." As these customary words flashed on the screen at the end of a feature picture at the New Harlan Theatre, Saturday night about 8 o'clock, they formed a perfect co-incidence with an act of real life. For preceding the words, "The End," there had been a happy scene where the stalwart hero took the lovable heroine in his strong arms, and—"they live happily ever after" and at the same time a wedding, back up in the motion picture booth of the theatre, had just been in progress and came to an end.
>
> Truly it may be said that this was one of the most unusual weddings ever officiated in Harlan. Miss Bessie Cooper . . . and Floyd E. Wilson, operator of the theatre, were married in the projection booth without any interruption of the running of the picture machines.[51]

In this case, the emphasis on the concurrence between the screen image and the projection room reality is striking.

For the funeral of Henry Johnson in 1882 at the Washington Opera House in Maysville, Kentucky, which was owned by the fire company, "The fire companies were all out in full force, and beside these a large attendance of ladies and citizens, to pay the sad offices of respect to the memory of the deceased."[52] The funeral services for Jack Bolen were held in 1905 at the Princess Theatre in Middlesborough, Kentucky, because "no church [was] large enough to accommodate the crowd."[53]

Sporting events also expose the implicit social understanding that obtained at the opera house. Sports that emphasized youth participation were considered acceptable fare, including basketball and roller-skating. Basketball was invented in the United States in 1891 and was widely popular by 1895. A basketball game involved high school students, family spectators, and town loyalty—all the

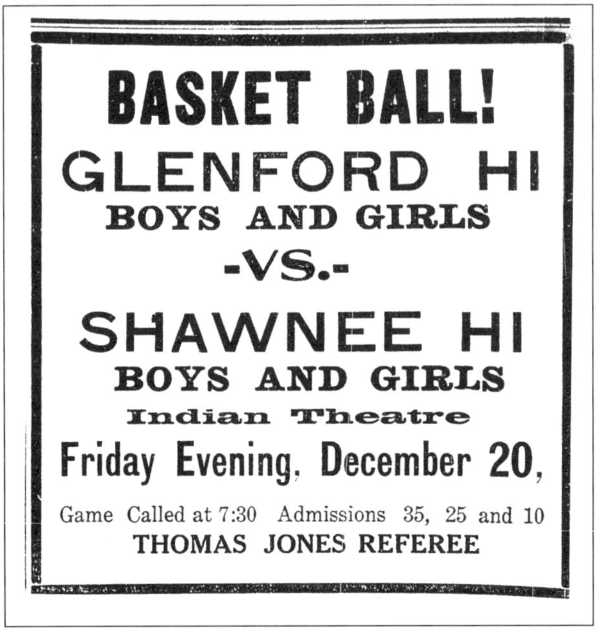

Advertisement for a basketball game at the Indian Theater (also known as the Red Men's Opera House), Shawnee, Ohio, 1929. From *Shawnee (OH) People's Advocate.*

ingredients for a perfect opera house event. Following the invention of ball-bearing skates, in 1884, roller-skating had its peak of popularity from 1885 to 1910. Roller-skating was common at opera houses with flat auditorium floors, and it functioned as a morally acceptable social interaction for sexually blooming boys and girls.

The novelty of roller-skating is evident in the 1883 report from Washington, Pennsylvania: "The Roller Skating Rink at the Town Hall last night was quite attractive. Quite a number of ladies were present and took their first lesson. They seemed to enjoy the exercuse [*sic*]."[54] The Athens Opera House, located in the city hall, probably had a flat floor, which may account for an 1883 *Messenger* article that reported "local juveniles of both sexes daily and nightly, in increasing number, availing themselves of the hilarious and health inspiring enjoyment" of skating.[55] In 1885, the moral underpinning of skating was reinforced: "A young people's roller skating club of large membership will hold their first meeting at the City Hall next Tuesday evening on which occasion new members of approved social standing will be received."[56] The emphasis on "approved social standing" shows that the organizers deemed it important to demonstrate the respectability and social rank of the activity, and that the opera house was a suitable location for such an activity.

Skating clearly existed in a nexus of other social activities. In Tarentum, Pennsylvania, the opera house (1886) was part of the largest commercial building in town, which housed a skating rink and dance hall in the rear of the building, as well as stores on the ground floor. In 1906, the newly built Tareco Opera House became the preeminent opera house in Tarentum, with the capacity to seat two hundred and a skating rink on the lower level.[57]

While opera houses were frequently adapted for skating, in a few cases the reverse occurred. In Oil City, Pennsylvania, the roller-skating rink was converted into an opera house after the existing opera house burned in 1884. The dimensions of the building were roughly comparable to other opera houses: 59 feet by 73 feet, 12 feet high at the sides, and 23 feet high at the center.[58] In Fairmont, West Virginia, a rink was built in the early 1880s as roller-skating was becoming popular; after its popularity subsided, it was converted into an opera house.[59]

Skating was often combined with other activities, and took place in a wide variety of opera house–like venues, including the Auditorium in Winchester, Kentucky, where people also played broomball[60] and basketball[61] in the first decade of the twentieth century. In Meyersdale, Pennsylvania, Reich's Auditorium in 1909 advertised skating, basketball, and dancing, and one could even combine activities: skating and watching movies.[62]

Sporting events that were presented for a working-class audience were subject to greater community regulation. An Athens, Ohio, women's club persuaded the county sheriff to cancel a scheduled professional boxing match that was to include James J. Jeffries, who was billed as "Champion of the World," in the neighboring mining town of Nelsonville. Miners came to Nelsonville on branch trains from all over the Hocking Valley, and without the fight to watch they flooded the bars. A riot ensued, leaving one man dead.[63] On the other hand, boxing matches in other towns that emphasized local participation were more acceptable. In New Straitsville, Ohio, in 1904, the *Record* announced, "The 'boys' of the town are preparing to pull off a boxing contest in the Opera House next Wednesday night. The participants will be local followers of the 'manly art' and none but friendly set-to's will be entered. A big crowd is expected from down the valley."[64]

As film entered the opera house in the early twentieth century, newsreels became a medium for rural Americans to see major national sporting events at the opera house, as they did in 1910 in Winchester, Kentucky: "OPERA HOUSE . . . World Series Baseball Games: CHICAGO VS. PHILADELPHIA. Showing some of the greatest fielding, base running, slugging and accurate throwing. Also 2000 FEET of comedy and dramatic pictures. Continuous Performance."[65] Spectators in Carlisle, Pennsylvania, in 1897 could see a Vitascope of a boxing match between Jim Corbett and Bob Fitzsimmons, which the newspaper transformed into acceptable opera house fare by noting that when the fight was shown in

Backstage poster for a boxing match at Stuart's Opera House, Nelsonville, Ohio, that was banned after pressure from a women's club. Reprinted with permission of Stuart's Opera House Archives, Nelsonville, Ohio.

Boston the audience consisted of ladies and gentlemen in evening dress; in addition the "fight" was only a motion picture, so the audience could see it without the "necessity of seeing men actually suffer."[66]

Social structures and the opera house converged in community preparation for World War I. In 1918, with Americans heading off to war, the Knights of Labor and Red Men Opera Houses in Shawnee, Ohio, held patriotic celebrations, farewell dances, Decoration Day services, and benefits. One announcement declared, "A patriotic entertainment will be given in the Indian opera house . . . for the benefit of our Allied Babies," with a program consisting of songs, bands, piano and speeches.[67] The following day, after holding a parade, "the Shawnee

Parade of veterans of the Grand Army of the Republic in 1888, gathered for a ceremonial photograph in front of the Wagner Opera House, Bradford, Pennsylvania (1876). Reprinted with permission of Bradford Landmark Society.

Chapter of the Red Cross gave an entertainment and banquet . . . in honor of the boys who will leave for camp Sunday." The event took place "in the K. of P. opera house."[68] The opera house also showed a film at about life at Camp Sherman.[69] The "Good Time Club" gave a farewell party and dance, also held at the Knights of Pythias Opera House, "in honor of the 14 Shawnee boys who leave here Saturday, May 25th for Camp Sherman."[70] In preparation for Decoration Day, the town held "Joint Memorial Services," consisting of patriotic songs, prayers, and music, at the opera house.[71] The prominence of the opera house is evident from the description of the parade route for the enlisting soldiers, which went "over the principal streets and halted on Main street in front of the K. of P. opera house, where a splendid program was rendered."[72]

Audiences at this particular time and place found these opera house events compelling because they involved audiences personally in the subjects of religion, education, jobs, politics, war, and sports. The presentations were so inclusive that everyone had a family member or a family event at the opera house. Cultural events at the opera house were subject to community regulation, and the dominant moral code was enforced. The community also gained a rich diversity of cultural programming.

CHAPTER NINE

Variety at the Opera House

The opera house offered its patrons an extraordinary variety of theatrical entertainment. To take but one example, there were 347 nights available for performances in the 1884–85 opera house season in Oil City, Pennsylvania (excluding the 57 Sundays). The opera house had events on 103 of these nights, including many nontheatrical events. Of the more conventional theatrical entertainment, 68 different touring companies provided 51 plays; 19 minstrel, variety, and concert performances; and 17 operas and operettas.[1]

One way of tracking the variety of events at the opera house is to note the multiple advertisements that appeared side by side on a given newspaper page. For example, in Athens, Ohio, on November 29, 1883, three notes appeared on the same page of the *Messenger* for events in the city hall, where the opera house was located:

> Miss Jennie Calef was warmly greeted with a large audience at the Athens City Hall . . . whom she uniformly, without apparent effort, agreeably impressed with her magnificent acting.
>
> The little girls of the Presbyterian S.S. infant class invite their friends to come to their Doll Show and Ironholder sale which they will hold at the W.C.T.U. room in the City Hall.
>
> The ladies of the Women's Christian Temperance Union of Athens will hold a prayer meeting in their new room in the City Hall building to-morrow.[2]

Backstage wall at Stuart's Opera House, Nelsonville, Ohio, covered with posters for many shows, indicating the variety of presentations at the opera house. Reprinted with permission of Stuart's Opera House Archives, Nelsonville, Ohio.

The important role of women at the opera house is demonstrated in the fact that all these events were held by, for, or about women.

In Shawnee, Ohio, articles appeared side by side on February 6, 1914, for a lyceum course and a Pythian minstrel show, both at the Knights of Pythias Opera House, and both typical of opera house variety shows:

> THE K. OF P. GOLDEN JUBILEE
>
> Golden Jubilee of the order of the Knights of Pythias
> A grand minstrel show, ball and supper will be given.
>
> A SPLENDID ENTERTAINMENT
>
> The K. of P. opera house was filled to its capacity Wednesday evening when the Hussar Quartet, fourth number of the Lyceum Course appeared. Agreeable to anticipation each member of the program was artistically and entertainingly rendered and the large audience in nowise failed to manifest its appreciation.[3]

Sixteen years later in Shawnee, a dinner dance and a musical comedy were advertised, both at the Knights of Pythias Opera House and both local benefits, another central feature of opera house fare:

ST. MARY'S CHURCH . . .
GOLDEN JUBILEE BAZAAR . . .
Chicken Dinner . . .
Dancing in The Evening . . .
A REUNION
Of Old Shawnee People

"COOL KNIGHTS"
A THREE ACT
MUSICAL COMEDY
(SPONCERED [*sic*] BY O.E.S.)
A Professional Show by People You Know.[4]

Finally, in Harlan, Kentucky, on April 7, 1923, a double ad for the New Harlan Theatre juxtaposed a mining movie and Oscar Wilde:

THE LITTLE CHURCH AROUND THE CORNER
A Special Coal Mining Picture with The Greatest All Star Cast
ever assembled in any one Picture

The Strollers Dramatic Club of University of Kentucky Presents
"LADY WINDERMERE'S FAN"
by Oscar Wilde[5]

The opera house was popular in the community because there was something for everyone. The period from the end of the Civil War to the end of the 1920s has been called the "golden age of popular entertainment in America." Popular entertainment flourished because of increased leisure time, improved transportation, and the rapid growth of cities. People had more time and money for amusement, and it was easier to take the family outside the home.[6]

In this golden age, Lawrence W. Levine argues, the twentieth-century distinction between "high" and "low" culture did not exist. During the nineteenth century, Shakespearean dramas and bel canto operas "were able to enjoy simultaneously high cultural status and mass popularity." In the nineteenth century, "Americans, in addition to whatever specific cultures they were a part of, shared a public culture less hierarchically organized, less fragmented into relatively rigid adjectival boxes than their descendants were to experience a century later." While Levine specifically addresses theaters, his comments also apply to small-town opera houses. Under the single roof of a single theater was "a microcosm of American society," with three to four social classes in the same theater at the same time; "and all of those classes had to be addressed." The events at a given theater therefore catered to "the entire spectrum of the population" and included "the complete range of entertainment from tragedy to farce, juggling to ballet, opera to minstrelsy. The theatre drew all ranks of people to one place." Levine argues that the shared culture that existed in early-nineteenth-century America had changed by the end of the century.[7] This assertion may hold up for larger towns and cities, in which, by century's end, there were several venues for entertainment, each specialized according to class and type of entertainment. But in the small towns of Appalachia, the opera house remained the single site of entertainment, and therefore the microcosm of shared culture was maintained longer than in major urban centers. Granted, the opera house audience may not always have been a microcosm of the mining town, in that some events were targeted toward women, men, children, or particular ethnic groups. On the other hand, events for all these groups took place in a common space.

Variety entertainments included saloon theater, minstrelsy, burlesque, museum theater, lyceum, chautauquas, medicine shows, and vaudeville. While there were subtle differences between these forms, they all shared a common structure, consisting of a series of unrelated, independent acts assembled into a single show. There was no plot to the whole, and the events had no thematic relationship to one another.[8]

The earliest variety shows in the United States took place in saloons in the 1840s, as owners provided free entertainment to attract and keep their customers, and to get them to buy more liquor. Concert saloons, which peaked in popularity from the Civil War through the next two decades, provided free or low-cost shows, primarily for men. Entertainment consisted of variety performances, including singers, dancers, musicians, comedians, and minstrelsy. Action within the audience consisted of drinking, coarse humor, gambling, smoking, and prostitution.

Many people felt that concert saloons promoted the related immoral acts of drinking, sex, and performance. "Waiter girls," who served drinks to men and sat with them, were often identified as prostitutes, but may have been barmaids or part-time performers. Some concert saloons also had private boxes or rooms for prostitution or other sexual assignations.[9] There was an effort in many cities to clean up saloon theaters in the 1860s, so they developed into "variety theaters," but still with men drinking alcohol while watching dancing girls.[10]

Some concert saloons were in former theaters, but most were in former saloons with a flat floor for tables and chairs, and a rudimentary stage at one end of the room. And while opera house promoters, with their moral project, would not care to admit to an influence from concert saloons, Brooks McNamara suggests that the small stage, flat floor, and small balcony at one end may have provided a model for opera house architecture.[11]

Roughly contemporaneous with saloon theaters were minstrel shows, which began in the early 1840s, with whites performing comedy and musical skits in blackface. The original minstrels claimed they were using authentic African American dialects, songs, dances, and jokes. But William Mahar argues that minstrelsy was not as simple as white appropriation or invention of an image of southern African American music and dance. Minstrelsy borrowed from a variety of sources, including English, French, and Italian musicals and a range of dramatic and literary sources. This European tradition was imported to the United States and was incorporated into the existing African American and Anglo-American tradition.[12]

Thomas D. Rice, credited with being the first minstrel performer, was an "Ethiopian delineator," a name for early blackfaced white entertainers. Rice claimed that he saw a crippled African American named Jim Crow singing and dancing, using a hopping and spinning motion. Rice said that he purchased the man's clothes, learned the song and dance, and embellished on it. He first performed the routine in 1828 and reached New York in 1832. Four performers, led by Dan Emmett, created the Virginia Minstrels in 1843; their show was billed as an evening of "oddities, peculiarities, eccentricities, and comicalities of that Sable Genius of Humanity." The use of "Virginia" made a claim to Southern authenticity, and "minstrels" was an attempt to capitalize on the recent successful tour of the "Tyrolese Minstrel Family," a group of European performers. In the 1840s, the Virginia Minstrels had many imitators, including E. P. Christy, who is credited with creating the common minstrel show structure.[13]

There is no question that minstrelsy was based on a racist construction of what whites perceived to be African American culture. Frederick Douglass famously referred to minstrels as "the filthy scum of white society, who have stolen from us a complexion denied to them by nature, in which to make money, and pander to the corrupt taste of their white fellow citizens."[14] And minstrelsy has remained infamous for perpetuating negative stereotypes of American blacks long after the performances ended. According to Eric Lott, "blackface minstrelsy's century-long commercial regulation of black cultural practices stalled the development of African-American public arts and generated an enduring narrative of racist ideology."[15] In addition to stereoptyping and oppressing African Americans, minstrelsy enforced a strict gender hierarchy. Mahar emphasizes that minstrelsy was primarily male entertainment for men; it defined acceptable standards for male sentimentality and marginalized women in songs and dramatic sketches "that restricted their sexual, domestic, and public roles in American society."[16]

Minstrelsy is nonetheless important, if for no other reason than that it was the most widespread form of entertainment in the United States from the 1850s through the 1880s, and was, alas, America's first original contribution to variety performance. Minstrelsy provided the basis for vaudeville, burlesque, radio, movies, and television. In addition, minstrel performers created popular and entertaining shows for the lower- and middle-class white audiences that attended opera houses in Appalachia. According to Don B. Wilmeth, "Minstrelsy was the first major stage entertainment to avoid the elitist reputation of legitimate drama and commit itself to the new common-man audience. It was immediate, unpretentious, and devoted to fun, the emotional outlet that its urban patrons needed so desperately."[17]

In the early days of minstrelsy, there was neither a fixed number of performers nor a fixed format for performance; instead the organization was "flexible and open-ended." As Mahar notes, minstrel shows included "a variety of acts and parts of longer performance routines and programs presented by different ensembles rather than a relatively rigid format in a tightly organized type of theater."[18] E. P. Christy later established the common structure, in which, for the first part, the performers stood in a semicircle facing the audience. The "interlocutor," or master of ceremonies, stood center stage, flanked by two comic "end men," Bruder Bones and Bruder Tambo, playing bones (flat clappers) and tambourine, respectively. The three engaged in repartee, with the end men mocking the pomposity of the interlocutor. This first part also consisted of jokes, serious and comic songs, dances, and specialty roles. The second part, called the "olio," was a series of variety acts in front of a curtain, allowing time for the final act to be set up behind. It consisted of song and dance; acrobats; men playing combs, porcupine quills, and glasses; and novelty acts; and concluded with a comic send-up of a political speech, full of malapropisms. The final part was a one-act skit.[19] The acts consisted of parodies of lectures or sermons, adaptations of scenes from operas and plays, and "Ethiopian" sketches and farces of plantation life, which were adaptable to other ethnic groups, such as the Irish.[20] Shows also dealt with social issues, such as the dangers of urban life, city living conditions, social and moral changes, and inequities in wealth.[21]

Like other variety entertainments, minstrelsy changed over time, and it incorporated other forms of entertainment after the Civil War, reaching its peak of popularity around 1870. In the late nineteenth century minstrelsy faced competition from variety shows, musicals, and burlesque, in addition to African American minstrel troupes, starting after the Civil War. Minstrels had lost their monopoly on American entertainment and had to reach markets in novel ways, employing new specialty acts and more lavish productions, with less emphasis on blacks and the South. As minstrel shows became more spectacular, refined,

Advertisement for a minstrel show in Athens, Ohio, in 1924, indicating the endurance of minstrel shows as benefits in small towns. From *Athens (OH) Messenger.*

and generalized, they grew farther from their roots.[22] While minstrelsy maintained a long life by incorporating other forms of entertainment, it also lost what made it unique, and it declined in popularity in the 1890s. By 1896 there were only ten touring minstrel companies left, and the form had been superseded by vaudeville. Minstrelsy lasted longer in small towns, however, including in the opera houses studied here. In its latter years, Robert C. Toll points out, minstrelsy "became nostalgic about its own past,"[23] especially in small towns, where the old songs, jokes, and dances were still popular.[24]

For example, John W. Vogel's Big City Minstrels presented a traditional minstrel show at Stuart's Opera House in Nelsonville, Ohio, about 1903, but with an emphasis on spectacle. The first part was "a grand scenic embellishment, entitled 'The Electric Velour First Part,' produced at an actual cost of $500,000," including "Terpsichorean movements by Gov. Bowen and assistants." There was the traditional Interlocutor, and Tambo and Bones, followed by skits entitled "Call a Cab and Send Me Home," "Oh My!" "That's a Habit I Never Had," and "The Preacher and the Bear." After the intermission, the olio included a series of variety acts unrelated to traditional minstrelsy:

> THE GREAT KNETZGER—Master Spirit of Ambidexterity.
> MARVELOUS MARSEILLES—The anatomical enigma—The most sensational act of the age direct from the Alhambra, London, England.
> FRED P. RUSSELL—Will tickle your risibilities.
> The Aeolian Voiced Soprano MASTER NEWTON SEE . . .
> THE FAMOUS D'ELMARS—Comedy Acrobatic Barrel Jumpers, performing seemingly impossible gymnastic feats.
> GOOD NIGHT.[25]

That minstrelsy was then in decline can be seen in the Stuart's program for Al. G. Fields Greater Minstrels in 1904. This "SCENIC SPECTACLE ENTITLED 'The Evolution of Minstrelsy,' ANCIENT, MEDIEVAL AND MODERN" implicitly accepted, and at the same time celebrated, the historic and anachronistic nature of the performance. The overture was called "a Merry Melange of Mirth and Music" and included such well-liked songs as "Lindy Lou," "The Songs My Mother Used to Sing," "Sweet Adeline," "Isabelly," and "Prohibition Party." After a "mammoth singing and dancing divertisement," variety performers appeared, including "THE QUAKER CITY QUARTETTE—Musical Blacksmith, in instrumental and vocal selections, interspersed with comedy" and "THE TWO AVOLOS—Originators of the greatest acrobatic and gymnastic novelty of the age. The only artists throwing double somersaults from perpendicular bars." The performance also used spectacle to appeal to the patriotic feelings of the audience:

> "WHILE OLD GLORY WAVES"—a review of the military service of the United States from the Colonial Days to the present.
> First Tableau—Washington crossing the Delaware
> Second Tableau—Hickory Jackson at New Orleans
> Third Tableau—The Alamo
> Fourth Tableau—The Destruction of the Maine
> Military Maneuqers [*sic*]—Tom McKenna introducing a corps of regular Soldiers.
> Tableau—"Old Glory."

Finally the show mocked the current president and rival candidate, with Spooneristic songs about "Pudge Jarker" and "Rosey Tedevelt."[26]

An 1883 review of a Hi. Henry's Minstrels performance in Athens, Ohio, also provides evidence of minstrelsy's declining popularity: "The performance in the main was excellent. The repertoire of the end men, however, was somewhat antiquated, and so excellent a leader as Mr. Henry should remedy this defect in the organization of his company if he wishes to retain the popular approval which has heretofore greeted his efforts in presenting to the public a first class entertainment."[27]

Burlesque, another variant of variety theater, was influenced by the saloon theaters, with their scantily clad female performers, and minstrelsy, when minstrel producers in the post–Civil War era sought to reinvigorate a flagging form by adding women. Burlesque consisted of variety acts, risqué jokes, comic sketches, musical numbers, and scantily clad women. *The Black Crook,* performed at New York's Niblo's Garden in 1866, with its combination of spectacle and dance, is usually credited as the first American burlesque. Lydia Thompson and Her British Blondes, which followed in 1869, included send-ups of current books and plays, along with the ubiquitous female performers. The first producer to exploit and standardize the form was M. B. Leavitt, who formed the Rentz-Santley Novelty and Burlesque Company in the 1870s. Mme. Rentz's Female Minstrels, first performing in 1879, combined minstrelsy, saloon theater, and popular theater. Leavitt made burlesque more respectable, taking it out of the saloons and into theaters. In the early twentieth century, the comic was the centerpiece of burlesque. Striptease, for which burlesque is most famous today, did not become part of burlesque until the 1920s and 1930s, with Izzy Herk's Mutual Association and the Minsky Brothers.[28] Since burlesque was identified with a lower-class, male audience, and the entertainment was considered morally suspect, there are few specific references to burlesque at the opera house. The opera house's moral agenda would have been compromised by the appearance of burlesque onstage.

In reaction to the perceived immorality of theater and its variety of performances, museums started offering "lectures" that were dramatic performances in all but name. "Dime museums" started in the mid-1840s and 1850s, with Moses Kimball's Boston Museum and P. T. Barnum's American Museum in New York. Dime museums flourished across the United States throughout the rest of the century, peaked in popularity between 1880 and 1900, and declined in the early 1900s. While other urban entertainment was separated according to class, dime museums brought the lower, middle, and upper classes together. Museums encouraged middle-class patronage, especially that of women and children, and created exhibitions and events that were respectable enough to preserve the reputations of their patrons, but cheap enough for everyone to attend.[29]

Dime museums contained a "lecture room," initially meant for natural-history lectures and science demonstrations; its use was then extended to magic-lantern shows and musical acts. Lecture rooms finally presented plays with a strong moral content, such as temperance plays, Biblical dramas, and *Uncle Tom's Cabin,* but they preserved the name "lecture room." These plays sold so well that the lecture rooms were regularly enlarged, seating up to three thousand by 1850; the plays were performed by museum stock companies, of which there may have been up to thirty-five by 1850.[30] Most spectators were native born, culturally Protestant, and middle class—"citizens especially vulnerable to status anxiety," according to Bruce McConachie.[31] The museum theaters, with their emphasis on morality and their avoidance of the term "theater," were forerunners of post–Civil War opera houses.

Lyceum was another form of educationally oriented variety entertainment. Like museum theaters, and later opera houses, this form emerged in deference to Protestant objections to theater. Josiah Holbrook founded the lyceum movement in 1826, with the name borrowed from an ancient Greek Temple of Apollo, Lyceus, where Aristotle taught. Lyceums were lecture-demonstrations; they were first given for textile workers in Massachusetts and then spread across the United States. The goals of these lectures and debates were self-improvement and scientific and literary study. After the Civil War, lyceums were controlled by large lecture bureaus, such as James Redpath's Boston Lyceum Bureau, that organized national tours of professional lecturers, including Susan B. Anthony, Henry Ward Beecher, William Jennings Bryan, Edward Everett Hale, Wendell Phillips, Charles Sumner, Henry M. Stanley, and Mark Twain. These bureaus added other entertainment, turning the lyceum into a form of variety show.[32]

John Heyl Vincent founded the chautauqua in 1874 in the upstate New York town of the same name, originally to improve Sunday school teaching. Influenced by the New York chautauqua, hundreds of midwestern towns created their own, using local talent and the lyceum form. Later, tent or circuit chautauquas toured all over America. By 1913, nationally managed touring lectures had largely replaced the locally organized chautauquas. Chautauquas were sold to communities in package form, providing entertainment and education for mass consumption. Chautauquas flourished in the late nineteenth century and reached their peak between 1920 and 1924, when ten thousand communities sponsored programs. In 1924, forty million Americans attended chautauqua events. The form declined quickly thereafter, with competition from film, radio, and automobiles, and died out after the stock market crash of 1929.[33]

There is great overlap between lyceums and chautauquas. Both consisted of a combination of singers, preachers, lecturers, performers, and musical acts. The same bureaus often managed both, and the same performers often appeared in both. In winter, managers booked acts into lyceums in opera houses, and in summer into chautauquas in huge brown tents. There was also great crossover between lyceums/chautauquas and family-oriented vaudeville, especially in the early 1900s. Lyceums and chautauquas might include readings of plays, including *Uncle Tom's Cabin* and plays by Shakespeare. Both forms also used projected entertainment, including in travelogue lectures, which consisted of dramatic readings with magic-lantern or early moving images. The reading created a mood or told about the slides, which provided visual images of exotic locales.[34]

Lyceums/chautauquas were central to small-town life in America, as an editor in Independence, Iowa, noted in 1867: "To be without a lecture course is considered a reproach to any progressive town of the West."[35] According to Atherton, "Lyceum series were justified on the grounds of instruction, moral uplift, the fostering of libraries, and entertainment, with entertainment becoming progressively more and more dominant." While famous names toured the larger opera houses, "little towns . . . had to be content with less expensive performers who discussed the need for prohibition, offered feats of magic with their dialogue, or told of travels in foreign lands."[36]

While chautauquas generally took place in tents during the summer, lyceums and lecture courses were common in opera houses. Some lectures seem delightfully silly, such as the 1881 lecture in Logan, Ohio: "Opera House for one night only . . . Robert J. Burdette of the Burlington Hawkeye in his famous lecture, entitled, 'Rise and Fall of the Mustache.'"[37] In Athens in 1894, "the fourth and last entertainment of the Epworth League" was announced, with "local talent" promising to be "varied and interesting." That the lecture series would combine teaching and pleasing is evident in an article from that year: "The Athens lecture course had a most gratifying close in the grand *concert* . . . which was enjoyably appreciated by the very large and refined audience present. . . . Professor Dunkle is already engaged in preparations to secure an even more interesting and edifying program for next season's course, which will include some of the best known platform attractions procurable."[38] Similarly, in Shawnee, Ohio, a lecture course opened in 1902 with Ritchie's Unique Entertainers at the Knights of Pythias Opera House,[39] and in neighboring New Straitsville, Ohio, a lecture course in 1902 included the Alice Carey Concert Company.[40]

Oil City, Pennsylvania, advertised in 1885 for the "STAR LYCEUM COURSE" at the New Opera House, with Miss Florence Marryat in "her Celebrated Musical and Dramatic Monologue entertainment, entitled, 'LOVE LETTERS.'" The price structure emphasized that the event was part of a series and encouraged ongoing participation: "Admission 50c; with Reserved Seat, 75c. Tickets for the Course: Admission to Three Entertainments, with Reserved Seat, $1.50."[41]

Some lectures were geared more toward business or promotional purposes. Miners in the model company town of Stearns, Kentucky, in 1932 could attend "GENTLEMEN PREFER BEEF . . . PICTURE-TALK: ADMISSION FREE . . . How to Select and Prepare Meat That Is Man's First Choice" at "Store No. 1."[42] A lecture in Winchester, Kentucky, sought to entice residents to migrate west on the railroads in 1911: "Dr. M. E. Broaddus, the official lecturer of the emigration department of the Frisco line," delivered a lecture at the Winchester, Kentucky, Auditorium, "followed by stereoptican views of the county, showing crops grown and how much to the acre and the wonderful development of the South West country in recent years. He told of the cheap twice a week rates via the Frisco line to home seekers." He was also supposed to give a lecture that night at the Court House, "but he failed to put in an appearance at that hour and the audience become discouraged and went home."[43] The goal, of course, was to entice people to purchase land along railway lines, providing a profit to the developer (most likely the railroad company) and providing business for the railroad.

Medicine shows toured throughout the United States from 1870 to 1930, with anywhere from two to thirty performers. A "professor" or "doctor" was the master of ceremonies, and sold medicines of dubious value, accompanied by a variety of entertainments. About one-third of the show was for the medicinal lecture, demonstrations, and sales, and the rest for variety entertainment.[44] The doctors made up their own tonics in bathtubs or, if it was a big-time operation, got them from national distributors. One such medicine man, T. P. Kelley, favored a particular state: "I made more money in small Ohio villages than I did in fair-sized towns in other states. . . . When the natives would raise their hands, holding bills and eager to buy my remedies, from the stage platform it would appear like a waving sea of currency was before me. It was a beautiful sight."[45]

Medicine shows toured to rural areas and small towns across America, performing in vacant lots, tents, and opera houses. There was usually no admission fee, because income came from sales of medicines and candies between the acts. In effect, a medicine show was a variety show with commercials. The entertainment consisted of Wild West shows, singing, dancing, acrobatics, fire eating, lectures, movies, magic, Punch and Judy, pantomime, menageries, and pie-eating contests; it ended with a comedy sketch from a minstrel show.[46] In Mechanicsburg, Pennsylvania, Professor Lorman rode into town selling Indian Oil in 1887 in a golden chariot pulled by four white horses, along with singers, a banjo player, and a ventriloquist, all preceded by a parade.[47]

Vaudeville was perhaps the broadest and most inclusive form of variety entertainment, consisting of a wide variety of acts, sketches, and short plays. One of the first to use the term "vaudeville" was H. J. Sargent, in 1871, with his "Sargent's Great Vaudeville Company" in Louisville, Kentucky. M. B. Leavitt's

Gigantic Vaudeville Stars followed in 1880. The roots of the word "vaudeville" are vague, but the term was chosen for that very vagueness, as well as its exoticism and gentility. "Variety" seemed more "crude and vulgar," while "vaudeville," with its French aura, seemed more "polished and refined."[48] Vaudeville provided light entertainment with no intellectual pretensions, aimed at a mass audience. It included slapstick, magic, comic routines, recitations, dramatic readings, trained animals, opera singers, sexual impersonators, ballet dancers, and ethnic humor.[49]

Tony Pastor is often credited as the father of vaudeville, though he preferred the term "variety." He promoted his performances as "decent," sold no liquor, and encouraged women to attend his theaters in New York City in the 1880s and 1890s. He sometimes offered door prizes to women, including sewing machines, hats, and silk dresses, or gave gifts, such as dress patterns or sewing kits, to all the women who attended a performance.[50]

Although Tony Pastor may have created vaudeville, it was B. F. Keith who made modern vaudeville into a nationwide industry. He institutionalized and popularized it, beginning with his first theater in Boston in 1887. Vaudeville theater became established as a form of variety theater made tasteful for the middle class, with none of the smoking, liquor, scantily clad women, or male atmosphere prevalent in saloon theaters, variety, or burlesque.[51]

By 1900, vaudeville had replaced minstrelsy as the most popular form of entertainment, with its heyday from the 1880s through the early 1930s. In the 1910s, there were ten to twenty thousand acts and five thousand vaudeville theaters, including eighty in big cities, the most famous of which was the Palace in New York City.[52] Vaudeville declined in the late 1910s and 1920s, with talent going to revues, musical comedies, burlesque, and then radio, records, and movies. The form was dead by 1932, when movies took over the Palace.[53]

While vaudeville borrowed from other forms, it did provide a new organization. The 1890s was the period of the commercialization of American entertainment, the era of trusts, monopolies, and conglomerates. As the legitimate theater was controlled by the Syndicate, so vaudeville was controlled by a few circuits run by E. F. Albee, B. F. Keith, Marcus Loew, F. F. Proctor, Alexander Pantages, and Martin Beck.[54]

Vaudeville was derivative and eclectic, relying on a combination of popular forms. Structurally vaudeville was virtually identical to variety: individual acts loosely strung together. It used elements of the minstrel show, especially the series of specialty acts in the olio half of the show and the humor of minstrelsy. From the circus it took the acrobats and trained animals. *The Black Crook,* the grandfather of modern musicals and burlesque, provided the structure of an assemblage of acts based on a flimsy plot. *Uncle Tom's Cabin* showed that a performance could be expanded and contracted with specialty acts. From variety shows, vaudeville took the skits, songs, dances, and comic monologues. The close relationships of all these entertainment forms are evident in the fact that performers readily moved from one form to another in early days of vaudeville.[55]

Although vaudeville seemed just a collection of acts, it was actually tightly structured to keep the audience's interest. Each act was short—only minutes long.[56] According to Robert C. Toll, "The show business form that seemed the most unstructured, that seemed little more than an entertainment hodgepodge, was in fact meticulously planned and highly structured to offer a balanced variety, to build excitement and expectation, to pulsate with its own rhythm, and to convey a sense of order and unity. The form of the vaudeville show was a new ritual for the new age."[57]

Vaudeville often had eight acts, with six acts leading up to the star's appearance in the next-to-last act.[58] The first act was called the "doormat of vaudeville," or the "dumb act," with no talking because of the many latecomers. This act might include dancers, jugglers, acrobats, bicycle riders, or animal acts. The second act's job was to settle the audience, and could be anything, such as a man and woman singing duo, provided it was more entertaining than the first. The third act's job was to wake the audience up, and could be a comedy sketch, a magician, a sister act, dancers, or a swimming act. Fourth was a big name or a spectacular scene, providing the first big "punch" of the show. Fifth was a big song and dance act, with a big star, to leave the audience buzzing during intermission. The sixth act, after intermission, was to keep the audience's interest, but not to be bigger than the seventh and most important act—the star. Finally came the "chaser," whose job it was to clear the auditorium but keep the audience happy.[59]

The key to vaudeville's wide appeal was its family orientation, and this is what made it prevalent at the opera house. Around the middle of the nineteenth century, theater owners realized that they needed to draw middle-class white women to their theaters in order to improve the reputations of the theaters. They promoted theatergoing as being educational, uplifting, and family oriented. Keith's strategy was to get women and children into his theaters so as to then attract the middle class as his target audience. According to Keith, "theatrical managers seemed to have quite ignored the wants of the average American family for theatrical amusements."[60] The audience had to be silenced and prostitution had to be curtailed in accord with what M. Alison Kibler terms the "sacralized, feminized culture" of the late nineteenth century.[61] Keith provided vaudeville with a strong moral tone, and he offered no objectionable material in what was known as the "Sunday School circuit." Keith believed that "the stage show must be free from vulgarisms and coarseness of any kind," so that the vaudeville auditorium would be "as 'homelike' an amusement resort as it was possible to make it."[62] He therefore censored his shows: "If there was one coarse, vulgar, or suggestive line or piece of stage business in the act, I cut it out." He had an "obsession with purity," and placed signs in his theaters such as "The use of 'Damn' and 'Hell' is forbidden on the stage of this theatre. If a performer cannot do without using them he need not open here." Other forbidden terms included "slob," "son of a gun," "liar," "devil," and "sucker."[63] A 1918 manual by Edward Renton on how to run a vaudeville theater stated,

> In advertising a group of classical dancers, the fact that their wardrobe is scant should not be featured; rather the aesthetic and beautiful points should be emphasized—and this may result in securing not only the patronage of those who might come with an idea of looking at nude limbs but as well of those who have a sincere appreciation for and knowledge of art and the beautiful. The latter *will not* be drawn by advertisements and stories of the attraction in which the feature of nudity is vulgarly or coarsely handled.[64]

Despite these attempts by management to control audiences in vaudeville, they were sometimes more lively and active than management would have liked. Specifically, Keith's control of audiences and performers was probably stronger in "big time" theaters than in small. While Keith boasts of his polite audiences, unpublished reports by local managers refer to a wide range of audience behavior.[65] In addition, vaudeville was more dependent on audience involvement than "legitimate" drama, in which audiences were to silently peer through the fourth wall. Managers wanted to control audiences, but vaudeville performers wanted audience members to participate in sing-alongs, volunteer for magic acts, and so on. According to Butsch, "The active audience . . . never entirely disappeared. It remained always a possibility if not a realization, even a necessity of the entertainer's success and the entrepreneur's profit. Rowdiness always survived on the margins."[66] (The struggle over onstage moral standards and audience behavior in opera houses is addressed in chapter 2.)

Variety entertainment, including vaudeville, was a major part of opera house fare. The Stuart's Opera House (Nelsonville, Ohio, 1904–5 season) program for *Buster Brown's Holiday,* a thematic variety show based on the cartoon series, emphasized the authenticity of this production as "The Only Production Authorized by the N.Y. Herald." The advertising stressed the family orientation of the entertainment:

> The one, the Only Play, Suited to All Ages and Every Eye
>
> THE ONLY COMEDY SURE TO MAKE
>
> GRANDMA GAY

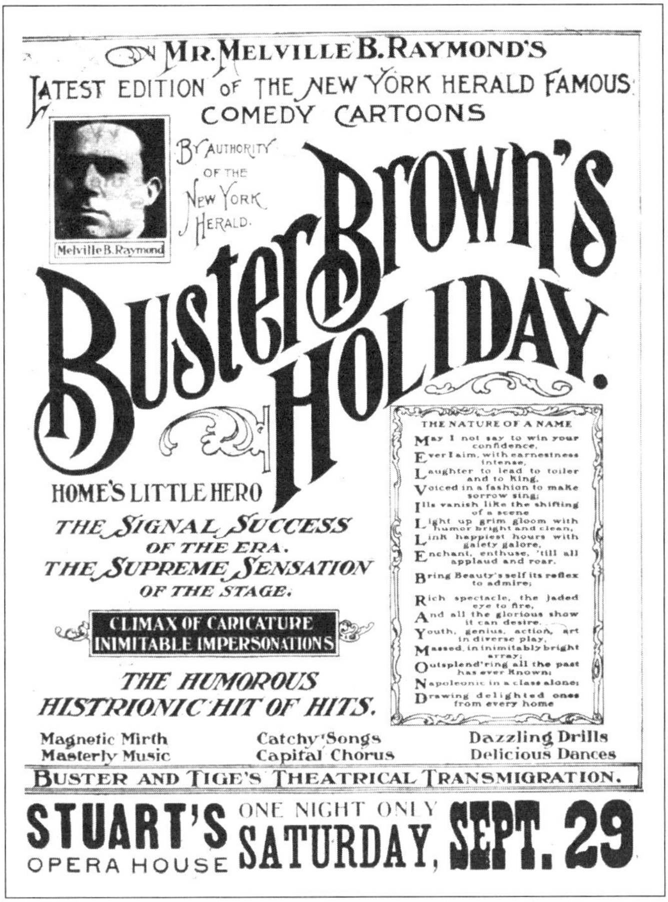

Program for *Buster Brown's Holiday* at Stuart's Opera House, Nelsonville, Ohio, an example of a vaudeville show at the opera house. Reprinted with permission of Stuart's Opera House Archives, Nelsonville, Ohio.

GRANDPA GRIN

MOTHER MOST MERRY

FATHER FEEL FUNNY

SEE IT NOW

IT WILL MAKE YOU YOUNG AGAIN[67]

Despite the moral emphasis of vaudeville, women were still a feature, as is evident in the presentation of *The Liberty Belles* in Nelsonville, Ohio, in 1905. The program promises:

Program for *The Liberty Belles* at Stuart's Opera House, Nelsonville, Ohio, a vaudeville performance at the opera house. Reprinted with permission of Stuart's Opera House Archives, Nelsonville, Ohio.

40—Singers-Dancers-Comedians—40
25—MUSICAL NUMBERS AND COMEDY FEATURES—25

The program includes pictures of "The pillow fight," "The original sextette," and "The prize beauty chorus."[68] The cast of *A Trip to Egypt,* at Stuart's in 1904, featured "PONY DANCING GIRLS," "OPERA GIRLS," and "SHOW GIRLS."[69] Similarly, Meyersdale, Pennsylvania, saw "Wood & Ward, with 18 helpers, mostly girls" in 1907.[70]

Variety featured exotic locales (as is evident in *A Trip to Egypt,* above), which provided an opportunity for spectacle and a framework for the different acts. Perhaps no locale is more exotic than that of *A Trip to the Moon,* presented in Nelsonville, Ohio, in 1905. The program entices with the list of characters:

> 250 Performers in this Spectacular Production 250.
> See! See!
> Little Bo-peep and all her Wee Wee Friends, Including Cinderella, Simple Simon and the Stingy Pie Man.

Chow Chow the Mischievous Chinaman.
The Wonderful Dwarfs, The Pigmies, and lots of them
The Old Woman That Sweeps the Cob-Webs from the Sky, and Hundreds of others from Fairyland.

Spectacle was essential to these shows, and *A Trip to the Moon* included

A Spectacle Surpassing in Grandeur all previous attempts of Illusion.
The Flight from the Moon to the Earth in a Parachute.
A Visit to the North Pole, inhabited by a Strange and Wonderful Race of People who inhabit the Moon.
The Master effort culminating in a Transformation Scene of rare Beauty, entitled "The Feast of the Dragon."

The synopsis describes one scene as follows: "Arrival of the Mysterious Astrologer, a student of the Sun, Moon and Stars who, through his wonderful Electromete, Projectophoto-Telephono-Tellegrapho-Tellawoman-o-Scope communicates with the Man in the Moon." The program adds a family touch:

SEE Your Mother-in-Law at the North Pole
Never before has an entertainment been offered to the public possessing such peculiar fascination for both young and old

Finally, it appeals to the citizens of Nelsonville directly:

Another scene represents the Fountain of Youth on New Years Eve. The Grandmothers and Grandfathers of Nelsonville, after being in spirit land 100 years, return to earth and note with great surprise the many changes that have taken place during their absence. The funny situations which arise can be appreciated only by witnessing the performance.
At Lancaster where it was presented last season, it took the people so by storm, that they packed the Avenue Theater for 3 consecutive performances.
At Athens where it was presented last it played to capacity, turning people away at each performance.
Don't Fail to Secure Seats in Advance[71]

Some vaudeville shows—such as *The Holy City,* presented in Nelsonville, Ohio, in 1905—took on a religious theme. The description makes clear that this was spectacular vaudeville fare:

Program for *A Trip to the Moon* at Stuart's Opera House, Nelsonville, Ohio, a vaudeville show at the opera house. Reprinted with permission of Stuart's Opera House Archives, Nelsonville, Ohio.

SEE

The Great Joppa Gate with its Wonderful Vision of the Spirit of John the Baptist

The Vision of the Holy Sepulchre, The Resurrection, The Flight of the Angels, The Gates of the New Jerusalem

The Temple of Jerusalem by Moonlight

The Vision of the Crucifixion

The Grand Hall of Judgement

The Storm on Galilee

The program stresses the show's religious value:

"THE HOLY CITY"

IS LIKE THE REGAL BLOOM OF THE CENTURY PLANT, PURE

Program for *The Holy City* at Stuart's Opera House, Nelsonville, Ohio, an example of a religiously oriented drama. Reprinted with permission of Stuart's Opera House Archives, Nelsonville, Ohio.

> AND PRECIOUS AS IT IS BEAUTIFUL. . . . NO ANTHEM SUNG IN DIM CATHEDRAL AISLES WAS EVER MORE DEVOUT THAN THIS GRAND DRAMA. . . . THE TRAGEDY OF ALL AGES. THE POWER TO GIVE TO THE WORLD OF ART SOMETHING NEW AND SUBLIME, IS THE BIRTH-RIGHT OF GENIUS—THE TRUE TEST OF ROYAL BLOOD THAT MARKS A KING OF THOUGHT. SUCH IS THE INFLUENCE OF
>
> —"THE HOLY CITY"—[72]

Wild West melodramas, and Buffalo Bill's shows in particular, were common at opera houses. When Buffalo Bill's show came to the opera house in Lock Haven, Pennsylvania, in 1874, the *Clinton Democrat* poked fun at his reputation in order to drum up ticket sales:

> Buffalo Bill is announced to appear at the Opera House on the evening of December 2d. It may be well for our citizens to see that their windows and doors are well secured that night, and their fire-arms and other instruments of destruction are in order for immediate use, for if

> that band of "red-skins," headed by the famous "William" don't happen to have a good house they may possibly turn in and massacre the whole populace. To keep them in good humor the best thing Lock Haven can do is to give them a full house. The play of Buffalo Bill and his talented company will be one of the finest ever presented to our citizens.[73]

His troupe also appeared in Maysville, Kentucky, in 1882: "Buffalo Bill and a party of real Indians will appear at the Opera House next Monday evening. Don't fail to see this great western celebrity. The street parade Monday morning should be witnessed by all as it will be well worth seeing."[74] Afterward, the *Daily Evening Bulletin* reported: "The Buffalo Bill troupe had a crowded house last night and many persons were turned away at the door. The play was of the dime novel order, with the usual amount of blood shed, hair breadth escapes, and harrowing situations. The Indians in their dances, Buffalo Bill's wonderful shooting, and Jule Keen's dutch impersonations were the most interesting features of the entertainment."[75] After the advent of film, Buffalo Bill's appearances were on the screen, such as at the Winchester (Kentucky) Opera House in 1910: "Buffalo Bill will be seen in motion pictures that are life-like and positively full size."[76]

A wide variety of other entertainments also appeared at the opera house. Maysville, Kentucky, saw a trained animal act, combined with puppets and juggling, in 1882: "Mrs. Jeannette DeLisle has on Exhibition at the opera house, an interesting collection of well-trained dogs, birds, goats etc., which do many seemingly wonderful things. There is besides a juggling exhibition and a Punch and Judy show which are interesting and amusing."[77]

Acrobatics, combined with music, was featured at the Winchester (Kentucky) Auditorium Theatre, in 1910:

> JAMES O'NEILL
>
> NOVELTY EQUILIBRIST AND ACROBAT
>
> One of the best of its kind.
>
> 2 MUSICAL GRACES
>
> Playing on the
>
> VIOLIN AND CELLA [*sic*]

In a sign of the changes coming to the opera house, the performance also included "Audiscope Pictures."[78]

Shooting acts were prevalent, and the Winchester (Kentucky) Opera House featured one in 1908: "Rose & Rose in their novelty shooting act gave some wonderful expert shooting; seldom missing the mark." Whether to ensure the safety of the performers or to add excitement to the show, the police banned part of the act: "The audience held their breath with excitement as Rose shot the targets arranged about Miss Rose's head and felt somewhat relieved when the city police would not allow the shooting of the small cork from her head." In another demonstration of the infiltration of movies into vaudeville, the article noted that a moving picture show followed the shooting act.[79]

Many vaudeville acts included parapsychology; the following advertisement was for a show at the Winchester, Kentucky, Opera House in 1910:

> GALLAND The man of Thought, Presenting Mind Reading,
> Hypnotism and Spiritualism.
> SEE the Sensational Blind and Old Carriage Drive, starting in front of
> the Opera House, Tuesday . . .
> SEE the Hypnotized Man Tuesday Night.
> SEE the Struggle for Life Wednesday Night.[80]

"Ita, the sixteen-year-old California girl mentalist," was heavily promoted for her appearance at the Winchester Opera House in 1911, along with "other high class vaudeville and two reels of feature pictures run nightly."[81] After the first performance, the *News* reported that there had been a "small crowd" for Ita, and described her act:

> Ita while blindfolded, was able to give correctly the sum of a column of six figures. She answered questions which had been written on slips of paper by various persons in the audience, and in many cases gave the names of the writers. She returned articles, such as a watch, ring, pencil or knife to the owners, although each article had been handed to her by another person. There was nothing in any answer given nor any statement made which could give offense, embarrass or humiliate.
>
> Ita does not claim to be infallible. She made several mistakes, but the great majority of her work was absolutely correct in every particular. . . .

Emphasizing the wholesomeness of the entertainment, advertisements billed the matinee as being "for ladies only," with the added inducement that Ita would "give a silver spoon to every lady who attends this performance."[82]

Special effects included electrical stunts—which would have been new and mysterious technology at the time—such as those at the Auditorium Theatre in Winchester, Kentucky, in 1910: "John Coughlan an electrical wonder, who does various astonishing stunts with electricity which makes the audience sit up and gasp. His first is the holding of two carbons between his teeth thereby completing a circuit and causing a bright light to blaze in his open mouth. He then lights up two very attractive Indian clubs with the current passing through his body and closes by an exhibition of how criminals are electrocuted at the Auburn."[83]

Vaudeville acts also had a local flavor, as this description of a show in Maysville, Kentucky, in 1882, demonstrates: "Portraits of prominent citizens and the streets of Maysville will be produced on canvas at Baron Seeman's entertainment this evening."[84] In Winchester, Kentucky, in 1908, at a performance by Mahan and Jackson's Vaudeville Company, Miss Isabella Verrey "caused much merriment in the crowd by casting her smiles, and addressing her love songs and throwing the light from a small mirrow [*sic*] on a certain well-known benedict in the audience."[85]

Variety was central to the opera house: variety among shows and variety interspersed in the midst of plays and local events. What made opera houses popular and a nexus of the community was precisely that they offered anyone in the town a wide variety of choices. One could also go to the opera house for a wide variety of motives: cultural, educational, entertainment related, political, social, and athletic.

CHAPTER TEN

Drama at the Opera House

Drama at the opera house reflected and gave voice to the anxieties of a country that was undergoing a cultural transformation of urbanization, development, immigration, and industrialization. According to Robert C. Toll, "All over the heartland of America, average citizens felt the bewilderment, the loss of control, the anxiety, and the frustration that accompanied the basic changes in the nature and quality of their lives. Their most cherished traditions, their values, and their morality all seemed to be threatened by the new industrial order." The opera house "reaffirmed traditional values" through melodramas that "centered on the conflict between virtuous plain people and immoral, conniving businessmen." In addition, opera house melodrama provided an escape into a mythological South through shows such as *Uncle Tom's Cabin* and into sentimental, nostalgic versions of the frontier through shows such as *Davy Crockett:* "In these and other perennial favorites that touring actors brought to the Beaver Dams of the nation lies at least part of the story of how average Americans reacted to and coped with the unsettling shocks of modernization."[1]

Melodrama best reflected this changing American culture, with its emphasis on respectability, work ethic, and family.[2] According to Martha Vicinus, it is significant that, in the midst of America's vast social and economic change, the focus of melodrama is domestic: "The ideal of domestic happiness, like myths of a past golden age, assuaged fears an audience might have about being too committed to the goals of an industrializing society. Melodrama provided a temporary resolution of conflicts between the home and outside world." Melodrama also addressed the fears of miners and their families in the midst of uncertain economics and employment circumstances, in that melodrama "seemed to demonstrate how difficult circumstances could be endured, and even turned to victory."[3]

Melodrama's moral clarity was a relief in complex changing times, as Toll points out: "Melodrama made evil and corruption easy to identify and solutions easy to find; it made heroes of common, simple people; and it made virtue and the virtuous triumph; it testified that, no matter how unfair life seemed, justice was not dead." Melodrama offered "welcome simplicity, reassurance, and hope . . . in a complex, uncertain, and disillusioning world." As with all matters of American melodrama, the clearest example is *Uncle Tom's Cabin,* the most famous and popular melodrama, which, in Toll's words, "offered a myth of a loving, rural American home life—the romanticized plantation. . . . It provided a full range of sentimental family images, from loving security to tragic destruction; it allowed insecure, frustrated whites to escape vicariously into the carefree world of stereotyped stage Negroes while at the same time feeling superior to the irresponsible, childish blacks."[4]

Guilbert de Pixérécourt, credited with writing the earliest melodramas in France, described the essence of the genre: "a villain, an unhappy virtuous woman, a good man who becomes her protector, and the comic character, who helps the good man rescue the heroine."[5] Other features of melodrama in America were stock characters, secrets, gimmicks, spectacle, sensational plots, topical subjects, and clear-cut, good-versus-evil morality. While "melodrama," largely misunderstood today, has become a term of derision, it was unquestionably the most popular dramatic form in nineteenth-century America. As McConachie states, "The relevant issue for theatre historians is not whether these diverse melodramas were any good. Judging plays solely on the basis of such formalistic concepts as complexity, style, and naturalness merely backs the historian into what Terry Eagleton has called 'the ideology of the aesthetic.'"[6] Melodrama endured and was widespread because it appealed to the needs and tastes of everyday Americans.[7]

Music was a major feature of melodrama, with identifying musical motives at the entrance or exit of main characters, such as a rumble for the villain, a trumpet fanfare for the hero, flute trills for the heroine, a crash of brass for the catastrophe, and soft music for love scenes. Spectacle included animals, ships, water, fire, and explosives, with an emphasis on new technology, such as railroads, steamships, and photography. The stage could be partially obscured with colored silk and gauze across the proscenium arch, like a modern scrim, for fairytale scenes, dream scenes, and fog. A panorama could be rolled across the rear of the stage to suggest movement, or a treadmill placed on stage for races.[8]

A flier for *Heart of Maryland,* performed in Nelsonville, Ohio, in 1905, emphasizes the machinery that was at the heart of melodrama's spectacular appeal: "Note: The engine effect is fully protected and patented by L. J. Carter, and anyone using same will be vigorously prosecuted."[9]

Variety also existed within melodrama, in that an evening's show included an afterpiece of a farce or a short comic opera, and between the acts were music, songs, dances, novelty acts, animal acts, and acrobats. Animals often appeared in plays, sometimes in leading roles; examples include talking magpies, lions, elephants, cats, monkeys, and apes.[10] Live horses pulled the chariots in *Ben-Hur* at the Grand Opera House in Paris, Kentucky.[11] In most cases, the variety acts between the acts of a melodrama were not directly related to the play at hand. But, far from being perceived as an interruption, they contributed to the overall effect of variety and spectacle.

Standard melodramas included *Richelieu* (1839), *Shore Acres* (1893), *Way Down East* (1898), and *Arizona* (1900). *Three of Us* (1914), with its focus on mining, would have had particular resonance for mining towns. Melodrama in small towns was often performed in cheap touring productions, often named for the ticket prices: ten-twenty-thirty ("ten-twent'-thirt'"). Cheap melodramas that may have been performed at opera houses included *In the Hands of the Enemy; Nellie, the Beautiful Cloak Model; Convict 99; Slaves of the Orient;* and *The Great Automobile Mystery.*[12]

The single most popular melodrama was *Uncle Tom's Cabin,* based on Harriet Beecher Stowe's novel. The most common adaptation, by George L. Aiken, was performed in its complete form first in Troy, New York, on November 15, 1852, and then in New York City on July 18, 1853.[13] While "Uncle Tom" is now an insulting reference to an obsequious African American, in the mid- to late nineteenth century the play and its portrayal of blacks was considered liberating and enlightening. While its ultimate effect was negative, the play initially broke the stage stereotype, reinforced by minstrel shows, of the black man as a lazy, shuffling fool.

It is hard today to comprehend the ubiquity of *Uncle Tom's Cabin.* It was not merely the most popular play of the second half of the nineteenth century; as Rosemarie Bank observes, "The extent of that popularity dwarfs superlatives."[14] In 1879, there were forty-nine "Tommer shows" in the United States, and in the 1890s that figure reached five hundred. In 1902 it was estimated that one million people in the United States, one out of thirty-five people, had seen a production in that year alone. By 1912, there had been an estimated 250,000 productions, and by 1952 there had been 100 million performances in the 100 years that the play had been performed.[15] According to Frank Rahill, "It had not merely outdrawn every other play; it had drawn more people into the theatre than the combined efforts of any other dozen plays."[16]

Backstage poster for *Uncle Tom's Cabin* at the Grand Opera House, Jackson, Ohio. Photo by author.

The significance of *Uncle Tom's Cabin* lies not only in the number of people attending but also in its appeal to people who otherwise would not have gone to a theater or opera house because of moral objections. These moral objections are identical to the ones that led to local halls being called opera houses. Adolphus Hart reported on a New York production he witnessed: "There was an air of sanctity in the upper tiers, which betokened that the work had a powerful influence in awakening the religious feelings of certain classes of the people."[17] And while blacks had been otherwise excluded from the theater, they were admitted to the National Theater in New York City, though in a segregated balcony.[18]

Productions of *Uncle Tom's Cabin* also became increasingly spectacular during the course of the nineteenth century. Minor scenes in the novel become important in the play for the sake of spectacle. For example, Eliza crossing the Ohio River, jumping from ice floe to ice floe while holding little Harry, constitutes two paragraphs in the novel; in the play it became one of the most important and famous scenes. Dogs (not in the novel) chased Eliza across ice; bloodhounds were used in the first productions and English mastiffs or Great Danes in later productions. Sometimes the actress playing Eliza carried meat in her clothing to get the dogs to chase her.[19] The need for hounds in the play was so great that kennels were established across the country just for breeding dogs for this play.[20] One show had a hundred ponies, and another had twenty-four hounds chasing Eliza across the Ohio River.[21]

While the Aiken adaptation was the most accepted, there were actually many versions of the play. One person claimed to have seen the show twenty-five times without ever seeing the same version twice, since each included different novelties such as hounds, ice floes, spirituals, jubilee songs, and black specialty acts. According to Toll, *Uncle Tom's Cabin* was not really a play, but "a catch phrase for a wide variety of shows . . . more an institution that evolved to suit its audiences than a relatively fixed production."[22] A 1903 production in Meyersdale, Pennsylvania, is evidence of this trend:

Stetson's Uncle Tom's Cabin Co., Under the Management of Leon W. Washburn

"THE BARNUM OF THEM ALL"

More Grand Novelties Than Ever

Gorgeous Scenery

Mechanical Effects

Prof. Gibson's Military Band

Colored Female Fife and Drum Corps

Blood Hounds

Beautiful Chariots and Tableaux

Wagons Drawn By Handsome Shetland Ponies

Genuine Cake Walks

Buck and Wing Dancers

Male and Female Quartets

Jubilee Singers

Grand Vision and Transformation Scenes

Eva and Her Golden Chariot

Watch for the Big Parade
It Beats Them All
Prices 25 and 50 cents[23]

In the 1920s and 1930s, there were fewer productions, and most were smaller. By 1927, only twelve Tommers were on tour; the final productions took place in the mid-1930s.[24]

As *Uncle Tom's Cabin* entered popular culture, whatever redeeming qualities the play might have had were stripped away, leaving remnants that reinforced white negative stereotypes of African Americans. While the novel and initial play may have tried to present a somewhat challenging image of blacks, as the characters entered minstrel and variety shows they were reintegrated into the older stage stereotypes. As Thomas F. Gossett states, "The 'happy' Uncle Tom content with slavery and faithful to 'ole massa' became a staple of the minstrel shows." After the Civil War, the antislavery themes of the play were weakened and the black characters became more stereotyped. Uncle Tom was not a man of dignity, but "a mere figure of pathos." Topsy and other black characters "were exaggerated to the point that they could scarcely be distinguished from those of the blacks of minstrel shows." Gossett concludes, "The play did more to hamper than to help the cause of blacks in the United States."[25]

Other plays also dealt with racial and Civil War issues, including *Shenandoah* (1888), *Held by the Enemy* (1886), *Secret Service* (1895), *The Octoroon* (1859), *Belle Lamar* (1874), *Norwood* (1867), and *The Heart of Maryland* (1895). An announcement in the *Athens (Ohio) Messenger* for "the widely famous comedy, entitled the 'Slave's Devotion'" promised to show audiences "every possible phase of plantation negro character."[26] The billing suggests, however, that the racial subject was more of a curiosity for the dominant white culture; this was not a play by, for, or about African Americans.

Melodramas on the dangers of alcohol, such as *The Drunkard* (1844), *Hot Corn* (1853), and *Ten Nights in a Bar Room* (1858), were also admired. These temperance plays were crowd-pleasers and, like *Uncle Tom's Cabin,* brought people into the theater who otherwise would not have gone. The clergy made a distinction between "worldly" plays and "moral" plays, and so attracted a churchgoing crowd to these latter plays. In turn, managers censored other plays to keep the newly attracted audience coming back to the theater and opera house. According to Judith McArthur, "With its unmistakable heroes and villains, tearful pleas, ringing declamations, and concluding triumph of good over evil, melodrama was a vehicle ideally suited to staging moral lessons on topical subjects such as temperance and slavery."[27] This maintenance of a moral code from one event to

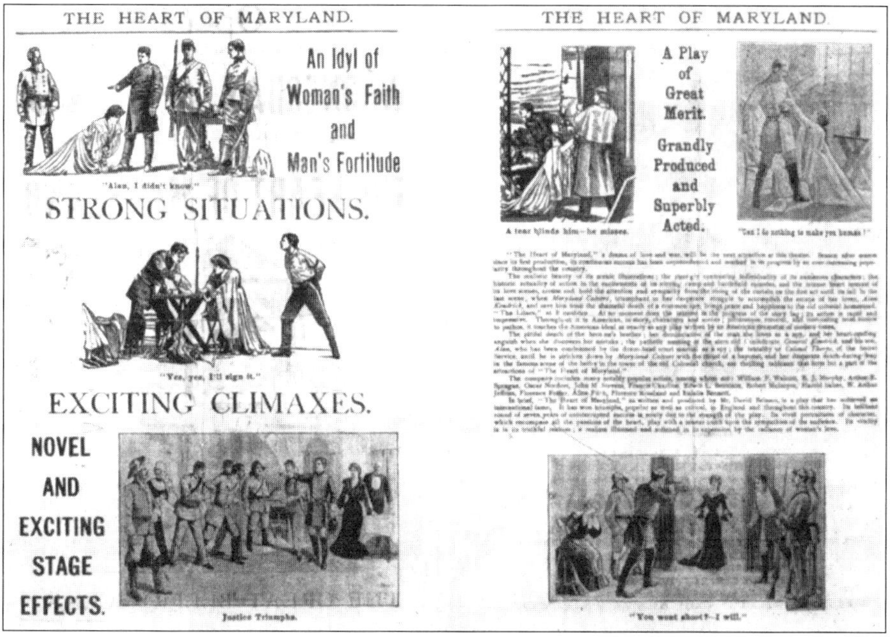

Program for *The Heart of Maryland* at Stuart's Opera House, Nelsonville, Ohio, a popular Civil War melodrama. Reprinted with permission of Stuart's Opera House Archives, Nelsonville, Ohio.

another, from melodrama to lectures, was also central to the opera house project of keeping the building a morally safe place for women and children.

Religious plays were well liked at the opera house; for example, *The Passion Play* was performed at the Carlisle Opera House in Pennsylvania in 1899. The advertisement in the *Evening Sentinel* proclaimed that it was "Endorsed highly by the Pulpit and Press throughout the universe."[28] In 1923, the New Harlan (Kentucky) Theatre screened the movie *Soldiers of the Cross*, for which "one of the local churches furnished the film and the management opened their doors to the public free of charge."[29]

Frontier melodramas reflected an idealized image of the American frontier at the same time that America was becoming a more urban culture and the frontier was being exploited by coal mining. According to Thomas Postlewait, frontier melodrama put onstage "a longing for the supposed lost harmony and innocence of country life."[30] The first frontier plays appeared between the 1830s and the 1850s, and the form was widespread after 1870. By the late nineteenth century, 5 to 10 percent of all touring productions were about the frontier, and some popular frontier plays toured for ten to thirty years. According to Roger A.

Hall, "The plays placed on stage vivid pictures of the western landscape, sometimes quite realistically presented, and they adorned those pictures with the garments and the paraphernalia of the region. Within those pictures, they brought to life the cowboys, outlaws, natives, horses, and gunfire of the border lands."[31]

Many frontier melodramas were set in the "West," but since the American frontier was constantly on the move, from the eastern seaboard, to the Ohio Valley, to the Mississippi, to the Great Plains, and finally to California, the locale of frontier plays also moved, as can be seen in the locales and dates of frequently performed plays: *Nick of the Woods* (Kentucky), 1838; *The Arkansas Traveler,* 1870; *Horizon* (California), 1871.[32] The result was that frontier, or border, plays might be set anywhere. In the case of Appalachia, even after lands far to the west had become the frontier in the late nineteenth century, Appalachia was still being discovered as an internal frontier.

Other popular frontier melodramas included *Davy Crockett* (1872), *My Partner* (1879), *The Girl of the Golden West* (1905), and *The Great Divide* (1906). Country plays, which offered a nostalgic and sentimental view of rural life, included *Rip van Winkle* (1866), *Shore Acres* (1893), *The Old Homestead* (1878), *Way Down East* (1898), and *The Country Fair* (1889). Regional life in America was also a favorite subject, as evidenced by the success of Augustus Thomas's plays *Alabama* (1891), *In Mizzoura* (1893), and *Arizona* (1899).[33]

Davy Crockett, for example, was performed at Stuart's Opera House in Nelsonville, Ohio (1905), starring James J. Jeffries, "Champion of the World," who was famous in Nelsonville for the banned boxing match (see chapter 8). A note in the program emphasized Jeffries' fighting talents: "At the conclusion of the last act Mr. Jeffries will give a physical culture exhibition with Joseph Kenney." The program also suggests that Jeffries himself was a latter-day Davy Crockett: "The skins, etc., used in this production were collected by Mr. Jeffries during his hunting trips."[34]

Some plays, such as *The Little Shepherd of Kingdom Come,* dealt specifically with local subjects. This play was advertised in the *Harlan (Kentucky) Enterprise* as

> The Biggest Play of the Century With All Live Folks Playing It!
>
> John Fox, Jr's Powerful Story Dramatized of the Kentucky Mountains
>
> A PLAY NOT A PICTURE[35]

Other "local" plays contained "hillbilly" characters that would have resonated with an Appalachian audience, such as the 1903 production of *Ye Deestreect Skewl,* presented by the Rathbone Sisters, with proceeds going to the Pythian orphans' home in New Straitsville, Ohio.[36]

Shakespeare was regularly performed in nineteenth-century America, and Levine argues that this popularity derived, in part, from his being considered a "moral" playwright: "Nineteenth-century Americans were able to fit Shakespeare into their culture so easily because he *seemed* to fit—because so many of his values and tastes were, or at least appeared to be, close to their own, and were presented through figures that seemed real and came to matter to the audience."[37] Shakespearean drama was so ubiquitous that Toll argues, "Shakespeare was the most popular playwright in the United States before the Civil War,"[38] and Levine states, "Shakespeare actually *was* popular entertainment in nineteenth-century America."[39] While this popularity waned in the latter half of the century, his plays were still widely produced at opera houses in Appalachia.

Performances of Shakespeare in nineteenth-century America were not straight renditions of the text, but were interpolated, as Toll notes, with "variety performers—jugglers, acrobats, song and dance acts, trained animals; 'freaks' like giants, midgets, and 'living skeletons'; and other peculiar specialties."[40] Integrating popular entertainment songs and dances into Shakespeare's plays did not dilute or denigrate the plays; instead, as Levine points out, the interpolations "may be understood more meaningfully as having *integrated* him into American culture. Shakespeare was presented as part of the same milieu inhabited by magicians, dancers, singers, acrobats, minstrels, and comics. He appeared on the same playbills and was advertised in the same spirit. . . . Shakespeare was presented as part of the culture they enjoyed, a Shakespeare rendered familiar and intimate by virtue of his context."[41]

Opera house Shakespeare was integrated into the usual opera house fare of community, sports, and benefits, as shown in a combination of *The Merchant of Venice* and football in Winchester, Kentucky:

Opera House Monday, December 14, 1908

Benefit College Athletic Ass'n.

Strong Cast of 40 People.

Football Game on Stage Adds Intense Interest.

Winchester Quartet will Sing Between Acts

Prices. 25c. 50c. and 75c.[42]

Shakespearean productions emphasized the spectacular quality of the plays, as an advertisement in the *Meyersdale (Pennsylvania) Republican* suggests: "King Richard The Third. New Fire-Proof Scenic Equipment, Novel Electrical Effects, Rich and Correct Costuming, Startling Battle Tableaux and Every Advantage."[43]

Program for *A Royal Slave* at Stuart's Opera House, Nelsonville, Ohio, a popular frontier melodrama. Reprinted with permission of Stuart's Opera House Archives, Nelsonville, Ohio.

As You Like It, also in Meyersdale, advertised "ALL SPECIAL SCENERY, MAGNIFICENT COSTUMES, AND STAGE SETTINGS."[44]

Romantic dramas were also performed often, and included *Francesca da Rimini, The Prisoner of Zenda, When Knighthood Was in Flower,* and *The Road to Yesterday,* in which an American girl goes to London and dreams of Elizabethan times. *A Royal Slave* is described in a Nelsonville, Ohio (1905), program as a "powerful romantic play." The audience was encouraged to experience the exotic spectacle:

> EVERY ACT a SCENIC MARVEL
> SEE
> The Ruins of the Old Monastery

The Royal Palace in the City of Mexico
The Robber's Cave Overlooking the Floating Islands
The . . . Volcano

The description emphasizes the luxurious Mexican locale:

> With the exception, perhaps of "Ben Hur," this has been the most successful. This charming story of the sunny south embodies all that is wooing in the song of the nightingale; all that is sweet in the shadow groves, the breath of the magnolias and bowers of the torrid bloom; all that is lovely in the tropical moonlight, the sighing palms and the soft vistas of purple leagues and distant snow-crowned peaks; all that is thrilling and romantic in the passionate hearts of the children of the Sun Land, Mexico, is to be found in the beautiful sensational success, "a ROYAL SLAVE."

Perhaps to differentiate the production from those that reused stock scenery, the program promises, "Every piece of Scenery used in the Production being Carried by the Company."[45]

Drama was a significant part of the opera house and provided entertaining shows for the communities in the mining regions of Appalachia. But the plays were more than entertainment. They operated in the context of the opera house project of morality and respectability, and the national context of massive social change and economic upheaval.

EPILOGUE

The Death (and Rebirth) of the Opera House

Opera houses declined in the 1920s and were close to death by the 1930s, for a number of reasons. Laws were enacted against second-story auditoriums. High schools built auditoriums and gymnasiums, draining off events from the opera house. Touring productions declined. Talent shows and other local events were no longer profitable; movies were cheaper. Radios and phonographs kept many at home. And the automobile made it possible for people to travel easily to big cities for entertainment.

Robert S. and Helen Merrell Lynd's examination of "Middletown," a typical American midwestern town, tracks the decline of the opera house. Jack Poggi extrapolated from their figures and found that in 1890, there were 125 performances in an opera house seating 800, mostly at capacity. The yearly attendance was 100,000, with a monthly average of 8,333. With a population of 12,000, the average monthly attendance was over two-thirds of the population. In 1923, the number of performances was down to 40; the yearly attendance was 32,000, and the monthly average attendance was 2,666, out of a population of 38,000. The average monthly attendance was now down to one-thirtieth of the population.[1] Opera houses were no longer the crossroads of the community. Opera houses were simply another place to go for entertainment or social and community gatherings.

The "road" for touring theatrical productions went downhill after 1910. The number of theaters outside large cities decreased between 1910 and 1925 from 1,549 to 674. Combination companies, which had

Advertisement for films of baseball games at the Winchester (Kentucky) Opera House in 1910. From *Winchester (KY) News.*

ruled American theater at the turn of the century, declined from 300 in the 1900–1901 season to 65 in the 1920s, and in the 1930s there were only 20 to 25 in existence in a given year. One reason for this decline was a glut of theaters and productions caused by competition between the Shuberts and the syndicate (see chapter 7). Audiences became disenchanted by too many poor productions that were puffed up with false advertising. Costs of production, railroad fees, and wages also increased for managers and producers. This combination led to a downward spiral of lower production standards and smaller audiences.[2]

Another cause for the decline of the opera house was the growing popularity and affordability of the automobile, combined with an increase in drivable roads. Driving was entertaining in itself, and spectators could travel easily and cheaply from small towns to big cities to see shows. According to the drama editor in Chillicothe, Ohio, "The automobile takes those who want the good legitimate shows to Columbus, 48 miles away. Twenty-five years ago this city played every star of any value, but now automobiles bring the big cities closer and the people will ride 100 miles to see a better show than they can get at home."[3]

The increase in radio programming and the availability of phonograph records in the 1920s also led to the decline of the opera house.[4] Many potential opera house spectators stayed at home as auditors, gathered around the radio or phonograph.

The construction of high school gymnasiums and auditoriums that could house basketball games, graduations, and other presentations removed the community foundation from the opera house. For example, between 1889 and 1894 the Ohio legislature passed laws allowing schools to rent school facilities for literary entertainments, exhibitions, recitals, and religious exercises. The result was that auditoriums became more common in urban schools at the turn of the century and were used for lectures, concerts, and theatrical performances.[5] In small towns and rural districts, there was a school building boom in the late 1910s and 1920s that frequently included auditoriums.[6] The community events that had been staged at the opera house now moved to the high school. Thus Meredith Willson's transplant of the Fourth of July celebration in *The Music Man* from the opera house to the high school gymnasium made sense to a mid-twentieth-century audience.

But the most significant factor in the decline of opera houses and traveling productions was the development of the movie industry between 1910 and 1920. Movies were much cheaper to attend, so the people with the lowest incomes left the opera house for the cinemas, leaving the galleries unfilled. Opera houses responded by incorporating film into the entertainment package (see chapter 9) or by converting entirely to showing movies. The movie industry also forced this changeover, in that it worked to gain exclusive rights for booking auditoriums, with the goal of driving out live theatrical productions.[7]

One way of looking at this shift from theater to film is in terms of a broader change from live entertainment to optical and mechanical entertainments, a shift beginning before the invention of film. Entertainment in the late nineteenth century placed increasing emphasis on painted and photographic images and less on live performance, with the development of the peep show, magic lantern, diorama, and panorama. In this sense, film has its roots in popular entertainment, and film used new technology to exploit an ongoing transition. For example, dioramas often used the same structure as standard plays, telling a story, while magic lanterns were organized like variety entertainments, with separate and unrelated groups of lantern slides.[8]

Shinnston Opera House, Shinnston, West Virginia (1910), showing an unrestored opera house currently used for storage. Photo by author.

Optical and mechanical entertainments were ubiquitous in the late nineteenth and early twentieth centuries. The magic lantern, which projected images from glass slides, was common in homes, schools, churches, and theaters. The post–Civil War era saw improvements in projectors and slides, as well as a reduction in their costs. Other popular entertainment technology included the phonograph and automated arcade machines. The panorama was an enormous painted canvas fastened inside a circular building; spectators stood or sat in semidarkness on a viewing platform in the center of the room, viewing a continuous, sometimes moving image. Panoramas often served as a form of documentary: battle scenes from the Civil War were common, as were religious subjects and historical accounts of tourist attractions, such as the Mississippi River. The diorama consisted of gigantic, often transparent pictures, shown under changing light in a theater, with background music or narration. These were also often documentaries, and were a step on the road to cinema.[9]

Edison's Kinetoscope was a mounted peep show device, viewed by only one person at a time, like the earlier handheld optical toys the Zoetrope and stereoscope. The Kinetoscope showed twenty-second movies, often accompanied by music from a phonograph, and was featured in professional Kinetoscope parlors beginning in 1891. Modern projected movies began in the 1890s and consisted of

Stuart's Opera House, Nelsonville, Ohio (1879), as it appeared about 1979, after having been shut in 1924, and before the fire of 1980. Reprinted with permission of Stuart's Opera House Archives, Nelsonville, Ohio.

vaudeville acts, sports events, dancers, acrobats, bodybuilders, comic skits, scenes from plays, and documentaries, usually accompanied by piano or orchestra.[10]

Early optical and mechanized entertainments appeared often in opera houses. One of the earliest records is from Carlisle, Pennsylvania, where in 1871 Rheem's Hall displayed

GRAND STEREOPTICON AND DISSOLVING VIEWS
The entertainment will consist of a choice selection of most
attractive view, enlarged on the screen from the finest photographs, the greater
part of them beautifully colored, and illuminated by the Oxy-calcium Light,
and will be made up of Scriptural, Historical, and Fancy Pictures, producing upon
canvas life-like and beautifully natural exhibitions of
PERSONS, PLACES AND OBJECTS.
Wm. B. Parker, Esq., will also give some Select Readings during the
evening, and the whole will be enlivened by
SELECT AIRS BY THE DEPOT BAND[11]

In 1882, Baron Seeman showed his "free exhibition of dissolving views in front of the opera house" in Maysville, Kentucky.[12] The following entertainment was featured in Athens, Ohio, in 1885:

> Moore's Calcichromopticon, Now making the 15th Annual Tour, will exhibit at ATHENS CITY HALL . . . FOR THE BENEFIT OF THE ATHENS Knights of St. George.
>
> The entertainment graphically illustrates the scenery of Ireland together with the customs and characteristics of its people. The splendid panoramic exhibition of notable scenes in Ireland is accompanied with wonderful transitions and dioramic effects, this with humorous and sentimental songs, together with new and startling illustrations by Prof. H.E. Moore, the prince of Conjurors, combine to make one of the most interesting and fascinating entertainments that has visited Athens within recent period.[13]

With the advent of Edison's inventions, opera houses incorporated the latest optical entertainment into their offerings. The Carlisle (Pennsylvania) Opera House advertised in 1896 for

> Edison's Wonderful
> PROJECTOSCOPE
> The society event of the season
> New Views[14]

The following year, another opera house in Carlisle, the Sentinel (in the same building as the newspaper, and sharing the same name), showed a wide variety of scenes that illustrate the continuity between early film and the vaudeville that was concurrently so popular. These movies were up-to-date, could be changed nightly, and provided a series of marvelous and astounding scenes:

> "Grand Old Falls of Niagara"
> America's Pride. See the tumbling, foaming whirling water.
> Comic Dance (Colored)
> Swimming School
> Battery park, N.Y.
> Elevated Railway Scene
> Moving trains, rushing throngs at Twenty-third street station, New York City.
> Shoot the Shutes.

Fire Rescue Scene.

New York's brave firemen rescuing little ones from the CRUEL FLAMES

Cartoonist

John Blackburn, N.Y. World

Umbrella Dance

By Leigh Sisters (Colored)

Sly Policeman Scene

How they act in a big city when the copper comes around. A fracas among the "boys."

Mounted Police Drill

View of Passaic Falls, N.J.

Mounted Police Charge.

New York City.

Monroe Doctrine.

Illustrated.

THE BUCKING BRONCHOS and disgruntled COWBOYS.

Cannon Artillery in Action

Fountain Scene

Central park, N.Y.

Scotch Dance

Rob Roy Trio.

A scene showing Layman man of one hundred faces in his changes. Aunty Miller (colored). Indian War Dance by band of Cheyenne and 57 other up-to-date pictures of the latest design. This is your only chance to see this wonderful "VITASCOPE."[15]

What vaudeville could not do, as this list makes clear, was to provide the apparent authenticity and travelogue flavor of these films. The Corry (Pennsylvania) Opera House in 1906 presented the "Friscoscope": "the only bona fide moving pictures" of the San Francisco earthquake. "In addition to the pictures a pleasing high class vaudeville entertainment of the leading American and European artists will be given."[16]

In Winchester, Kentucky, audiences at the opera house in 1909 could

GO WITH

LYMAN H. HOWE

TO

Egypt

and

Stuart's Opera House, Nelsonville, Ohio (1879), as it appeared about 1979. Reprinted with permission of Stuart's Opera House Archives, Nelsonville, Ohio.

Russia.
EXTRAORDINARY SCENES OF
Sicily
Before and after the
Earthquake
A THRILLING RIDE ON A RUNAWAY TRAIN.
WRIGHT'S WONDERFUL AEROPLANE FLIGHTS.
GREAT MOSCOW FLOODS
THE JUGGLING FLY.
20 OTHER BIG FEATURES
Each a Living Reality[17]

In 1924, perhaps with some form of 3-D glasses, the New Harlan Theatre offered:

The NEWEST Thing In Motion Pictures
PLASTOGRAMS

> The figures "come off the screen" and approach you so realistically you want to dodge them.
>
> The Third Dimention [*sic*] Movie[18]

The popularity of these projected entertainments led to purpose-built sites for their enjoyment. The first motion picture theater was built in McKeesport, Pennsylvania, in 1905; only four years later there were eight thousand movie theaters in the United States, and by 1913 there were thirty thousand.[19] Newspapers from Winchester, Kentucky, attest to the change from live entertainment to movies. In 1909, the *News* announced,

> PICTURE THEATER IS NEARLY COMPLETED
>
> Work on the new moving picture theater that is to be located in the Auditorium Skating Rink is progressing rapidly. . . . The theatre when completed will be one of the prettiest and must [*sic*] up-to-date in Central Kentucky.[20]

The following year, the *News* announced the upcoming combination of movies and live vaudeville: "Messrs. Marshall Prewitt and Hub Bush of this city will start out in a few days with their moving picture and vaudeville show. They have purchased their moving picture outfit and are waiting for the films to arrive."[21] Within one month, however, movies had edged out live entertainment:

> VAUDEVILLE TO BE DISCONTINUED
>
> Management of Auditorium Has Closed Contract With Leading Moving Picture Company.
>
> The vaudeville season at the Winchester Auditorium will close Saturday night. . . . The crowds have been good but the opening of the opera house for the winter season will cut off attendance to such an extent that Messrs. Bloomfield & Ratliff, the proprietors, have decided to close the vaudeville show.
>
> They have closed a contract with the leading picture film company of the country for licensed pictures and beginning next Monday will start a moving picture show. . . . The people of Winchester will have the opportunity for the remainder of the winter to see high class moving picture shows.[22]

Similarly, in Carlisle, Pennsylvania, movies were shown at the opera house beginning in 1904, and by 1908 they were a nightly occurrence.[23] In Mount Sterling, Kentucky, movies were first used as fillers during the live performances, but had taken over the entire evening by 1911.[24] Other opera houses closed and

Stuart's Opera House, Nelsonville, Ohio (1879), as it appeared about 1979. Reprinted with permission of Stuart's Opera House Archives, Nelsonville, Ohio.

reopened as movie theaters, including the Academy of Music (Meadville, Pennsylvania, 1885), which became the Paramount Theatre in 1924, and the Tareco Opera House (Tarentum, Pennsylvania, 1906), which became a movie house in 1926.

The competition between forms of entertainment is clear in two adjacent headlines in the *Harlan (Kentucky) Enterprise* in 1922. Referring to a site for live entertainment, one headline declared, "CUMBERLAND THEATRE WILL CLOSE FOR THREE MONTHS," in order to avoid loss during the summer "carnival season." The next headline, referring to the opening of Harlan's New Theatre movie house, read: "NEW THEATRE OPENS WITH FULL HOUSE."[25]

Most opera houses closed, or ceased functioning as opera houses, in the 1920s, while some endured into the 1930s. Many were converted to movie theaters, many were converted to nontheatrical purposes, and many burned down.

Some opera houses are still extant, but are used for storage, with no signs of restoration. The Shinnston Opera House (West Virginia, 1910) became a movie theater and, after a fire, was converted to a skating rink. It is now used for general storage. The Coll Opera House (Jackson, Ohio, 1883) closed in the late 1920s, was briefly reopened in the 1930s for community theater, and closed permanently in 1937. It is now used for automobile parts storage for a car dealership downstairs. The Knights of Pythias Opera House in Shawnee, Ohio (1881), closed in 1929, and when the Knights of Pythias went bankrupt in 1943, the building was sold to Hannah Brothers Furniture, which uses it for storage. Similarly, the Nova Theatre (Cumberland, Kentucky, 1937) closed in 1985 and is now used for furniture storage.

Other opera houses were converted beyond recognition to nontheatrical purposes. The Elkins Opera House (West Virginia, 1898) was converted to apartments and stores. The Mannington Opera House (West Virginia, 1894) was converted to an apartment building in the late 1930s, and the building burned down in 1968. In Blairsville, Pennsylvania, Einstein's Opera House (1904) closed in 1916 because of competition from cinemas and was converted to apartments. Tabb Opera House (Mount Sterling, Kentucky, 1910) hosted a local minstrel troupe through 1961, but it closed in 1963 and was converted to a discount-clothing store, and then burned down in the 1970s. Most of the Wagner Opera House (Bradford, Pennsylvania, 1876) was destroyed in a fire in 1966, and the remainder was converted to a McCrory's discount store. The store has since closed, and the building is now owned by the city. The Fairmont Opera House (West Virginia, 1902) was renovated in 1916, then closed and sold to the Odd Fellows in 1920, when it was totally revamped for lodge purposes. The building was razed for a parking lot in 1980. The Ridgway Opera House (Pennsylvania, 1897) was converted to the Strand Theatre, a cinema that closed in 1983. The building, which now houses a Keystone Hardware, is slated for demolition. The Tarentum Opera House (Pennsylvania, 1886) became a skating rink, then a furniture store, and is now a drugstore. The Armstrong Opera House (1893) in Johnsonburg, Pennsylvania, was converted to the Palace Theatre for movies, and then closed in 1962. A bowling alley was put into the basement in the 1960s, and the building is now a garage.

Other opera houses have simply been torn down. The Northeast Opera House (Pennsylvania, 1886) was set to become a movie theater in 1915, but the safety requirements for a second-story movie theater were too expensive, so the opera house closed and the building was razed in 1943 for a parking lot. Grandin Opera House (Tidioute, Pennsylvania, 1872) was condemned in the 1920s and remained empty until it was razed in 1980. The Academy of Music (1893) in Tyrone, Pennsylvania, was razed, along with many other historic buildings, for an interstate highway in 1994.

Many opera houses burned down. Fire was a major danger for opera houses around the turn of the century, and many new opera houses proclaimed their fire safety procedures when they opened. Architects, engineers, and planners addressed this problem in the late nineteenth century. In *Modern Opera Houses and Theatres,* a book widely accepted as authoritative when it was published (1896–98), Edwin O. Sachs calculated the average life of a theater built between

Marlinton Opera House, Marlinton, West Virginia (1909), as it appears today in the process of restoration. Photos by author.

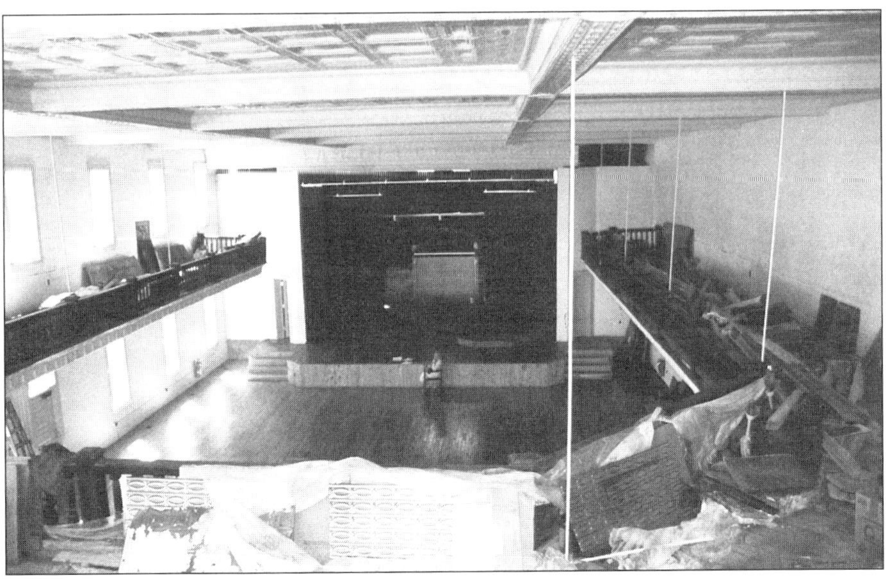

1797 and 1896 in Europe or the United States at twelve to eighteen years. Most of these theaters and opera houses burned down; most of the fires whose origins could be determined started in the stage house, from gas or electric lighting, heating, or special effects. About one-third of the fires ignited during or within two hours of a performance. Sachs also pointed out the rapid increase in the frequency of theater fires during the late nineteenth century: one-third of the total number of fires occurred during the last ten years of that period, at a rate of thirty-six fires per year.[26]

A few years later, John R. Freeman addressed the issue of fire safety and prevention in theaters specifically in his book *On the Safeguarding of Life in Theaters* (1906). In particular, he examined the horrendous Iroquois Theatre fire of 1903 in Chicago, which killed 571 people. The fire started with a spark from an electric arc light that touched a stage drapery, and then spread to the hanging scenery. Most of the scenery was on fire within one to two minutes, and the smoke poured into the auditorium, suffocating audience members. There were 1,830 spectators in the auditorium for the standing-room-only holiday matinee, and about one-third were killed, most within five minutes of the outbreak of the fire. Freeman took pains to identify the dangerous places in the theater: 400 of those killed were in the gallery, or, put another way, 70 percent of the gallery patrons died; 125 people died in the balcony, or 30 percent of those seated there. Of the 900 people in the gallery and balcony, only 300 got out alive. On the main floor, however, only 7 people died, mostly as a result of people jumping from the gallery. Ironically, the theater was new and had been advertised as having "fireproof construction," and in fact there was little damage to the building; only the scenery, decoration, and upholstery burned. Freeman concluded that the greatest danger was from fires started onstage, with deaths overwhelmingly occurring in the balconies: "In the great theater fires of history the loss of life has commonly resulted from the rapid spread of flame on a stage covered with scenery, followed within two or three minutes by an outpouring of suffocating smoke through the proscenium arch into the top of the auditorium, before those in the galleries could escape. Death has come chiefly to those in the balconies, and often within less than five minutes of the first flame." Freeman recommended such safeguards as "automatic, quick-opening smoke vents over the stage," automatic sprinklers, and "especially ample exits and stairways from the gallery."[27] Many of these reforms were enacted around the country in the following years, and led to the decline of second-story opera houses, which were considered a greater safety hazard.

A look at just the oil region of Pennsylvania can provide evidence of the short life of opera houses and of the frequency with which they burned down:

Red Men's Opera House, Shawnee, Ohio (1907), showing its restored exterior. Photo by author.

Titusville:

Crittenden Hall, 1860, burned 1861

Bliss Opera House, 1865, then furniture store, burned 1939

Corinthian Hall (Academy of Music), 1865, then furniture store in 1946

Parshall Opera House, 1870, burned 1882

Emery Opera House, 1886, burned 1887

Titusville Opera House, 1887, became Grand Theater in 1920s, torn down 1930–31

Pithole City:

Murphy's Theatre, 1865, dismantled and moved to Pleasantville, razed 1872

Metropolitan Theatre, 1865, burned 1865

Pleasantville:

St. Nicholas Opera House, 1868, burned 1871

Holeman Opera House, 1872–73, condemned 1913, used occasionally until 1928, top removed 1951, burned 1992

Petroleum Centre:

Metropolitan Theatre, 1866, burned 1866

Sobel's Opera House, 1872–73, burned 1878

Akin's Opera House, 1866, burned 1867

Community redevelopment and historic preservation efforts in the late twentieth century saved many opera houses that did survive; some have been restored and reopened. Ironically, the very poverty of Appalachia in the post-coal, postindustrial era saved many of the area's opera houses. In many cases, the opera house was simply boarded over. There was no money available to redevelop the space for other uses, and so the opera house sat abandoned—forgotten by all but a few old-timers. In the late twentieth and early twenty-first centuries, communities have come to realize the value of their historic architecture and have tried to save, restore, and reopen opera houses. These efforts have usually been led by a few quixotic individuals with a blind, dogged determination to overcome any obstacle. The first step is usually to stabilize the building, putting on a new roof, solidifying the foundation, and shoring up the walls. These are the most expensive steps, but are the least visible and have the least tangible payoff, leading many in the communities to wonder where all that money is going. Only after such stabilization can opera house advocates begin to think of making the auditorium and stage safe and usable for audiences and performers.

Stuart's Opera House (Nelsonville, Ohio, 1879) was packed in 1924 for what turned out to be its last performance. The following morning shopkeepers on the first floor were unable to open their doors, and the rumor spread that the building was in danger of collapse. Another explanation was that extremely humid weather had caused doors all over town to stick, including those in the opera house building. While the opera house was closed for inspection, the Ohio legislature passed stringent new fire and safety laws that outlawed opening a new second-floor theater or reopening one that was closed. The opera house remained closed until 1979. During this dormant phase the theater still contained its full array of seats, draperies, lights, light board, scenery, props,

Red Men's Opera House, Shawnee, Ohio (1907), showing an unrestored interior in which the plaster has fallen off the lathe walls and ceiling. Photo by author.

hemp rigging, asbestos curtain, and posters. The opera house reopened briefly in 1979, but a major fire destroyed most of the building the following year. Following the fire, the mayor, echoed by many letters to the editor, advocated demolishing the remains of the building in favor of a parking lot. Community members led a twenty-year effort, supported by a trickle of private and government grants, to rebuild the opera house. The opera house reopened in 1997 and is now used for community theater and concerts.

In McConnelsville, Ohio, showboats traveled the Muskingum River, but the town lacked a permanent theater. In addition, it lacked a town hall for council meetings, and so one building was proposed to meet both needs. The result, in 1892, was the Town Hall and Opera House, built on the town's central square. The opera house, which sat seven hundred people, was situated on the ground floor; the architect is credited with predicting that second-floor theaters would soon be outlawed. The building is a town landmark, topped with a 108-foot tower and weather vane, and is still the tallest building in McConnelsville. The opera house was renovated in 1936, with the provision for showing movies, but sank into disrepair and underuse in the 1950s and 1960s. In 1968 the space was slated for conversion to office space, and the opera house manager ran for mayor on just one plank: "Save the Opera House!" He won by a two-to-one margin. His dedication to the theater included living in a grand silken pavilion

Red Men's Opera House, Shawnee, Ohio (1907). Photo by author.

constructed onstage behind the projection screen. The theater was renovated again in 1973, and a federal grant in 1984 provided money for a major restoration. It is now used for movies, concerts, and community theater.

In Charles Town, West Virginia, the New Opera House opened in 1911 with a "home talent" production, which was a benefit by the Daughters of the Confederacy for indigent Confederate veterans. The opera house was subsequently used for vaudeville, movies, conventions, religious lectures, boxing, church services, basketball, and finally as a movie theater. It closed in 1948 and was scheduled to be torn down for a parking lot, as is so often the case with an abandoned opera house. In 1973 community senior citizen volunteers carried out thirty-five truckloads of pigeon droppings and saved the opera house. The owner was so impressed with their work that he donated the opera house to the volunteers. The "Old Opera House Theatre Company" formed in 1973 and now operates the restored opera house as a community theater.

Opera houses in Pennsylvania and Kentucky have also been restored for current use as theaters. In Warren, Pennsylvania, the Struthers Library Theatre (1883) was converted for showing movies in 1919 and closed briefly in 1983. Community volunteers raised the money to reopen the theater later that year, and it has been in continuous operation since for community productions. The Acad-

Marlin's Opera House, Brookville, Pennsylvania (1886), has remained intact and in pristine condition since it was shuttered in 1901. Photo by author.

emy Theatre (Meadville, Pennsylvania, 1885) was in use as a movie theater from the 1920s through the 1980s, when it closed. The Meadville Redevelopment Authority, as part of a citywide redevelopment effort, purchased the building in 1988, and the Academy Theatre Foundation formed in 1989. The Academy Theatre reopened in 1992 and is now used for community theater. Garman's Opera House (Bellefonte, Pennsylvania, 1890) was used for movies from the 1920s through 1961 and then became a furniture warehouse. It was nearly torn down for a parking lot but was bought by local people who wanted to save the structure, and it reopened for movies and community theater in 1997. The Maysville Players, a community theater group, bought the Washington Opera House (Maysville, Kentucky, 1898) in 1965, and it remains in operation. In Altoona, Pennsylvania, the Mishler Theatre (built and largely destroyed by fire in 1906, rebuilt in 1907) was converted to a cinema in 1923 and remained in operation through 1965. It was slated to be torn down for a parking lot but was purchased by the Altoona Community Theatre and the Blair County Arts Foundation. The Mishler Theatre is now used for community theater and dance.

At other opera houses, restoration plans are still in progress or have not yet begun. The Marlinton Opera House (West Virginia, 1909) was used for roller-skating and basketball, among other activities. The building then was used, in turn, as a community center, as a car dealership, and for lumber storage. The

Marlin's Opera House, Brookville, Pennsylvania (1886). Photo by author.

opera house was finally purchased by the historical society in 1991, and is now in the process of restoration for a community performing arts center. Cotrill's Opera House (1902) in Thomas, West Virginia—an active mining town from 1912 to 1920, with lodges including Woodmen of the World, Improved Order of Red Men, Masons, Knights of Pythias, Knights of Modern Maccabees, Eagles, Sons of Lithuania, Croatian Society, Sons of Italy, Saint John's Society, Saint Stephen's Society, and African American lodges of Masons and Pythias—was converted to a movie theater in the 1940s and closed in 1973. Restoration efforts began in 1979, with a goal to turn it into a regional theater.

In Shawnee, Ohio, the Red Men's Opera House survived because of the addition of the Linda Theatre for movies downstairs. The Linda closed in 1955 and the building was abandoned. It was about to be sold for five hundred dollars for the reclamation value of its internal I-beams when community activists raised the money to save the building. The building now has a new roof and solid foundation, and is kept occupied with a library and an apartment. Long-term plans have been drawn up for restoring the theater, to be renamed the Tecumseh Theatre. The Benham Theatre (Kentucky, 1922) was used as a youth center until the late 1970s, when it was closed because of a leaking roof. The building has been stabilized and the community has plans to restore it as part of an emphasis on its coal-mining history. Marlin's Opera House (Brookville, Pennsylvania, 1883) was closed in 1901 but was still owned by the Marlin family. It was briefly reopened in 1923 for use as an indoor driving range to provide winter golf practice: golfers used coconut doormats for tees, with old carpets lining the walls for protection. In 1983 Regis and Phyllis McCabe bought the building, and they hope to restore the intact opera house. In Harrodsburg, Kentucky, the opera house was in the Odd Fellows Hall, which was sold to the Masons and then rented in 1955 by a radio station. The radio station still uses the opera house but hopes to restore it to its original architecture.

In Vandergrift, Pennsylvania, the Casino Theater (1900) was the centerpiece of a planned community designed by Frederick Law Olmstead. The theater became a cinema and then closed in 1981. In the 1990s, community efforts began to restore the theater. Since the closing of the Harmony Opera House (Pennsylvania, 1887–90), the building has housed a restaurant, a bowling alley, a dance hall, a basketball court, a garage, a fan factory, a bottling works, and an antique shop. The building is privately owned, and the owner hopes to restore the opera house to its original condition. Finally, the Pierce Opera House (Sharpsville, Pennsylvania, 1872) was used as a movie theater in the 1910s and 1920s, and it remained empty from 1928 through 1940; fraternal organizations and churches then used it from 1961 through 2000. It is now owned by a community redevelopment organization that plans to restore it.

The role the opera house can play in the future is found in its past. The opera house was never used exclusively for theatrical performance. It was a part of the fabric of the community and was used for anything and everything that a large indoor space could provide for. The key to saving these treasures, then, is for the community once more to have a stake in the buildings. If the opera house can again present events that the community deems important, the opera house will survive.

APPENDIX

List of Opera Houses Studied

Kentucky

Ashland	Ashland Opera House	1890
Benham	Benham Theatre	1921
Carlisle	Mozart's Hall	1883
Cumberland	Corlee Theatre	1925
	Cumberland Theatre	1928
	Novo Theatre	1937
Danville	James Hall	1869
Elizabethtown	Stewart Opera House	1907
Evans City	Glenn Opera House	1900
Harlan	New Harlan Theater	c. 1924
Harrodsburg	Odd Fellows Lodge	1905
Lynch	Victory Theatre	1919
Maysville	Washington Opera House	1898
Middlesboro(ough)	Middlesborough (aka Princess/Manring) Theater	1889
Mount Sterling	Grand Opera House	1890
	Tabb Opera House	1910
Paris	Odd Fellows Hall	1855
	Grand Opera House	1890
Richmond	Green's Opera House	1872
Sanford	Walton's Opera House	Unknown
Somerset	Gem Opera House	Unknown
Stearns	Stearns Opera House	c. 1910
Winchester	Winchester Opera House	1880

Ohio

Athens	Athens Opera House	1874
Chesterhill	Chesterhill Opera House	1908
Chillicothe	Masonic Opera House aka Majestic Theater	1876
Corning	Monahan's Opera House	Unknown
Gallipolis	Gallipolis Opera House aka Ariel Theatre	1895
Glouster	Glouster Opera House	Unknown
Ironton	New Masonic Opera House	Unknown
Jackson	Crescent Opera House	1885
	Grand Opera House aka Coll Opera House	1893
McConnelsville	Twin City Opera House	1892
Nelsonville	Stuart's Opera House	1879
Pomeroy	Pomeroy Opera House	Unknown
Portsmouth	Grand Opera House	Unknown
Shawnee	Knights of Labor Opera House aka Knights of Pythias Opera House	1881
	Red Men's Opera House	1907
Zaleski	Fisher Opera House	1884

Pennsylvania

Altoona	Mishler Theatre	1906
Bellefonte	Garman's Opera House	1890
Blairsville	Einstein Opera House	1904
Bradford	Music Room	1865
	Wagner Opera House	1876
Brookville	Marlin's Opera House	1886
Carlisle	Sentinel Opera House aka Rheem's Hall	1898
	Carlisle Opera House	1898
Connellsville	Newmeyer Opera House	1881
Corry	Wright's Theatre	1865
DuBois	DuBois Opera House	1886
Greenville	Laird's Opera House	1873
Harmony	Harmony Opera House	1875
Hollidaysburg	Condron's Opera House	c. 1868
Jamestown	Gibson's Opera House	1860
Johnsonburg	Armstrong Opera House	1890
Johnstown	Union Hall	1867
	Park's Opera House	1869
	Adair Opera House	1889
	Johnstown Opera House	1892
	Majestic Theatre	1907

Kittanning	Kittanning Opera House	1874
Latrobe	Mozart Hall	1890
Latrobe	Showalter Hall	1883
Lock Haven	Lock Haven Opera House	1869
Meadville	Academy of Music	1885
Mercer	Mercer Opera House	1873
Meyersdale	Slicer Opera House	1883
	Grand Opera House	1900
	Donges Theatre	1904
	Reich's Auditorium	1909
Northeast	Short's Opera House	1887
Oil City	Bascom's Hall	1865
	Love's Opera House	1872
	New Opera House	1884
	Oil City Opera House	1885
Petroleum Center	Metropolitan Theatre	1866
	Akin's Opera House	1866
	Sobel's Opera House	1872
Pithole	Murphy Theatre	1865
	Metropolitan	1865
	Athenaeum	Torn down 1867
Pleasantville	St. Nicholas Opera House	1868
	Holeman Opera House	1873
Renovo	P. H. Sullivan's Opera House	1885
	Renovo Opera House	1893
	Spangler's Opera House	Torn down 1893
Reynoldsville	Reynolds Opera House	1875
Ridgway	Ridgway Opera House	1897
Sharpsville	Pierce Opera House	1871
Smethport	Kittredge Opera House	1880
Tarentum	Tarentum Opera House	1886
	Tareco Opera House aka Nixon/Harris	1906
Tidioute	Grandin Opera House	1872
Titusville	Critenden Hall	1861
	Bliss Opera House	1865
	Corinthian Hall	1865
	Parshall Opera House	1870
	Opera House	1887
Tyrone	Academy of Music	1893
Uniontown	Grand Opera House	1883
Vandergrift	Casino Theatre	1900
Warren	Roscoe Hall	1868
	Struthers Library Theatre	1883
	Woodward Theater	1912
Washington	Washington Opera House	1859

West Virginia

Buckhannon	Opera House / Town Hall	1854
	Burr Opera House	1886
	Buckhannon Opera House	1903
Charles Town	Charles Town Opera House	1911
Elkins	Elkins Opera House	1898
Fairmont	Town Hall Theatre	1870
	The Rink	1885
	Grand Opera House	1902
Logan	Logan Theatre	Unknown
Mannington	Mannington Opera House	1894
Marlinton	Marlinton Opera House	1909
Martinsburg	Apollo Theatre	1913
Point Pleasant	Hoof's Opera House	1889
Shinnston	Shinnston Opera House	1910
Shepherdstown	Shepherdstown Opera House	1909
Spencer	Wells Opera House	1903
	Robey Theater	1907
Thomas	Cotrill's Opera House	1902
Wellsburg	Barth's Opera House	1880
West Union	West Union Opera House	1900

NOTES

Chapter 1

1. Meredith Willson, *The Music Man* (New York: Putnam's, 1958), 51–66.

2. David Naylor and Joan Dillon, *American Theaters: Performance Halls of the Nineteenth Century* (New York: John Wiley, 1997), 11.

3. *Athens (OH) Messenger,* December 1, 1881.

4. "The Name Opera House," *Dramatic Mirror,* March 7, 1885.

5. Jonas Barish, *The Antitheatrical Prejudice* (Berkeley and Los Angeles: University of California Press, 1981), 1.

6. Arthur Hornblow, *A History of the Theatre in America from Its Beginnings to the Present Time,* vol. 1 (Philadelphia: Lippincott, 1919), 172–73.

7. Bruce McConachie, "American Theatre in Context, from the Beginnings to 1870," in *The Cambridge History of American Theatre,* 2 vols., ed. Don B. Wilmeth and Christopher Bigsby (New York: Cambridge University Press, 1998–99), 1:126.

8. *Mirror of Taste* 1 (January 1810): 51; *Kentucky Gazette,* May 12, 1812, qtd. in David Grimsted, *Melodrama Unveiled: American Theater and Culture, 1800–1850* (Berkeley and Los Angeles: University of California Press, 1987), 34.

9. Lewis Atherton, *Main Street on the Middle Border* (Bloomington: Indiana University Press, 1954), 113, 117–18, 142.

10. *Curtain Up: New Life for Historic Theaters,* Information Ser. 72 (Washington, DC: National Trust for Historic Preservation, 1993), 6.

11. *Maysville (KY) Daily Evening Bulletin,* January 4, 1883.

12. Grace Doherty Library, Danville, KY.

13. *Connellsville (PA) Courier,* May 29, 1881.

14. *Paris Kentuckian Citizen,* December 31, 1890.

15. *Renovo (PA) Record,* December 23, 1892.

16. *Renovo (PA) Record,* March 24, 1893.

17. *Paris Kentuckian Citizen,* February 15, 1854.

18. *Paris Kentuckian Citizen,* July 14, 1886.

19. *Paris Kentuckian Citizen,* July 22, 1886.

20. *Paris Kentuckian Citizen,* April 1, 1889.

21. *Paris Kentuckian Citizen,* December 27, 1890.

22. *Paris Kentuckian Citizen,* January 15, 1891.

23. *Paris Kentuckian Citizen,* January 15, 1893.

24. *Maysville (KY) Daily Evening Bulletin,* June 26, 1884.

25. John L. Marsh, "Troupers at Tidioute," *Players* 47 (1972): 138.
26. Drake Well Museum, Titusville, PA.
27. Randolph County Historical Society, Elkins, WV.
28. Warren County Historical Society, Warren, PA.
29. *Athens (OH) Messenger,* September 4, 1879.
30. December 29, 1870, Drake Well Museum, Titusville, PA.
31. February 15, 1906, Altoona Area Public Library, Altoona, PA.
32. *Renovo (PA) Record,* July 23, 1885.
33. *Renovo (PA) Record,* August 6, 1885.
34. *Renovo (PA) Record,* December 23, 1892.
35. *Harlan (KY) Enterprise,* September 29, 1922.
36. *Harlan (KY) Enterprise,* April 20, 1923.
37. *Harlan (KY) Enterprise,* May 12, 1922.
38. *Cumberland (KY) Tri-City News,* December 23, 1937.
39. *Cumberland (KY) Tri-City News,* January 9, 1938.
40. *Cumberland (KY) Tri-City News,* December 23, 1937.
41. *Paris Kentuckian Citizen,* September 28, 1886.
42. *Paris Kentuckian Citizen,* November 16, 1895.
43. *Carlisle (PA) Evening Sentinel,* Cumberland County Historical Society and Hamilton Library Association, Carlisle, PA.
44. *Harlan (KY) Enterprise,* May 16, 1924.
45. *Maysville (KY) Daily Evening Bulletin,* November 30, 1881.
46. Stuart's Opera House Archives, Nelsonville, OH.

Chapter 2

1. Atherton, *Main Street,* 13, 117–18, 142.
2. Richard Butsch, *The Making of American Audiences: From Stage to Television, 1750–1990* (New York: Cambridge University Press, 2000), 67.
3. Bruce McConachie, *Melodramatic Formations: American Theatre and Society, 1820–1870* (Iowa City: University of Iowa Press, 1992), 157.
4. Randolph County Historical Society, Elkins, WV.
5. December 29, 1870, Drake Well Museum, Titusville, PA.
6. *Paris Kentuckian Citizen,* December 31, 1890.
7. *Harlan (KY) Enterprise,* May 12, 1922.
8. *Harlan (KY) Enterprise,* May 18, 1923.
9. Warren County Historical Society, Warren, PA.
10. Bradford Landmark Society, Bradford, PA.
11. *New Straitsville (OH) Record,* November 21, 1902.
12. *Meyersdale (PA) Republican,* December 14, 1913.
13. *Meyersdale (PA) Republican,* September 15, 1913.
14. *Meyersdale (PA) Republican,* August 14, 1913.
15. *Shawnee (OH) People's Advocate,* March 1, 1918.
16. *Paris Kentuckian Citizen,* October 8, 1879.

17. *Paris Kentuckian Citizen,* November 8, 1882.

18. *Athens (OH) Messenger,* December 24, 1885.

19. *Winchester (KY) News,* May 27, 1911.

20. *Shawnee (OH) People's Advocate,* October 6, 1933, qtd. in Rob Dishong and John Winnenberg, *Shawnee: Reflections upon the First 125 Years, 1873–1998* (Nelsonville, OH: Tribune, 1998), 115.

21. *Gallipolis (OH) Tribune,* April 23, 1899, qtd. in M. Jane Daniel, "Nineteenth-Century Opera Houses of Gallipolis, Ohio" (master's thesis, Marshall University, Huntington, WV, 1992), 137.

22. *Middlesborough (KY) Weekly News,* March 1, 1902.

23. *Gallipolis (OH) Tribune,* January 7, 1896, qtd. in Daniel, "Nineteenth-Century," 96.

24. *New Straitsville (OH) Record,* November 6, 1903.

25. *Maysville (KY) Daily Evening Bulletin,* March 31, 1882.

26. March 12, 1892, Washington County Historical Society, Washington, PA.

27. *Harlan (KY) Enterprise,* May 12, 1922.

28. *Winchester (KY) News,* March 9, 1911.

29. *Meyersdale (PA) Republican,* October 31, 1912.

30. *Harlan (KY) Enterprise,* March 13, 1925.

31. *Harlan (KY) Enterprise,* April 24, 1924.

32. *Harlan (KY) Enterprise,* May 11, 1923.

33. *Harlan (KY) Enterprise,* September 8, 1922.

34. Drake Well Museum, Titusville, PA.

35. Lawrence W. Levine, *Highbrow/Lowbrow: The Emergence of Cultural Hierarchy in America* (Cambridge: Harvard University Press, 1988), 192, 197–98.

36. Mary Ann Clawson, "Spectatorship and Masculinity in the Scottish Rite," in *Theatre of the Fraternity: Staging the Ritual Space,* ed. C. Lance Brockman (Jackson: University Press of Mississippi, 1996), 61.

37. Levine, *Highbrow/Lowbrow,* 198.

38. Butsch, *Making,* 68, 72, 80.

39. M. Alison Kibler, *Rank Ladies: Gender and Cultural Hierarchy in American Vaudeville* (Chapel Hill: University of North Carolina Press, 1999), 46.

40. Clawson, "Spectatorship," 61.

41. Levine, *Highbrow/Lowbrow,* 196.

42. Edwin Milton Royle, "The Vaudeville Theatre," *Scribner's* 26 (October 1899): 488, qtd. in Robert W. Snyder, *The Voice of the City: Vaudeville and Popular Culture in New York* (New York: Oxford University Press, 1989), 32.

43. B. F. Keith, "The Vogue of Vaudeville," *National Magazine* 9 (November 1898): 146–53, qtd. in Charles W. Stein, ed., *American Vaudeville as Seen by Its Contemporaries* (New York: Knopf, 1984), 17.

44. Clawson, "Spectatorship," 61.

45. Clawson, "Spectatorship," 61.

46. *Jackson (OH) Standard Journal,* May 26, 1883.

47. *New Straitsville (OH) Record,* March 18, 1904.

48. *Brookville (PA) Jeffersonian Democrat,* April 9, 1890.

49. *Brookville (PA) Jeffersonian Democrat,* June 11, 1890.

50. *Brookville (PA) Jeffersonian Democrat,* March 5, 1891.

51. *Brookville (PA) Jeffersonian Democrat,* June 11, 1891.

52. *Brookville (PA) Jeffersonian Democrat,* June 11, 1891.

53. *Athens (OH) Messenger,* October 21, 1886.

54. *Athens (OH) Messenger,* July 12, 1883.

55. Daniel, "Nineteenth-Century," 125–26.

56. *Maysville (KY) Daily Evening Bulletin,* November 21, 1882.

57. *Maysville (KY) Daily Evening Bulletin,* February 19, 1883.

58. *Maysville (KY) Daily Evening Bulletin,* November 27, 1900.

59. Levine, *Highbrow/Lowbrow,* 191.

60. *Maysville (KY) Daily Evening Bulletin,* December 2, 1899.

61. *Louisville (KY) Courier-Journal,* Patty M. Biddle personal collection, Paris, KY.

62. *Paris Kentuckian Citizen,* December 31, 1890.

63. *Brookville (PA) Jeffersonian Democrat,* September 11, 1890.

64. Laurence Senelick, *The Changing Room: Sex, Drag and Theatre* (London: Routledge, 2000), 295–97.

65. Senelick, *Changing,* 298, 311.

66. *Maysville (KY) Daily Evening Bulletin,* March 2, 1882.

67. *Maysville (KY) Daily Evening Bulletin,* January 23, 1883.

68. *Winchester (KY) News,* March 31, 1909.

69. *Oil City (PA) Derrick,* November 24, 1914.

70. *Gallipolis (OH) Tribune,* October 17, 1898, qtd. in Daniel, "Nineteenth-Century," 128–29.

71. *Gallipolis (OH) Tribune,* January 10, 1899, qtd. in Daniel, "Nineteenth-Century," 132–33.

72. Spencer Steenrod, *A History of Stuart's Opera House, Nelsonville, Ohio* (Nelsonville, OH: Tribune, 1978), 44.

Chapter 3

1. John Brinckerhoff Jackson, *Discovering the Vernacular Landscape* (New Haven: Yale University Press, 1984), 8.

2. Paul Groth, "Frameworks for Cultural Landscape Study," in *Understanding Ordinary Landscapes,* ed. Paul Groth and Todd W. Bressi (New Haven: Yale University Press, 1997), 1.

3. D. W. Meinig, "Reading the Landscape: An Appreciation of W. G. Hoskins and J. B. Jackson," in *The Interpretation of Ordinary Landscapes: Geographical Essays,* ed. D. W. Meinig (New York: Oxford University Press, 1979), 228.

4. D. W. Meinig, introduction to Meinig, *Interpretation,* 5.

5. Peirce F. Lewis, "Axioms for Reading the Landscape: Some Guides to the American Scene," in Meinig, *Interpretation,* 24.

6. Groth, "Frameworks," 1.

7. Groth, "Frameworks," 3.

8. Peirce F. Lewis, "Axioms," 12.

9. Peirce F. Lewis, "Axioms," 18.

10. Richard V. Francaviglia, *Main Street Revisited: Time, Space, and Image Building in Small-Town America* (Iowa City: University of Iowa Press, 1996), 80.

11. Jackson, *Discovering,* 18, 75; Francaviglia, *Main,* xix.

12. John Brinckerhoff Jackson, *Landscapes: Selected Writings of J. B. Jackson,* ed. Ervin H. Zube (Amherst: University of Massachusetts Press, 1970), 127.

13. Richard V. Francaviglia, *Hard Places: Reading the Landscape of America's Historic Mining Districts* (Iowa City: University of Iowa Press, 1991), 30.

14. Francaviglia, *Hard,* 117–18.

15. Francaviglia, *Hard,* 84.

16. Francaviglia, *Hard,* 35, 40, 85.

17. Peirce F. Lewis, "Axioms," 34.

18. Kevin Lynch, *The Image of the City* (Cambridge, MA: Technology Press, 1960), 47–48.

19. *Shawnee (OH) People's Advocate,* June 28, 1918.

20. *Harlan (KY) Enterprise,* May 15, 1922.

21. Kentucky Coal Mining Museum, Benham, KY.

22. Marvin Carlson, *Places of Performance: The Semiotics of Theatre Architecture* (Ithaca, NY: Cornell University Press, 1989), 105–7.

23. Francaviglia, *Main,* 2–4.

24. Francaviglia, *Main,* 65.

25. Carlson, *Places,* 79.

26. Carlson, *Places,* 68.

27. Roubo *fils, Traité de la construction des théâtres et des machines théâtracles* (Paris, 1777), 24, qtd. in Carlson, *Places,* 79.

28. Drake Well Museum, Titusville, PA.

29. Allegheny-Kiski Valley Historical Society, Tarentum, PA.

30. Blair County Genealogical Society, Hollidaysburg, PA.

31. Francaviglia, *Main,* 28.

32. Francaviglia, *Hard,* 43.

33. Francaviglia, *Main,* 29.

34. Francaviglia, *Main,* 32.

35. Francaviglia, *Main,* 36.

36. *Maysville (KY) Daily Evening Bulletin,* February 12, 1885.

37. Cumberland County Historical Society and Hamilton Library Association, Carlisle, PA.

38. Drake Well Museum, Titusville, PA.

Chapter 4

1. Bruce Ergood, "Toward a Definition of Appalachia," in *Appalachia: Social Context Past and Present,* ed. Bruce Ergood and Bruce E. Kuhre (Dubuque, IA: Kendall/Hunt, 1991), 45.

2. Henry D. Shapiro, "Appalachia and the Idea of America: The Problem of the Persisting Frontier," in Ergood and Kuhre, *Appalachia,* 75.

3. Darlene Wilson, "A Judicious Combination of Incident and Psychology: John Fox Jr. and the Southern Mountain Motif," in *Confronting Appalachian Stereotypes: Back Talk from an American Region,* ed. Dwight B. Billings, Gurney Norman, and Katherine Ledford (Lexington: University Press of Kentucky, 1999), 100.

4. Ronald D. Eller, foreword to Billings, Norman, and Ledford, *Confronting,* x.

5. George W. Knepper, *Ohio and Its People* (Kent, OH: Kent State University Press, 1989), 287.

6. Walter Precourt, "The Image of Appalachian Poverty," in Ergood and Kuhre, 176, 180.

7. Crandall A. Shifflett, "Coal Towns: The Company Town and Southern Appalachian History," in Ergood and Kuhre, 195–96.

8. Shifflett, "Coal Towns," 195–96.

9. Ronald L. Lewis, "Beyond Isolation and Homogeneity: Diversity and the History of Appalachia," in Billings, Norman, and Ledford, *Confronting,* 35.

10. John Winnenberg, *Our Journey Continues: The History of New Straitsville, Ohio, Volume 1: 1870–1925* (Logan, OH: Fine Print, 1995), 12.

11. Ivan Tribe, *Little Cities of Black Diamonds: Urban Development in the Hocking Coal Region, 1870–1900* (Athens, OH: Athens Ancestree, 1986), 95.

12. David Alan Corbin, *Life, Work, and Rebellion in the Coal Fields: The Southern West Virginia Miners, 1880–1922* (Chicago: University of Illinois Press, 1981), 8; Price V. Fishback, *Soft Coal, Hard Choices: The Economic Welfare of Bituminous Coal Miners, 1890–1930* (New York: Oxford University Press, 1992), 172–74.

13. Thomas A. Kelemen, "A History of Lynch, Kentucky, 1917–1930," *The Filson Club History Quarterly* 48 (1974): 160; Harry Caudill, *Theirs Be the Power: The Moguls of Eastern Kentucky* (Urbana: University of Illinois Press, 1983), 98; Mabel Brown Ellis, "Children of the Kentucky Coal Fields," *The American Child,* 1920, 290.

14. Ronald D. Eller, *Miners, Millhands, and Mountaineers: Industrialization of the Appalachian South, 1880–1930* (Knoxville: University of Tennessee Press, 1982), 74.

15. *McCreary County (KY) Record,* March 26, 1929.

16. Corbin, *Life,* 1.

17. Eller, *Miners,* 170.

18. Ronald L. Lewis, "Beyond," 36.

19. Ronald L. Lewis, "Beyond," 36.

20. Fishback, *Soft,* 174.

21. Eller, *Miners,* 174.

22. Tribe, *Little,* 105–15; Ivan Tribe, *Sprinkled with Coal Dust: Life and Work in the Hocking Coal Region, 1870–1900* (Athens, OH: Athens County Historical Society and Museum, 1989), 61–62, 96–97.

23. R. M. Gibson, *The 1907 Photographic History of New Straitsville* (Newark: Ohio Advertising Co., 1907), qtd. in Winnenberg, *Our Journey,* 13.

24. Ellis, "Children," 339.

25. Charles R. Towson, "Replacing the Saloon in Mining Communities," *Coal Age* 8 (1915): 265.

26. Corbin, *Life,* 62, 66.

27. Eller, *Miners,* 170; Fishback, *Soft,* 174, 183; Francaviglia, *Hard,* 103.

28. Caudill, *Theirs,* 9, 10, 12; Eller, *Miners,* xxi–xxii, 54–56, 64; Corbin, *Life,* 4.

29. Walter Precourt, "The Image of Appalachian Poverty," in *Appalachia and America: Autonomy and Regional Dependence,* ed. Allen W. Batteau (Lexington: University Press of Kentucky, 1983), 104.

30. Eller, *Miners,* xxi.

31. Paul Frederick Cressy, "Social Disorganization and Reorganization in Harlan County, Kentucky," *American Sociology Review* 14 (1949): 392.

32. Winthrop Lane, "Black Avalanche," *Survey* 47 (March 25, 1922): 1002, qtd. in Corbin, *Life,* 1.

33. Precourt, "Image," in Batteau, 104.

34. Harry M. Caudill, *Night Comes to the Cumberlands* (Boston: Little, Brown, 1962), qtd. in Helen Matthews Lewis and Edward E. Knipe, "The Colonialism Model: The Appalachian Model," in *Colonialism in Modern America: The Appalachian Case,* ed. Helen Matthews Lewis et al. (Boone, NC: Appalachian Consortium, 1978), 15.

35. Robert Blauner, "Internal Colonialism and Ghetto Revolt," *Social Problems* 16 (Spring 1969): 395–96.

36. Precourt, "Image," 181.

37. Jack Weller, "Appalachia: America's Mineral Colony," in Lewis et al., *Colonialism,* 48.

38. Cressy, "Social," 390.

39. Precourt, "Image," 180.

Chapter 5

1. Eller, *Miners,* 156.

2. Crandall A. Shifflett, *Coal Towns: Life, Work, and Culture in Company Towns of Southern Appalachia, 1880–1960* (Knoxville: University of Tennessee Press, 1991), 30.

3. Eller, *Miners,* 87, 95.

4. Francaviglia, *Hard,* 135.

5. Francaviglia, *Hard,* 73.

6. Ronald L. Lewis, "Beyond," 33.

7. Francaviglia, *Hard,* 76.

8. W. L. Slout, *Theatre in a Tent: The Development of a Provincial Entertainment* (Bowling Green: Bowling Green University Popular Press), 1.

9. Shifflett, *Coal Towns: Life,* 34; Corbin, *Life,* 9.

10. Cressy, "Social," 389–90.

11. Robert F. Munn, "The Development of Model Towns in the Bituminous Coal Fields," *West Virginia History* 40 (1979): 244.

12. Shifflett, *Coal Towns: Life,* xv.

13. Munn, "Development," 244–45.

14. Shifflett, *Coal Towns: Life,* xiii, 35, 162.

15. John S. Garner, introduction to *The Company Town: Architecture and Society in the Early Industrial Age* (New York: Oxford University Press, 1992), 4.

16. Ronald L. Lewis, "Beyond," 34.

17. Ellis, "Children," 322.

18. Amy E. Schertz, *Harlan County Coal Camps: Lynch and Benham, Kentucky; Cultural Transition from Rural to Urban Communities; Industrial Documentary Photography, 1912–1948* (Lexington: University of Kentucky Press, 1987), 2.

19. Billings, Norman, and Ledford, *Confronting,* 34.

20. Fishback, *Soft,* 4–5.

21. Cressy, "Social," 391.

22. Munn, "Development," 252.

23. Schertz, *Harlan County,* 3.

24. Kelemen, "History," 165.

25. Shifflett, "Coal Town," 195.

26. L. E. Perry, *McCreary Conquest: A Narrative History* (Whitley City, KY: L. E. Perry, 1979), 114–16.

27. Kelemen, "History," 158, 173.

28. Caudill, *Theirs,* 99.

29. *Harlan (KY) Enterprise,* December 15, 1922.

30. Howard N. Eavenson, "Building Complete Thousand-Dwelling Town for a Mining Population of 7,000 at Lynch, Ky.," *Coal Age* 20 (1921): 532.

31. Eller, *Miners,* 179.

32. Corbin, *Life,* 10.

33. Eller, *Miners,* 197.

34. Thomas F. Ford, "The Passing of Provincialism," in Ergood and Kuhre, *Appalachia,* 86.

35. Caudill, *Theirs,* 113.

36. Perry, *McCreary,* 121, 125–26.

37. *Shawnee (OH) People's Advocate,* February 17, 1893.

38. Fishback, *Soft,* 21, 88.

39. Knepper, *Ohio,* 302.

40. Tribe, *Coal,* 51–52.

41. Corbin, *Life,* 10.

42. Tribe, *Coal,* 50–55.

43. Eller, *Miners,* 188.

44. Eller, *Miners,* 33.

45. Kelemen, "History," 162–63.

46. Shifflett, *Coal Towns: Life,* 57.

47. Kentucky Coal Mining Museum, Benham, KY.

48. Eavenson, "Building," 535.

49. Munn, "Development," 249–50.

50. E. E. Bach, "Social and Religious Organizations as Factors in the Labor Problem," *Transactions* 59 (1918): 592.

51. "Theater for Miners," *Dramatic Mirror* 80 (August 7, 1919): 1227; "The Cabin Creek YMCA, Decota," *Coal Age* 4 (November 15, 1913): 741–42, qtd. in Corbin, *Life,* 126–27.

52. Testimony of Langdon Bell, U.S. Congress, Senate Committee on Interstate Commerce, *Conditions on the Coal Fields of Pennsylvania, West Virginia and Ohio,* 70th Cong., 1st sess., 2 vols. (Washington, D.C., 1928), 2:1845; "The Cabin Creek YMCA, Decota," *Coal Age* 4 (November 15, 1913): 742, qtd. in Corbin, *Life,* 126–27.

53. *Harlan (KY) Enterprise,* April 7, 1923.

54. Ellis, "Children," 368–69.
55. Eller, *Miners,* 156.
56. Caudill, *Theirs,* 124–26.
57. Eller, *Miners,* 158.
58. Munn, "Development," 252–53.
59. Shifflett, *Coal Towns: Life,* xii–xiii.

Chapter 6

1. Mary Ann Clawson, *Constructing Brotherhood: Class, Gender and Fraternalism* (Princeton: Princeton University Press, 1989), 88, 124.
2. Lynn Dumenil, *Freemasonry and American Culture, 1880–1930* (Princeton: Princeton University Press, 1984), xi.
3. Clawson, *Constructing,* 123; Dumenil, *Freemasonry,* xi; Kenneth L. Ames, "The Lure of the Spectacular," in Brockman, *Theatre,* 19; Mark C. Carnes, *Secret Rituals and Manhood in Victorian America* (New Haven: Yale University Press, 1989), 1, 151.
4. C. Lance Brockman, introduction to Brockman, *Theatre,* 13.
5. Clawson, *Constructing,* 112.
6. Dumenil, *Freemasonry,* 18–19.
7. William D. Moore, "From Lodge Room to Theatre: Meeting Spaces of the Scottish Rite," in Brockman, *Theatre,* 33, 35.
8. Dumenil, *Freemasonry,* 30.
9. Dumenil, *Freemasonry,* 180.
10. Dumenil, *Freemasonry,* xii, 30, 72–73.
11. Dishong and Winnenberg, *Shawnee,* 21.
12. Dumenil, *Freemasonry,* xii, 23.
13. Clawson, *Constructing,* 17–18, 239.
14. Clawson, *Constructing,* 110.
15. Clawson, *Constructing,* 131–32.
16. C. A. Cabell, "Building a Mining Community," *West Virginia Review,* April 1927, 210, qtd. in Corbin, *Life,* 74–75.
17. *Paris Kentuckian Citizen,* March 10, 1880.
18. Dumenil, *Freemasonry,* 25.
19. Clawson, *Constructing,* 178–80.
20. Ames, "Lure," 22–23.
21. Dumenil, *Freemasonry,* 89–91, 110.
22. Clawson, *Constructing,* 178–80.
23. Dumenil, *Freemasonry,* 25.
24. Clawson, *Constructing,* 94, 138, 144.
25. Dishong and Winnenberg, *Shawnee,* 21.
26. Atherton, *Main Street,* 189–90.
27. *Paris Kentuckian Citizen,* October 6, 1869; October 8, 1879; July 18, 1885.
28. *Shawnee (OH) People's Advocate,* March 7, 1902.
29. *Shawnee (OH) People's Advocate,* November 21, 1902.

Chapter 7

1. Philip Graham, *Showboats: The History of an American Institution* (Austin: University of Texas Press, 1951), 185.

2. Betty Bryant, *Here Comes the Showboat!* (Lexington: University Press of Kentucky, 1994), 3.

3. Bryant, *Here Comes*, 2–16; Graham, *Showboats,* 42–45; Mary C. Henderson, *Theater in America: 250 Years of Plays, Players, and Productions* (New York: Abrams, 1996), 20–21.

4. Stuart's Opera House Archives, Nelsonville, OH.

5. Stuart's Opera House Archives, Nelsonville, OH.

6. Quoted in Mary C. Henderson, "Scenography, Stagecraft, and Architecture in the American Theatre, Beginnings to 1870," in Wilmeth and Bigsby, *Cambridge History* (New York: Cambridge University Press, 1998), 1: 387; Jack Poggi, *Theater in America: The Impact of Economic Forces, 1870–1976* (Ithaca, NY: Cornell University Press, 1968), 6; Thomas Postlewait, "The Hieroglyphic Stage: American Theatre and Society, Post–Civil War to 1945," in Wilmeth and Bigsby, *Cambridge History* (New York: Cambridge University Press, 1999), 2:154.

7. John Frick, "A Changing Theatre: New York and Beyond," in Wilmeth and Bigsby, *Cambridge History,* 2:200–205; Poggi, *Theater,* 4–5.

8. Frick, "Changing," 201; Poggi, *Theater,* 7.

9. Frick, "Changing," 202–3.

10. *New Straitsville (OH) Record,* December 19, 1902.

11. Frick, "Changing," 203; Henderson, *Theater,* 25.

12. Poggi, *Theater,* 10–13, Frick, "Changing," 212–14.

13. Frick, "Changing," 212–13; Poggi, *Theater,* 26.

14. Poggi, *Theater,* 14–20.

15. Garrett H. Leverton, *The Production of Later Nineteenth Century American Drama: A Basis for Teaching* (New York: Teachers College, Columbia University, 1936), 8–9.

16. George Lipsitz, "Theatre Space as Social Space: The Twin City Scenic Collection," in *The Twin City Scenic Collection: Popular Entertainment, 1895–1929,* by University Art Museum, University of Minnesota, Minneapolis, 46–47 (Minneapolis: The Museum, 1987); Leverton, *Production,* 20–27; C. Lance Brockman, "Creating Scenic Illusion for the Theatre and the Fraternity," in Brockman, *Theatre,* 97.

17. *Berrien County Record,* May 7, 1889, qtd. in Willis Frederick Dunbar, "The Opera House as a Social Institution in Michigan," *Michigan History Magazine* 27 (1943): 668.

18. Henderson, "Scenography," 415.

19. Tracy Cunning, *Iowa Opera Halls and Opera Houses: Evolution of Stage-Focused Structures in Iowa* (n.p.: Bureau of Historic Preservation, Iowa State Historical Society, n.d.), 33–34.

20. Leverton, *Production,* 36–37, 42–52.

21. Leverton, *Production,* 36–37, 42–52.

22. Frank M. Clark, "The Roller Skating Rink Opera House of Oil City, Pennsylvania: The 1884–1885 Theater Season," *Western Pennsylvania Historical Magazine* 66 (1883): 232–33.

23. Benjamin McArthur, *Actors and American Culture, 1880–1920* (Philadelphia: Temple University Press, 1984), 12–16.

24. Benjamin McArthur, *Actors,* 23–24.

25. Benjamin McArthur, *Actors,* 27–29.

26. Benjamin McArthur, *Actors,* 29–30.

27. *Winchester (KY) News,* October 21, 1908.

Chapter 8

1. *Athens (OH) Messenger,* May 31, 1894.

2. *Athens (OH) Messenger,* September 4, 1879.

3. Patty M. Biddle, "Paris Opera House: A Grand Landmark for More Than 60 Years" (unpublished essay, n.d.).

4. *Brookville (PA) Jeffersonian Democrat,* April 30, 1890.

5. *Maysville (KY) Daily Evening Bulletin,* June 18 and 21, 1883.

6. *Glouster (OH) Tribune,* October 15, 1896.

7. *Athens (OH) Messenger,* June 21, 1883.

8. *Winchester (KY) News,* January 30, 1911.

9. *Paris Kentuckian Citizen,* May 3, 1911.

10. *Winchester (KY) News,* October 31, 1908.

11. *Winchester (KY) News,* October 31, 1908.

12. Atherton, *Main Street,* 307.

13. *Bradford (PA) Era,* April 25, 1892.

14. *Athens (OH) Messenger,* May 31, 1894.

15. *New Straitsville (OH) Record,* October 30, 1903.

16. *Athens (OH) Messenger,* September 4, 1879.

17. *Winchester (KY) News,* October 21, 1908.

18. *Athens (OH) Messenger,* November 13, 1879.

19. *Winchester (KY) News,* October 30, 1908.

20. Cumberland County Historical Society and Hamilton Library Association, Carlisle, PA.

21. *Bradford (PA) Era,* November 11, 1924.

22. Bob Vore and Bill Lawson, eds., *Nostalgic Nelsonville* ([Nelsonville, OH?], [1973?]), 37.

23. "Lynched on Stage, Shots Came from Pit," *New York Times,* April 21, 1911, 1, qtd. in Kirk W. Fuoss, "Lynching Performances, Theatres of Violence," *Text and Performance Quarterly* 19 (1999): 2.

24. Fuoss, "Lynching," 1–2, 28.

25. Dishong and Winnenberg, *Shawnee,* 23.

26. *Shawnee (OH) People's Advocate,* February 1, 1918.

27. *Harlan (KY) Enterprise,* February 17, 1922.

28. *Harlan (KY) Enterprise,* March 3, 1922.

29. *Shawnee (OH) People's Advocate,* March 6, 1908.

30. October 17, 1919, Corry Area Historical Society, Corry, PA.

31. *Brookville (PA) Jeffersonian Democrat,* April 30, 1890.

32. *Winchester (KY) News,* January 19, 1911.

33. *Winchester (KY) News,* March 9, 1911.

34. *Maysville (KY) Daily Evening Bulletin,* November 3, 1877.

35. *Meyersdale (PA) Republican,* October 2, 1913.
36. *Meyersdale (PA) Republican,* February 7, 1907.
37. *Meyersdale (PA) Republican,* January 24, 1907.
38. *Meyersdale (PA) Republican,* May 23, 1907.
39. *Ten Nights in a Bar Room,* flier, March 16, 1906, Stuart's Opera House Archives, Nelsonville, OH.
40. *Maysville (KY) Daily Evening Bulletin,* April 18, 1882.
41. *Harlan (KY) Enterprise,* May 30, 1924.
42. *Winchester (KY) News,* May 1, 1911.
43. *Winchester (KY) News,* May 6, 1911.
44. *Winchester (KY) News,* May 1, 1911.
45. *Athens (OH) Messenger,* April 1, 1880, 5.
46. *Athens (OH) Messenger,* February 8, 1885; February 18, 1886.
47. Green Clay, *Madison County Chronicles* (Richmond, KY, n.d.), 114–15.
48. *Athens (OH) Messenger,* May 16, 1903.
49. *Athens (OH) Messenger,* April 4, 1924.
50. *Oil City (PA) Derrick,* January 19, 1885.
51. *Harlan (KY) Enterprise,* February 1, 1924.
52. *Maysville (KY) Daily Evening Bulletin,* January 2, 1882.
53. *Middlesborough (KY) Weekly News,* October 6, 1905.
54. February 7, 1883, Washington County Historical Society, Washington, PA.
55. *Athens (OH) Messenger,* April 19, 1883.
56. *Athens (OH) Messenger,* March 5, 1885.
57. Allegheny-Kiski Valley Historical Society, Tarentum, PA.
58. Clark, "Roller Skating," 228.
59. Marion County Historical Society Museum, Fairmont, WV.
60. *Winchester (KY) News,* December 16, 1908.
61. *Winchester (KY) News,* December 17, 1910.
62. Meyersdale Public Library, Meyersdale, PA.
63. Edna Oliver, interview with Spencer Steenrod, in *History,* 60–61.
64. *New Straitsville (OH) Record,* May 6, 1904.
65. *Winchester (KY) News,* November 23, 1910.
66. Cumberland County Historical Society and Hamilton Library Association, Carlisle, PA.
67. *Shawnee (OH) People's Advocate,* April 12, 1918.
68. *Shawnee (OH) People's Advocate,* April 19, 1918.
69. *Shawnee (OH) People's Advocate,* May 3, 1918.
70. *Shawnee (OH) People's Advocate,* May 10, 1918.
71. *Shawnee (OH) People's Advocate,* May 24, 1918.
72. *Shawnee (OH) People's Advocate,* June 28, 1918.

Chapter 9

1. Drake Well Museum, Titusville, PA.
2. *Athens (OH) Messenger,* November 29, 1883.
3. *Shawnee (OH) People's Advocate*, February 6, 1914.

4. *Shawnee (OH) People's Advocate*, November 21, 1930.

5. *Harlan (KY) Enterprise*, April 7, 1923.

6. Brooks McNamara, "Popular Entertainment," in Wilmeth and Bigsby, *Cambridge History*, 2:378.

7. Levine, *Highbrow/Lowbrow*, 9, 25, 56, 233.

8. McNamara, "Popular," 380.

9. Brooks McNamara, *The New York Concert Saloon: The Devil's Own Nights* (New York: Cambridge University Press, 2002), xvii, 1.

10. Don B. Wilmeth, *Variety Entertainment and Outdoor Amusements: A Reference Guide* (Westport, CT: Greenwood, 1982), 130–31.

11. McNamara, *New York*, 117.

12. William Mahar, *Behind the Burnt Cork Mask: Early Blackface Minstrelsy and Antebellum American Popular Culture* (Urbana: University of Illinois Press, 1999), 1–2.

13. Wilmeth, *Variety*, 119; Don B. Wilmeth, "Stage Entertainment," in *Handbook of American Popular Culture*, vol. 1, ed. Thomas M. Inge (Westport: Greenwood Press, 1989), 295; Robert C. Toll, *Blacking Up: The Minstrel Show in Nineteenth-Century America* (New York: Oxford University Press, 1974), 30.

14. Frederick Douglass, "Gavitt's Original Ethiopian Serenaders," *North Star*, June 29, 1849, qtd. in Eric Lott, *Love and Theft: Blackface Minstrelsy and the American Working Class* (New York: Oxford University Press, 1993), 15.

15. Lott, *Love*, 17.

16. Mahar, *Behind*, 1–2, 268–69, 331.

17. Wilmeth, "Stage," 295.

18. Mahar, *Behind*, 332.

19. Wilmeth, "Stage," 295; Toll, *Blacking*, 52–56.

20. Mahar, *Behind*, 59, 101, 157, 195.

21. Robert C. Toll, "Social Commentary in Late-Nineteenth-Century White Minstrelsy," in *Inside the Minstrel Mask: Readings in Nineteenth-Century Blackface Minstrelsy*, ed. Annemarie Bean, James V. Hatch, and Brooks McNamara (Hanover, NH: Wesleyan University Press, 1996), 102–3.

22. Wilmeth, "Stage," 296; Wilmeth, *Variety*, 121; Toll, *Blacking*, 135.

23. Toll, *Blacking*, 155.

24. Atherton, *Main Street*, 129.

25. John W. Vogel's Big City Minstrels, playbill, n.d., Stuart's Opera House Archives, Nelsonville, OH.

26. Al. G. Field's Greater Minstrels, program, n.d., Stuart's Opera House, Nelsonville, OH, file.

27. *Athens (OH) Messenger*, October 25, 1883.

28. McNamara, "Popular," 395.

29. Andrea Stulman Dennett, *Weird and Wonderful: The Dime Museum in America* (New York: New York University Press, 1997), 5–6.

30. Dennett, *Weird*, 34–35, 90.

31. Bruce McConachie, "Museum Theatre and the Problem of Respectability for Mid-Century Urban Americans," in *The American Stage: Social and Economic Issues from the Colonial Period to the Present*, ed. Ron Engle and Tice L. Miller (New York: Cambridge University Press, 1993), 66–68.

32. McNamara, "Popular," 397–98; John E. Tapia, *Circuit Chautauqua: From Rural Education to Popular Entertainment in Early Twentieth Century America* (Jefferson, NC: McFarland, 1997), 8, 12–15.

33. Tapia, *Circuit*, 7–9, 25; McNamara, "Popular," 397–98.

34. McNamara, "Popular," 397–98; Tapia, *Circuit*, 8, 18–19, 70–72.

35. Independence, Iowa, *Cannon County Bulletin and Garden*, May 17, 1867, qtd. in Atherton, *Main Street*, 140–41.

36. Atherton, *Main Street*, 141.

37. *Athens (OH) Messenger*, November 10, 1881.

38. *Athens (OH) Messenger*, April 5, 1894.

39. *Shawnee (OH) People's Advocate*, October 1, 1902.

40. *New Straitsville (OH) Record*, December 12, 1902.

41. *Oil City (PA) Derrick*, January 20, 1885.

42. *McCreary County (KY) Record*, January 26, 1932.

43. *Winchester (KY) News*, February 13, 1911.

44. Brooks McNamara, *Step Right Up: An Illustrated History of the American Medicine Show* (Jackson: University Press of Mississippi, 1995), 43–44.

45. Thomas P. Kelley Jr., *The Fabulous Kelley* (Richmond Hill, Ont.: Simon and Schuster, 1968), 101–2, qtd. in McNamara, *Step*, 46.

46. McNamara, "Popular," 396–97; McNamara, *Step*, 16.

47. Cumberland County Historical Society and Hamilton Library Association, Carlisle, PA.

48. Albert F. McLean Jr., *American Vaudeville as Ritual* (Lexington: University of Kentucky Press, 1965), 18–19; Toll, *Show*, 265; Stein, *American*, 3.

49. Toll, *Show*, 276; Wilmeth, *Variety*, 133.

50. Toll, *Show*, 269.

51. Snyder, *Voice*, 12.

52. Wilmeth, *Variety*, 132; Stein, *American*, xiii; Toll, *Show*, 272.

53. Wilmeth, *Variety*, 134; McLean, *American*, 24.

54. McNamara, "Popular," 392; Wilmeth, *Variety*, 132.

55. McLean, *American*, 16–18, 22, 25, 33; Snyder, *Voice*, 12.

56. Wilmeth, *Variety*, 133.

57. Toll, *Show*, 276.

58. Stein, *American*, xiii.

59. John E. DiMeglio, *Vaudeville U.S.A.* (Bowling Green, KY: Bowling Green University Popular Press, 1973), 35–37.

60. "Profits in Clean Vaudeville," *Literary Digest* 43 (October 1911): 603–5, qtd. in McLean, *American*, 69.

61. Kibler, *Rank*, 7.

62. B. F. Keith, "The Vogue of Vaudeville," *National Magazine* 9 (November 1898): 146–53, qtd. in Levine, *Highbrow/Lowbrow*, 195–96.

63. "Profits in Clean Vaudeville"; Brett Page, *Writing for Vaudeville* (Springfield, MA, 1915), 105, qtd. in McLean, *American*, 69–70.

64. Edward Renton, *The Vaudeville Theatre; Building, Operation, Management* (New York: Gotham Press, 1918), qtd. in Snyder, *Voice*, 144.

65. Kibler, *Rank*, 13, 18, 24.

66. Butsch, *Making,* 109, 115–17, 120.

67. *Buster Brown's Holiday,* program, n.d., Stuart's Opera House Archives, Nelsonville, OH.

68. *Liberty Belles,* program, September 6, 1905, Stuart's Opera House Archives, Nelsonville, OH.

69. *A Trip to Egypt,* playbill, November 2, 1904, Stuart's Opera House Archives, Nelsonville, OH.

70. *Meyersdale (PA) Republican,* March 28, 1907.

71. *A Trip to the Moon,* program, June 16, 1905, Stuart's Opera House Archives, Nelsonville, OH.

72. *The Holy City,* program, September 2, 1904, Stuart's Opera House Archives, Nelsonville, OH.

73. *Lock Haven (PA) Clinton Democrat,* November 20, 1874.

74. *Maysville (KY) Daily Evening Bulletin,* October 11, 1882.

75. *Maysville (KY) Daily Evening Bulletin,* October 17, 1882.

76. *Winchester (KY) News,* December 27, 1910.

77. *Maysville (KY) Daily Evening Bulletin,* May 31, 1882.

78. *Winchester (KY) News,* November 4, 1910.

79. *Winchester (KY) News,* October 13, 1908.

80. *Winchester (KY) News,* October 28, 1910.

81. *Winchester (KY) News,* May 23, 1911.

82. *Winchester (KY) News,* May 23, 1911.

83. *Winchester (KY) News,* October 20, 1910.

84. *Maysville (KY) Daily Evening Bulletin,* June 27, 1882.

85. *Winchester (KY) News,* October 13, 1908.

Chapter 10

1. Robert C. Toll, *On with the Show: The First Century of Show Business in America* (New York: Oxford University Press, 1976), 146–47.

2. Toll, *Show,* 148–49.

3. Martha Vicinus, "'Helpless and Unfriended': Nineteenth-Century Domestic Melodrama," in *When They Weren't Doing Shakespeare,* ed. Judith Fisher and Stephen Watt (Athens: University of Georgia Press, 1989), 177.

4. Toll, *Show,* 147, 155–57.

5. Qtd. in Henderson, *Theatre,* 44.

6. McConachie, *Melodramatic,* x.

7. Wilmeth, "Stage," 299.

8. Rahill, *Melodrama,* 121, 172, 299.

9. *Heart of Maryland,* playbill, December 28, 1905, Stuart's Opera House Archives, Nelsonville, OH.

10. Grimsted, *Melodrama,* 99, 102.

11. Biddle, "Paris."

12. McNamara, "Popular," 399.

13. Thomas F. Gossett, *Uncle Tom's Cabin and American Culture* (Dallas: Southern Methodist University Press, 1985), 269.

14. Rosemarie Bank, *Theatre Culture in America, 1825–1860* (New York: Cambridge University Press, 1997), 148.

15. Gossett, *Uncle,* 372.

16. Frank Rahill, "America's Number One Hit," *Theatre Arts* 36 (1952): 18.

17. Adolphus M. Hart, *Uncle Tom in Paris; or, Views of Slavery Outside the Cabin, Together with Washington's Views of Slavery* (Baltimore: Taylor & Co., 1854), 5–6, qtd. in Gossett, *Uncle,* 270.

18. Gossett, *Uncle,* 271.

19. Gossett, *Uncle,* 268.

20. Glenn Hughes, *A History of the American Theatre, 1700–1950* (New York: French, 1954), 302.

21. Gossett, *Uncle,* 370–72.

22. Toll, *Show,* 152.

23. *Meyersdale (PA) Republican,* March 12, 1903.

24. Gossett, *Uncle,* 385.

25. Gossett, *Uncle,* 276, 367, 387.

26. *Athens (OH) Messenger,* September 20, 1883.

27. Judith McArthur, "Demon Rum on the Boards: Temperance Melodrama and the Tradition of Antebellum Reform," *Journal of the Early Republic* 9 (1989): 524–26.

28. Cumberland County Historical Society and Hamilton Library Association, Carlisle, PA.

29. *Harlan (KY) Enterprise,* March 23, 1923.

30. Postlewait, "Hieroglyphic," 148.

31. Roger A. Hall, *Performing the American Frontier, 1870–1906* (New York: Cambridge University Press, 2001), 1, 3, 12.

32. Garff Wilson, *Three Hundred Years of American Drama and Theatre: From Ye Bare and Ye Cubb to Chorus Line* (Englewood Cliffs, NJ: Prentice Hall, 1982), 221.

33. Postlewait, "Hieroglyphic," 148; Tice Miller, "Plays and Playwrights: Civil War to 1896," in Wilmeth and Bigsby, *Cambridge History,* 2:256; Rahill, *Melodrama,* 258–59; Hughes, *History,* 297.

34. *Davy Crockett,* playbill, April 29, 1905, Stuart's Opera House Archives, Nelsonville, OH.

35. *Harlan (KY) Enterprise,* September 29, 1922.

36. *New Straitsville (OH) Record,* January 1, 1903.

37. Levine, *Highbrow/Lowbrow,* 35.

38. Toll, *Show,* 9.

39. Levine, *Highbrow/Lowbrow,* 4.

40. Toll, *Show,* 9.

41. Levine, *Highbrow/Lowbrow,* 23.

42. *Winchester (KY) News,* December 11, 1908.

43. *Meyersdale (PA) Republican,* September 1905.

44. *Meyersdale (PA) Republican,* April 7, 1903.

45. *A Royal Slave,* program, September 16, 1905, Stuart's Opera House Archives, Nelsonville, OH.

Epilogue

1. Poggi, *Theater,* 40.

2. Poggi, *Theater,* 28–39; Postlewait, "Hieroglyphic," 164–65.

3. *Billboard*, Aug. 14, 1926, in Poggi, *Theater,* 33–39.

4. McNamara, *Step,* 149.

5. Virginia McCormick, *Educational Architecture in Ohio: From One-Room Schools and Carnegie Libraries to Community Education Villages* (Kent, OH: Kent State University Press, 2001), 93–94.

6. Virginia McCormick, e-mail to author, March 11, 2003.

7. Poggi, *Theater,* 40–42.

8. McNamara, "Popular," 383.

9. McNamara, "Popular," 403–4.

10. McNamara, "Popular," 404.

11. *Carlisle (PA) Evening Sentinel,* January 5, 1871.

12. *Maysville (KY) Daily Evening Bulletin,* June 26, 1882.

13. *Athens (OH) Messenger,* December 3, 1885.

14. *Carlisle (PA) Evening Sentinel,* December 31, 1896.

15. *Carlisle (PA) Evening Sentinel,* March 23, 1897.

16. June 1, 1906, Corry Area Historical Society, Corry, PA.

17. *Winchester (KY) News,* April 13, 1909.

18. *Harlan (KY) Enterprise,* July 11, 1924.

19. Wilmeth, *Variety,* 134.

20. *Winchester (KY) News,* March 4, 1909.

21. *Winchester (KY) News,* October 20, 1910.

22. *Winchester (KY) News,* November 22, 1910.

23. Cumberland County Historical Society and Hamilton Library Association, Carlisle, PA.

24. Mt. Sterling Library, Mt. Sterling, KY.

25. *Harlan (KY) Enterprise,* May 26, 1922.

26. Edwin O. Sachs and Ernest A. E. Woodrow, *Modern Opera Houses and Theatres* (1896–98; reprint, New York: Arno, 1981), 3:127–28.

27. John R. Freeman, *On the Safeguarding of Life in Theaters; Being a Study from the Standpoint of an Engineer* (New York, 1906), 5, 10–13.

BIBLIOGRAPHY

Books, Articles, Other Secondary Sources

Ames, Kenneth L. "The Lure of the Spectacular." In Brockman, *Theatre,* 19–29.

Atherton, Lewis. *Main Street on the Middle Border.* Bloomington: Indiana University Press, 1954.

Bach, E. E. "Social and Religious Organizations as Factors in the Labor Problem." *Transactions* 59 (1918): 590–611.

Bank, Rosemarie. *Theatre Culture in America, 1825–1860.* New York: Cambridge University Press, 1997.

Barish, Jonas. *The Antitheatrical Prejudice.* Berkeley: University of California Press, 1981.

Batteau, Allen W., ed. *Appalachia and America: Autonomy and Regional Dependence.* Lexington: University Press of Kentucky, 1983.

Bean, Annemarie, James V. Hatch, and Brooks McNamara, eds. *Inside the Minstrel Mask: Readings in Nineteenth-Century Blackface Minstrelsy.* Hanover, NH: Wesleyan University Press, 1996.

Biddle, Patty M. "Paris Opera House: A Grand Landmark for More Than 60 Years." Unpublished essay, n.d.

Billings, Dwight B., Gurney Norman, and Katherine Ledford, eds. *Confronting Appalachian Stereotypes: Back Talk from an American Region.* Lexington: University Press of Kentucky, 1999.

Blauner, Robert. "Internal Colonialism and Ghetto Revolt." *Social Problems* 16 (1969): 393–408.

Brockman, C. Lance. "Creating Scenic Illusion for the Theatre and the Fraternity." In Brockman, *Theatre,* 92–109.

———. Introduction to Brockman, *Theatre,* 12–16.

———, ed. *Theatre of the Fraternity: Staging the Ritual Space.* Jackson: University Press of Mississippi, 1996.

Bryant, Betty. *Here Comes the Showboat!* Lexington: University Press of Kentucky, 1994.

Butsch, Richard. *The Making of American Audiences: From Stage to Television, 1750–1990.* New York: Cambridge University Press, 2000.

Carlson, Marvin. *Places of Performance: The Semiotics of Theatre Architecture.* Ithaca, NY: Cornell University Press, 1989.

Carnes, Mark C. *Secret Rituals and Manhood in Victorian America.* New Haven, CT: Yale University Press, 1989.

Caudill, Harry. *Theirs Be the Power: The Moguls of Eastern Kentucky.* Urbana: University of Illinois Press, 1983.

Clark, Frank M. "The Roller Skating Rink Opera House of Oil City, Pennsylvania: The 1884–1885 Theater Season." *Western Pennsylvania Historical Magazine* 66 (1883): 223–36.

Clawson, Mary Ann. *Constructing Brotherhood: Class, Gender and Fraternalism.* Princeton, NJ: Princeton University Press, 1989.

———. "Spectatorship and Masculinity in the Scottish Rite." In Brockman, *Theatre,* 52–71.

Clay, Green. *Madison County Chronicles.* Richmond, KY, n.d.

Corbin, David Alan. *Life, Work, and Rebellion in the Coal Fields: The Southern West Virginia Miners, 1880–1922.* Chicago: University of Illinois Press, 1981.

Cressy, Paul Frederick. "Social Disorganization and Reorganization in Harlan County, Kentucky." *American Sociology Review* 14 (1949): 389–94.

Cunning, Tracy. *Iowa Opera Halls and Opera Houses: Evolution of Stage-Focused Structures in Iowa.* N.P.: Bureau of Historic Preservation, Iowa State Historical Society, n.d.

Daniel, M. Jane. "Nineteenth-Century Opera Houses of Gallipolis, Ohio." Master's thesis, Marshall University, Huntington, WV, 1992.

Dennett, Andrea Stulman. *Weird and Wonderful: The Dime Museum in America.* New York: New York University Press, 1997.

DiMeglio, John E. *Vaudeville U.S.A.* Bowling Green, KY: Bowling Green University Popular Press, 1973.

Dishong, Rob, and John Winnenberg. *Shawnee: Reflections upon the First 125 Years, 1873–1998.* Nelsonville, OH: Tribune, 1998.

Dramatic Mirror. "The Name Opera House." March 7, 1885.

Dumenil, Lynn. *Freemasonry and American Culture, 1880–1930.* Princeton, NJ: Princeton University Press, 1984.

Dunbar, Willis Frederick. "The Opera House as a Social Institution in Michigan." *Michigan History Magazine* 27 (1943): 661–72.

Eavenson, Howard N. "Building Complete Thousand-Dwelling Town for a Mining Population of 7,000 at Lynch, Ky." *Coal Age* 20 (1921): 532–36.

Eller, Ronald D. Foreword to Billings, Norman, and Ledford, *Confronting,* ix–xi.

———. *Miners, Millhands, and Mountaineers: Industrialization of the Appalachian South, 1880–1930.* Knoxville: University of Tennessee Press, 1982.

Ellis, Mabel Brown. "Children of the Kentucky Coal Fields." *The American Child,* 1920, 285–405.

Engle, Ron, and Tice L. Miller, eds. *The American Stage: Social and Economic Issues from the Colonial Period to the Present.* New York: Cambridge University Press, 1993.

Ergood, Bruce. "Toward a Definition of Appalachia." In Ergood and Kuhre, *Appalachia,* 39–49.

Ergood, Bruce, and Bruce E. Kuhre, eds. *Appalachia: Social Context Past and Present.* Dubuque, IA: Kendall/Hunt, 1991.

Fishback, Price V. *Soft Coal, Hard Choices: The Economic Welfare of Bituminous Coal Miners, 1890–1930.* New York: Oxford University Press, 1992.

Fisher, Judith, and Stephen Watt, eds. *When They Weren't Doing Shakespeare.* Athens: University of Georgia Press, 1989.

Ford, Thomas F. "The Passing of Provincialism." In Ergood and Kuhre, *Appalachia,* 80–103.

Francaviglia, Richard V. *Hard Places: Reading the Landscape of America's Historic Mining Districts.* Iowa City: University of Iowa Press, 1991.

———. *Main Street Revisited: Time, Space, and Image Building in Small-Town America.* Iowa City: University of Iowa Press, 1996.

Freeman, John R. *On the Safeguarding of Life in Theaters; Being a Study from the Standpoint of an Engineer.* New York, 1906.

Frick, John. "A Changing Theatre: New York and Beyond." In Wilmeth and Bigsby, *Cambridge History,* 2:196–232.

Fuoss, Kirk W. "Lynching Performances, Theatres of Violence." *Text and Performance Quarterly* 19 (1999): 1–37.

Garner, John S. Introduction to *The Company Town: Architecture and Society in the Early Industrial Age.* New York: Oxford University Press, 1992.

Glenn, George D., and Richard L. Poole. *The Opera Houses of Iowa.* Ames: Iowa State University Press, 1993.

Gossett, Thomas F. *Uncle Tom's Cabin and American Culture.* Dallas: Southern Methodist University Press, 1985.

Graham, Philip. *Showboats: The History of an American Institution.* Austin: University of Texas Press, 1951.

Grimsted, David. *Melodrama Unveiled: American Theater and Culture, 1800–1850.* Berkeley: University of California Press, 1987.

Groth, Paul. "Frameworks for Cultural Landscape Study." In Groth and Bressi, *Understanding,* 1–21.

Groth, Paul, and Todd W. Bressi, eds. *Understanding Ordinary Landscapes.* New Haven, CT: Yale University Press, 1997.

Hall, Roger A. *Performing the American Frontier, 1870–1906.* New York: Cambridge University Press, 2001.

Henderson, Mary C. "Scenography, Stagecraft, and Architecture in the American Theatre, Beginnings to 1870." In Wilmeth and Bigsby, *Cambridge History,* 1:373–423.

———. *Theater in America: 250 Years of Plays, Players, and Productions.* New York: Abrams, 1996.

Hornblow, Arthur. *A History of the Theatre in America from Its Beginnings to the Present Time.* Vol. 1. Philadelphia: Lippincott, 1919.

Hughes, Glenn. *A History of the American Theatre, 1700–1950.* New York: French, 1954.

Inge, Thomas M., ed. *Handbook of American Popular Culture.* Westport: Greenwood Press, 1989.

Jackson, John Brinckerhoff. *Discovering the Vernacular Landscape.* New Haven, CT: Yale University Press, 1984.

———. *Landscapes: Selected Writings of J. B. Jackson.* Ed. Ervin H. Zube. Amherst: University of Massachusetts Press, 1970.

Kelemen, Thomas A. "A History of Lynch, Kentucky, 1917–1930." *The Filson Club History Quarterly* 48 (1974): 156–76.

Kibler, M. Alison. *Rank Ladies: Gender and Cultural Hierarchy in American Vaudeville.* Chapel Hill: University of North Carolina Press, 1999.

Knepper, George W. *Ohio and Its People.* Kent, OH: Kent State University Press, 1989.

Leverton, Garrett H. *The Production of Later Nineteenth Century American Drama: A Basis for Teaching.* New York: Teachers College, Columbia University, 1936.

Levine, Lawrence W. *Highbrow/Lowbrow: The Emergence of Cultural Hierarchy in America.* Cambridge: Harvard University Press, 1988.

Lewis, Helen Matthews, et al., eds. *Colonialism in Modern America: The Appalachian Case.* Boone, NC: Appalachian Consortium, 1978.

Lewis, Helen Matthews, and Edward E. Knipe. "The Colonialism Model: The Appalachian Model." In Lewis et al., *Colonialism,* 9–31.

Lewis, Peirce F. "Axioms for Reading the Landscape: Some Guides to the American Scene." In Meinig, *Interpretation,* 11–32.

Lewis, Ronald L. "Beyond Isolation and Homogeneity: Diversity and the History of Appalachia." In Billings, Norman, and Ledford, *Confronting,* 21–43.

Lhamon, W. T. *Raising Cain: Blackface Performance from Jim Crow to Hip Hop.* Cambridge, MA: Harvard University Press, 1998.

Lipsitz, George. "Theatre Space as Social Space: The Twin City Scenic Collection." In University Art Museum, University of Minnesota, Minneapolis, *Twin City,* 17–36.

Lott, Eric. *Love and Theft: Blackface Minstrelsy and the American Working Class.* New York: Oxford University Press, 1993.

Lynch, Kevin. *The Image of the City.* Cambridge: Technology Press, 1960.

Lynd, Robert S., and Helen Merrell Lynd. *Middletown: A Study in American Culture.* New York: Harcourt, 1956.

Mahar, William. *Behind the Burnt Cork Mask: Early Blackface Minstrelsy and Antebellum American Popular Culture.* Urbana: University of Illinois Press, 1999.

Marsh, John L. "Frank Coltman: Trouper from Tidioute." *Theatre Survey* 16 (1975): 121–35.

———. "Troupers at Tidioute." *Players* 47 (1972): 138–44.

McArthur, Benjamin. *Actors and American Culture, 1880–1920.* Philadelphia: Temple University Press, 1984.

McArthur, Judith. "Demon Rum on the Boards: Temperance Melodrama and the Tradition of Antebellum Reform." *Journal of the Early Republic* 9 (1989): 518–40.

McConachie, Bruce. "American Theatre in Context, from the Beginnings to 1870." In Wilmeth and Bigsby, *Cambridge History,* 1:111–81.

———. *Melodramatic Formations: American Theatre and Society, 1820–1870.* Iowa City: University of Iowa Press, 1992.

———. "Museum Theatre and the Problem of Respectability for Mid-Century Urban Americans." In Engle and Miller, *American Stage,* 65–80.

McCormick, Virginia. *Educational Architecture in Ohio: From One-Room Schools and Carnegie Libraries to Community Education Villages.* Kent, OH: Kent State University Press, 2001.

———. E-mail to the author. March 11, 2003.

McLean, Albert F., Jr. *American Vaudeville as Ritual.* Lexington: University of Kentucky Press, 1965.

McNamara, Brooks. *The New York Concert Saloon: The Devil's Own Nights.* New York: Cambridge University Press, 2002.

———. "Popular Entertainment." In Wilmeth and Bigsby, *Cambridge History,* 2:378–410.

———. *Step Right Up: An Illustrated History of the American Medicine Show.* Jackson: University Press of Mississippi, 1995.

Meinig, D. W., ed. *The Interpretation of Ordinary Landscapes: Geographical Essays.* New York: Oxford University Press, 1979.

———. "Reading the Landscape: An Appreciation of W. G. Hoskins and J. B. Jackson." In Meinig, *Interpretation,* 195–244.

Miller, Tice. "Plays and Playwrights: Civil War to 1896." In Wilmeth and Bigsby, *Cambridge History,* 2:233–61.

Moore, William D. "From Lodge Room to Theatre: Meeting Spaces of the Scottish Rite." In Brockman, *Theatre,* 30–51.

Munn, Robert F. "The Development of Model Towns in the Bituminous Coal Fields." *West Virginia History* 40 (1979): 243–51.

National Trust for Historic Preservation. *Curtain Up: New Life for Historic Theaters.* Information Ser. 72. Washington, DC: National Trust for Historic Preservation, 1993.

Naylor, David, and Joan Dillon. *American Theaters: Performance Halls of the Nineteenth Century.* New York: Wiley, 1997.

Perry, L. E. *McCreary Conquest: A Narrative History.* Whitley City, KY: L. E. Perry, 1979.

Poggi, Jack. *Theater in America: The Impact of Economic Forces, 1870–1976.* Ithaca, NY: Cornell University Press, 1968.

Postlewait, Thomas. "The Hieroglyphic Stage: American Theatre and Society, Post–Civil War to 1945." In Wilmeth and Bigsby, *Cambridge History,* 2:107–95.

Precourt, Walter. "The Image of Appalachian Poverty." In Batteau, *Appalachia and America,* 86–110.

———. "The Image of Appalachian Poverty." In Ergood and Kuhre, *Appalachia,* 173–85.

Rahill, Frank. "America's Number One Hit." *Theatre Arts* 36 (1952): 18–24.

———. *The World of Melodrama.* University Park: Pennsylvania State University Press, 1967.

Sachs, Edwin O., and Ernest A. E. Woodrow. *Modern Opera Houses and Theatres.* 1896–98; reprint, New York: Arno, 1981.

Schertz, Amy E. *Harlan County Coal Camps: Lynch and Benham, Kentucky; Cultural Transition from Rural to Urban Communities; Industrial Documentary Photography, 1912–1948.* Lexington: University of Kentucky Press, 1987.

Senelick, Laurence. *The Changing Room: Sex, Drag and Theatre.* London: Routledge, 2000.

Shapiro, Henry D. "Appalachia and the Idea of America: The Problem of the Persisting Frontier." In Ergood and Kuhre, *Appalachia,* 74–80.

Shifflett, Crandall A. *Coal Towns: Life, Work, and Culture in Company Towns of Southern Appalachia, 1880–1960.* Knoxville: University of Tennessee Press, 1991.

———. "Coal Towns: The Company Town and Southern Appalachian History." In Ergood and Kuhre, *Appalachia,* 194–98.

Slout, W. L. *Theatre in a Tent: The Development of a Provincial Entertainment.* Bowling Green, OH: Bowling Green University Popular Press, 1972.

Snyder, Robert W. *The Voice of the City: Vaudeville and Popular Culture in New York.* New York: Oxford University Press, 1989.

Steenrod, Spencer. *A History of Stuart's Opera House, Nelsonville, Ohio.* Nelsonville: Tribune, 1978.

Stein, Charles W., ed. *American Vaudeville as Seen by Its Contemporaries.* New York: Knopf, 1984.

Tapia, John E. *Circuit Chautauqua: From Rural Education to Popular Entertainment in Early Twentieth Century America.* Jefferson, NC: McFarland, 1997.

Toll, Robert C. *Blacking Up: The Minstrel Show in Nineteenth-Century America.* New York: Oxford University Press, 1974.

———. *On with the Show: The First Century of Show Business in America.* New York: Oxford University Press, 1976.

———. "Social Commentary in Late-Nineteenth-Century White Minstrelsy." In Bean, Hatch, and McNamara, *Inside,* 86–109.

Towson, Charles R. "Replacing the Saloon in Mining Communities." *Coal Age* 8 (1915): 264–66.

Tribe, Ivan M. *Little Cities of Black Diamonds: Urban Development in the Hocking Coal Region, 1870–1900*. Athens, OH: Athens Ancestree, 1986.

———. *Sprinkled with Coal Dust: Life and Work in the Hocking Coal Region, 1870–1900*. Athens, OH: Athens County Historical Society and Museum, 1989.

University Art Museum, University of Minnesota, Minneapolis. *The Twin City Scenic Collection: Popular Entertainment, 1895–1929*. Minneapolis: The Museum, 1987.

Vicinus, Martha. "'Helpless and Unfriended': Nineteenth-Century Domestic Melodrama." In Fisher and Watt, *When*, 174–86.

Vore, Bob, and Bill Lawson, eds. *Nostalgic Nelsonville*. [Nelsonville, OH?], [1973?].

Waller, Gregory A. *Main Street Amusements: Movies and Commercial Entertainments in a Southern City, 1896–1930*. Washington, DC: Smithsonian, 1995.

Weller, Jack. "Appalachia: America's Mineral Colony." In Lewis et al., *Colonialism*, 47–55.

Willson, Meredith. *The Music Man*. New York: Putnam's, 1958.

Wilmeth, Don B. "Stage Entertainment." In Inge, *Handbook*, 293–322.

———. *Variety Entertainment and Outdoor Amusements: A Reference Guide*. Westport, CT: Greenwood, 1982.

Wilmeth, Don B., and Christopher Bigsby, eds. *The Cambridge History of American Theatre*. 2 vols. New York: Cambridge University Press, 1998–99.

Wilson, Darlene. "A Judicious Combination of Incident and Psychology: John Fox Jr. and the Southern Mountain Motif." In Billings, Norman, and Ledford, *Confronting*, 98–118.

Wilson, Garff. *Three Hundred Years of American Drama and Theatre: From Ye Bare and Ye Cubb to Chorus Line*. Englewood Cliffs, NJ: Prentice-Hall, 1982.

Winnenberg, John. *Our Journey Continues: The History of New Straitsville, Ohio, Volume 1: 1870–1925*. Logan, OH: Fine Print, 1995.

Witham, Barry B., ed. *Theatre in the United States: A Documentary History. Volume 1: 1750–1915; Theatre in the Colonies and United States*. New York: Cambridge University Press, 1996.

Historical Societies, Libraries, and Opera House Archives

Note on sources: In many cases, newspaper clippings have come from small-town libraries, historical societies, opera houses, and private collections. In cases in which not all bibliographical information was preserved, I have provided the source of the clipping.

KENTUCKY

Benham, Cumberland, Lynch: Kentucky Coal Mining Museum, Benham.
Danville: Grace Doherty Library, Centre College, Danville.
Harlan: Southeast Community College Library, Harlan County.
Maysville: Mason County Museum, Maysville.
Middlesborough (Middlesboro): Bell County Public Library, Middlesboro.

Mount Sterling: Mt. Sterling Library, Mt. Sterling.
Paris: Mrs. Patty M. Biddle personal collection, Paris.
Richmond: Eastern Kentucky University Libraries, Richmond.
Winchester: Clark County Public Library, Winchester.

OHIO

Athens, Nelsonville: Stuart's Opera House Archives, Nelsonville.
Gallipolis: Ariel Opera House, Gallipolis.
New Straitsville, Shawnee: Tecumseh Theater, Shawnee.

PENNSYLVANIA

Altoona: Altoona Area Public Library, Altoona.
Blairsville: Historical Society of the Blairsville Area, Blairsville.
Bradford: Bradford Landmark Society, Bradford.
Brookville: Jefferson County Historical Society, Brookville.
Carlisle: Cumberland County Historical Society and the Hamilton Library Association, Carlisle.
Connellsville: Connellsville Historical Society, Connellsville.
Corry: Corry Area Historical Society, Corry.
Hollidaysburg: Blair County Genealogical Society, Hollidaysburg.
Johnsonburg, Ridgway: Elk County Historical Society, Ridgway, PA; Ridgway Public Library, Ridgway.
Lock Haven: Annie Halenbrake Ross Library, Lock Haven.
Meadville: Academy Theatre, Meadville; Crawford County Historical Society, Meadville.
Meyersdale: Meyersdale Public Library, Meyersdale.
Northeast: Erie County Historical Society and Museums, Northeast.
Oil City, Pithole, Tidioute, Titusville: Drake Well Museum, Titusville.
Renovo: Renovo Area Public Library, Renovo.
Tarentum: Allegheny-Kiski Valley Historical Society, Tarentum.
Tyrone: Tyrone-Snyder Twp Library, Tyrone.
Warren: Warren County Historical Society, Warren.
Washington: Washington County Historical Society, Washington.

WEST VIRGINIA

Elkins: Randolph County Historical Society, Elkins.
Fairmont: Marion County Historical Society Museum, Fairmont.
Mannington: Mannington Public Library, Mannington.
Point Pleasant: Mason County Library, Point Pleasant.

INDEX

Page numbers in italic type refer to pages that contain illustrations.